Henry Richard Fox Bourne

English Seamen Under the Tudors

Vol. I

Henry Richard Fox Bourne

English Seamen Under the Tudors
Vol. I

ISBN/EAN: 9783337004040

Printed in Europe, USA, Canada, Australia, Japan

Cover: Foto ©ninafisch / pixelio.de

More available books at **www.hansebooks.com**

ENGLISH SEAMEN UNDER THE TUDORS.

VOL. I.

LONDON: PRINTED BY W. CLOWES AND SONS, STAMFORD STREET AND CHARING CROSS.

ENGLISH SEAMEN

UNDER

THE TUDORS.

BY

H. R. FOX BOURNE,
AUTHOR OF "A MEMOIR OF SIR PHILIP SIDNEY," "ENGLISH MERCHANTS," ETC.

IN TWO VOLUMES.

VOLUME I.

LONDON:
RICHARD BENTLEY, NEW BURLINGTON STREET,
Publisher in Ordinary to Her Majesty.
1868.

PREFACE.

THE great deeds of England's heroes on the sea during the memorable period of Tudor rule have furnished material for many volumes of special biography, and for numberless briefer memoirs in biographical dictionaries, in antiquarian repertories, and in miscellaneous publications. They have also yielded topics for brilliant episodes and instructive generalizations in histories of all sorts. But nowhere, I believe, except in John Campbell's *Lives of the British Admirals* (1761), in the *Lives of the British Admirals* begun by Robert Southey and continued by Robert Bell (1833—1840), and in the *Memoirs of the Naval Worthies of Queen Elizabeth's Reign* by Mr. John Barrow (1845), has any complete or consecutive account of these deeds been attempted; and there seems to be fair excuse for supplementing these good books with another and a differently planned work.

Preface.

I have here attempted to set forth all that is most memorable in the careers of the great leaders of English navigation and English sea-fighting under the Tudors, so far as they had anything to do with naval affairs; but, instead of writing a number of short biographies, it seemed to me better to make the biographical details subordinate to the history of the famous enterprises to which they belong. After a short introductory chapter, and three other chapters which, relating to the reigns of Henry VII., Henry VIII., and Edward VI., may also be looked upon as introductory to the fuller narrative of English sea-going under Elizabeth, I have therefore so arranged my materials as to present, in each of the following volumes, a separate historical episode. In the first is given, as concisely as seemed possible with due regard to the interest of the subject, the story of the efforts made by Elizabethan navigators to reach the Indies and acquire their wealth by arctic voyaging, and of the efforts issuing therefrom, by which were begun the English colonization of America, and the English mastery of India. In the second, the same memorable half-century has been traversed, chiefly to show the way in which, while trading enterprise and bold love of adventure were being peaceably exercised by the arctic explorers and the founders of our colonial empire, another set of men, or the same men applying themselves to a different object, went to sea with the determination of wresting the wealth of the Spanish Main and the Southern Seas from the nation which had learnt to think them exclusively her own. The outcome of these efforts was the Great Armada Fight, and the naval supremacy of England over all the nations of Europe.

The authorities for the statements made in the following pages have been carefully indicated in footnotes. Among recent works, I am especially indebted to the many publications of the Hakluyt Society, and to the excellent Calendars of State Papers prepared under the direction of the Master of the Rolls. But it is hardly necessary to state that my largest debts are due to Hakluyt's *Voyages*, and Purchas's *Pilgrims*, and to the journals and other illustrative documents, not included in those voluminous collections, which are preserved in the British Museum Library, the Record Office, and elsewhere. Having a wonderful gathering of personal narratives to work from, I have purposely made free use of the quaint and eloquent words and sentences of the original writers, generally sharers and often leaders in the several enterprises which they describe. My effort has been simply and concisely to relate the story of some great achievements by which the little island of Britain was helped to become a rich and powerful nation. To that end I have, as far as possible, abstained from interpolating the narrative with comments and criticisms of my own. History, I venture to think, is always best taught, and its lessons are always made most plain, by straightforward relating of facts; and interpretations and expositions would be especially out of place where the history is so eloquent and the lessons are so transparent as in the case of the heroic undertakings which are the theme of these volumes.

H. R. Fox Bourne.

4th March, 1868.

CONTENTS OF VOLUME I.

CHAPTER I.

THE ANTECEDENTS OF TUDOR SEAMANSHIP.

Introduction—The Primitive Shipping of Britain—Celtic and Roman Shipping—Anglo-Saxon and Danish "Wave-traversers"—Improvements in English Shipping under Alfred the Great and his Successors—The Rise of the Cinque Ports—Chaucer's "Schipman"—Plantagenet Ships and Sailors—Crusaders on the Sea—Sea-fighting under Richard I. and King John—The Decay of Plantagenet Shipping—The Water-walls of England   1

CHAPTER II.

THE VOYAGES OF THE CABOTS.

[1485—1517.]

Early English Maritime Discovery—Saint Brendan, Madoc, and Macham—The Fabled Wonders of Cathay, and their Issue—Christopher Columbus and John Cabot—John Cabot's Life in Venice and in Bristol—His Cathayan Project—His North-western Voyage, and his New-found-lands—Sebastian Cabot's North American Explorations—The first English Settlements in America—Sebastian Cabot's later Expeditions—His Services to Spain   24

CHAPTER III.

HENRY THE EIGHTH'S NAVY.

[1511—1546.]

The Beginnings of the English Navy—The Work of the Howards—Their Punishment of **Andrew Barton** and the Scottish Pirates—Lord Thomas **Howard** in Spain—**Sir** Edward Howard off Brittany—The Improvement of the Navy under Henry VIII. and Wolsey—Sir Edward Howard and Prester John—Sir Edward Howard's **last Fight**—**Henry VIII.'s** Ship-building and its **Effect**—**His last War** with France—**The Battle** at Spithead, and the Loss of the *Mary Rose* 46

CHAPTER IV.

SEBASTIAN CABOT'S LATER WORK.

[1527—1557.]

Robert Thorne's Projects for Arctic Voyaging—The Voyages of Captain Rut and Master Hore—Sebastian Cabot's last Cathayan Project—Sir Hugh Willoughby and Richard Chancelor—Their North-eastern Voyage towards Cathay—Willoughby's Death—The Muscovy Company and its Work—Chancelor's last Work—Sebastian Cabot's Death 81

CHAPTER V.

THE PROMOTERS OF CATHAYAN ENTERPRISE UNDER QUEEN ELIZABETH.

[1558—1575.]

Early Explorers of the North American Coast: Cortereal, Vermzano, and Sebastian Gomez—English Followers of the Cabots: Arthur Jenkinson and Humphrey Gilbert—Gilbert's Employments in Ireland and in Flanders—His *Discourse to Prove a Passage to Cathay*—Michael Lock—Martin Frobisher—His Voyages to Africa and elsewhere—The Beginnings of his Cathayan Enterprise 103

CHAPTER VI.

MARTIN FROBISHER'S THREE VOYAGES IN THE DIRECTION OF CATHAY.

[1575—1579.]

Frobisher's First Voyage—His Discovery of Meta Incognita and Observations thereon—His Gold-finding, and its Results—The Cathay Company—Frobisher's Second Voyage—The rude People of Orkney—The Exploration of Frobisher's Straits—The Inhabitants of Meta Incognita, and English Dealings with them—Frobisher's Third Voyage—His Visit to Greenland—The Perils of an Arctic Storm—Frobisher's Discovery of Hudson's Straits—His last Researches and Experiences in Meta Incognita—Relics of his Stay therein—His Return to England—His Rivals and Enemies—Proposals for a Fourth Voyage—The Troubles of Dame Isabel Frobisher 124

CHAPTER VII.

THE COLONIZING PROJECTS OF SIR HUMPHREY GILBERT.

[1574—1583.]

Gilbert's Projects against Spain—His Charter for American Colonization—Walter Raleigh's Early History—His Share in Gilbert's Project—The first unfortunate Issue of that Project—The Occupations of Gilbert and Raleigh in Ireland and in England—The Renewal of the Colonizing Project—Gilbert's Second Expedition—Troubles in Newfoundland and on the Homeward Voyage—The Death of Sir Humphrey Gilbert . . . 178

CHAPTER VIII.

SIR WALTER RALEIGH'S VIRGINIA.

[1584—1590.]

Raleigh's Charter for American Colonization—The Exploring Voyage of Philip Amadas and Arthur Barlow—Their Observations in North Carolina—The primitive Country of Virginia and its simple People—Raleigh's First Colony—Sir Richard Grenville and Ralph Lane—The Misconduct of the English Colonists—The Troubles of the Indians in Virginia—The Original of Caliban—The Failure of the First Colony—Grenville's abortive Expedition for its Relief—Raleigh's Second Colony—Its unfortunate History—John White's Search for its Members—The later Colonization of Virginia 200

CHAPTER IX.

JOHN DAVIS'S THREE VOYAGES IN THE DIRECTION OF CATHAY.
[1585—1587.]

The North-eastern Voyage of Arthur Pet and Charles Jackman—Later Projects for North-western Voyaging—The Fellowship of New Navigations—Davis's First Voyage—His Exploration of Greenland—The Land of Desolation—Discovery of Davis's Straits and Cumberland Island—Davis's Second Voyage—The unworthy Exploits of Richard Pope—Davis at Gilbert's Sound—His Intercourse with the Greenlanders—His Researches along the Coasts of Cumberland Island and Labrador—His Third Voyage—Quarrels with the Greenlanders—Further Discoveries in Davis's Straits and Baffin's Bay—The End of Davis's Northern Voyaging 245

CHAPTER X.

THE END OF THE CATHAYAN QUEST.
[1579—1603.]

The First Voyagers to the East Indies: Thomas Stevens; Fitch and Newberry—The East Indian Expedition under George Raymond and James Lancaster—The Mischances of the Outward Voyage and the Shipwreck of Raymond—Lancaster's Adventures in the Indian Seas—The Mischances of his Homeward Voyage—Dutch Voyages to the East Indies, with John Davis and William Adams for Pilots—The Formation of the East India Company—Lancaster's Second East Indian Expedition—His Stay in Africa—The Beginnings of English Trade with Sumatra and Java—Fresh Projects for North-western Voyaging towards India—George Waymouth's Disastrous Expedition . 275

LIST OF MAPS.

The Arctic Regions . . . . *Facing page* 33

The Arctic Regions (reduced from a map prepared by Michael Lock) . . . . ,, ,, 126

Frobisher's Straits (from a map prepared by Captain C. F. Hall, and published in his *Life with the Esquimaux*, 1864) . . . . . ,, ,, 129

The Countess of Warwick's Sound, Frobisher's Straits (from the same) . . . . . ,, ,, 129

Davis's Straits . . . . ,, ,, 250

THE RISE OF ENGLISH SEAMANSHIP

UNDER THE EARLIER TUDORS;

AND

THE PROGRESS OF MARITIME DISCOVERY AND COLONIAL ENTERPRISE

UNDER QUEEN ELIZABETH.

ENGLISH SEAMEN UNDER THE TUDORS.

CHAPTER I.

THE ANTECEDENTS OF TUDOR SEAMANSHIP.

ENGLISH sailors were first great under the Tudors. The fame of their seafaring began in the reign of Henry VII. with the voyages of those Bristol merchants, under the Cabots, who discovered North America. The fame of their sea-fighting began in the reign of Henry VIII. with the employment of a national navy, under Sir Edward Howard, against the French.

But from the time when our Anglo-Saxon forefathers first visited these shores, we may trace, both in sea-fighting and in seafaring, an almost steady growth of skill and courage. The earliest indications of skill and courage belong, indeed, to a period lasting for centuries, perhaps thousands of years, before the Anglo-Saxon settlement.

The very first inhabitants of our island must have been sailors, expert enough to make and guide the crafts which brought them from their older continental homes. These may have been very rude and very fragile; but, if so, there is evidence that the primitive knowledge was soon improved upon. In various parts of England and Scotland, so deep underground, and so far from the present limits of the sea that long ages must have elapsed since they were used, boats have been discovered, very similar to the canoes still built by the North American Indians and the natives of the Pacific Islands, and adapted for trading and fishing expeditions. Some are only five or six feet long, and hardly able to hold more than a single man; others are five or six times as large, and with room enough for a little company of voyagers. Most of them are shaped, as if by fire, out of solid blocks of oak; a few are made of separate pieces, fastened by wooden pins; and one, considerably larger than the others, and probably of a much later date, has copper instead of wooden nails.*

All but the smallest bear resemblance to the vessels in which the Celts of Gaul, aided, as we are told, by the Celts of Britain, attempted to withstand the conquering force of Julius Cæsar; and Cæsar's honest praise, corroborated by the discoveries of archæologists, gives us a tolerably clear insight into the maritime condition of the Celtic races near the beginning of the Christian era. "In agility and a ready command of oars," he says, "we had the advantage; but in other respects, considering the situation of the coast and the assaults of storms, all things ran very

* *Archæologia*, vol. xxvi. (1836), pp. 257—264; Wilson. *Pre-historic Annals of Scotland* (2nd ed., 1863), vol. i., pp. 43—47, 52—56, 360.

much in their favour. For neither could our ships injure them in their prows, so great was their strength and firmness; nor could we easily throw in our darts, because of their height above us, for which reason also we found it extremely difficult to grapple with the enemy and bring them to close fight. Add to all this, that, when the sea began to rage, and they were forced to submit to the winds, they could both weather the storm better and more securely trust themselves among the shallows, because they feared nothing from the rocks and cliffs upon the ebbing of the tide."*

These oaken galleys, slow-going and not very manageable, flat-bottomed and with high prows and sterns, supplied with leather sails and iron cables, were the chief causes of trouble to Cæsar in his naval fighting with the Celtic races. The Celts were also famed for the long slender boats, akin to the modern pinnace, provided with light-blue sails and keels of the same colour, so as to be hardly distinguishable, at a little distance, from the sea and sky, in which, during war-time, they darted noiselessly upon the enemy, and glided swiftly from place to place, seeking and giving information.† And for peaceful avocations they had vessels, of size intermediate between the galleys and the boats, made partly of wood and partly of wicker covered with ox-hide, and provided with a few oars and a single sail a-piece, in which merchants conveyed their goods from one home port to another, or across the narrow seas that

---

* Cæsar, *De Bello Gallico*, lib. iii., cap. 13.
† Flavius Vegetius, *De Re Militari*, lib. iv., cap. 37.

separated Gaul from Britain and Britain from Hibernia.*

The Britons appear to have made no progress in maritime affairs after the Roman conquest. They learnt nothing from their rulers, who, indeed, found it more convenient, for warfare in the northern seas, to copy the Celtic fashions than to use their own style of shipping; and under the weakening influences of a foreign civilization they lost much of their ancient skill. Yet for some centuries it does not seem that Teutonic and Scandinavian shipping was much superior to that of the Celtic nations which it was the chief means of mastering. Braver hearts and stouter hands guided them; but the Norse and Anglo-Saxon boats were as small and as ill-constructed as those of the Britons. In some respects perhaps they were even ruder. When Beowulf, hero of the fine old poem which is the earliest treasure of English literature, heard of the troubles by which Hrothgar, the king of the West Goths, was harassed, and resolved to cross the seas for his assistance,

> "He bade for him a wave-traverser
> Good be prepared;"

but it was only large enough to hold a very few of the brave warriors eager to join in his expedition.

> "With some fifteen
> The floating wood he sought.
> A water-crafty man,
> A warrior, pointed out
> The shores and shoals.

---

* CÆSAR, lib. i., cap. 54; SELDEN, *Mare Clausum* (1635), lib. ii., cap. 2.

Anglo-Saxon Shipping.

> Then speedily
> The floater was on the waves,
>   The boat under the mountain.
> The ready warriors
>   On the prow stept.
> Into the bark's brow
>   The warriors bore
> Clear-shining weapons,
>   Sumptuous war-gear,
> And on the welcome voyage
>   The men pressed forth.
> Departed then, o'er the wavy sea,
>   By the wind impelled,
> The floater foamy-necked,
>   To a bird most like."*

Not much larger, it is probable, were the vessels in which the Teutonic conquerors of Britain arrived. The traditions which have assigned a few precise dates to the migration that must have proceeded slowly and steadily through some centuries would lead, if we accept them, to a different conclusion. Hengist and Horsa are said to have come, in 449, with three long-ships or keels; Ella and his sons, in 477, with three others; Cerdic and Cynric, in 495, with five; Port and his two sons, in 501, with two; and the leaders of the West Saxons, in 514, with three.† But we have no ground for supposing that any Anglo-Saxon ".wave-traverser" before the time of Alfred the Great, whether styled a ship or a keel, a hulk or a boat, was of more than fifty tons' burthen, or had room for more than half a hundred men. All appear to have been built after the same fashion, with planks laid one over the other, and stretching from

---

* BEOWULF, ed. by THORPE (1855), lines 399, 400, 420—442.
† *Anglo-Saxon Chronicle*, ed. by THORPE (1861), *sub annis*.

prow to stern. Both prow and stern rose high above the middle part of the vessel, the former, or sometimes both, being adorned with a rude figure-head, and the latter being provided with a long broad oar, to be used by the captain or pilot in directing the course of the voyage. Rowers were placed at the sides, and, with a favourable wind, the progress was greatly aided by a large square sail suspended from a yard at the top of a single slender mast, and fastened at the bottom to the edges of the vessel. The keels, apparently, were longer and narrower, lighter and swifter than the ships, while the hulks were broader and more compact, being intended for the transport of stores and merchandize, and the boats were adapted for river-transit and passage between the larger crafts. We find no mention, however, of vessels too large to be rowed by one or two dozen men, or to be pushed by hand from the shore when they were required for use.*

It was in vessels of this sort that the people whom

* STRUTT, *Chronicle of England* (1777), vol. i., p. 337; NICOLAS, *History of the Royal Navy* (1847, vol. i., pp. 8—11. " A very interesting account," says the latter authority, " is given by the northern historians of the Danish fleets which so frequently harassed this country. The crews obeyed a single chief, whom they styled their king, and who also commanded them on land; who was always the bravest of the brave; who never slept beneath a raftered roof, nor ever drained the bowl by a sheltered hearth—a glowing picture of their wild and predatory habits. To these qualities a celebrated sea-chieftain, called Olaf, added extraordinary eloquence and great personal strength and agility. He was second to none as a swimmer, could walk upon the oars of his vessel while they were in motion, could throw three darts into the air at the same time and catch two of them alternately, and could, moreover, hurl a lance with each hand; but he was impetuous, cruel, and revengeful, and 'prompt to dare and do.' "

we call Anglo-Saxons came to our shores during the fourth and fifth centuries; and the vessels in which they were attacked, during the ninth and tenth centuries, by their rougher kinsmen, known as Danes, were of the same description.* King Alfred has the credit of effecting the first great improvement in English shipping. In 897, says the contemporary historian, he caused long ships to be built. "They were twice as long as the others. Some had sixty oars, some had more. They were swifter, steadier, and higher than the rest, shapen neither like the Frisian nor like the Danish, but as seemed to him most useful."† But even the new large ships were so small and light that they could, at high tide, sail in water which, when it ebbed, left them dry upon the shore; and from the frequent records of their foundering, we must infer that they were neither very well managed nor very manageable.‡

Alfred's zeal in naval matters was inherited by several of his successors. Athelstan not only obtained such a thorough victory over the Danes, in 937, that they gave no further trouble to the English for half a century, but he was able, in 933, to invade Scotland by sea, and, in 939, to send a fleet to the King of France for the purpose of resisting his rebellious nobles and the

---

* A boat, supposed to have been used by the Danish or Norman freebooters in France—"heavy, stout, and clumsy, the keel hollowed out of a single piece of timber"—was found in the valley of the Seine, near Paris, in 1806.—PALGRAVE, *History of Normandy and England*, vol. i., pp. 615, 747.

† *Anglo-Saxon Chronicle, sub anno.*   ‡ *Ibid.*

King of Germany. Yet more famous was Athelstan's son Edgar, of whom it is said that, in 973, "he led all his ship-forces to Chester, and there came to meet him six kings, and they all plighted their troth to him that they would be his fellow-workers by sea and by land."* To that fact the mediæval chroniclers added the fiction of his having been rowed up the Dee by the Kings of Scotland, Cumberland, Anglesea, Wales, Galloway, and Westmoreland; and out of both fact and fiction have been constructed wonderful reports of Edgar's maritime greatness. But no fables were needed to exalt his fame as a naval reformer.

> "Was no fleet so insolent,
> No host so strong,
> That in the Angle race
> Took from him aught
> The while this noble King
> Ruled in the royal seat." †

Even Ethelred the Unready has a place in naval history. Though he was unable to put it to good use, he collected, in 1009, a fleet of nearly eight hundred vessels, "so many as never before had been among the English nation in any king's days."‡ The levying of ship-money by which this was effected, being continued by Canute and his sons, enabled them to make further improvement in English shipping, and to leave it in a state from which there appears to have been little fresh advance for nearly a century and a half.

The ship-money was abolished by Edward the Confessor; but when William the Norman conquered Eng-

* *Anglo-Saxon Chronicle, sub anno.*   † *Ibid.*   ‡ *Ibid.*

land, he found and kept in force certain provisions for naval service. The burgesses of Dover, for instance, were bound to provide twenty ships, carrying twenty-one men each, for fifteen days each year, in return for exemption from sac and soc and from toll throughout all England; and by the people of Sandwich similar services were rendered in return for similar privileges. Every time that the King sent ships to sea, the burgesses of Lewes had to contribute twenty shillings towards the wages of the crews. Warwick had to find four seamen, or pay four pounds in lieu, and twenty burgesses of Oxford had to attend the King on each expedition, or, in default, twenty pounds were to be paid for substitutes. Lands were held in the hundred of Maldon, in Essex, on agreement to supply wood for building the King's ships, and Gloucester had to furnish iron for nails to be used in making the same.* Of like sort were many other miscellaneous imposts, some of which continue, in modified forms, to the present day, the most important of all being the scheme of service by which the Cinque Ports were enabled to take an influential part in English maritime history throughout the middle ages.

The origin of these Cinque Ports is referred to a period long antecedent to the Norman Conquest. The Romans are supposed to have established five fortresses under a Comes Littoris Saxonici—Regulbium, near the site of Reculvers in Thanet; Rutupiæ, now

---

* *Domesday Book, passim;* MACPHERSON, *Annals of Commerce* (1805), vol. i., pp. 293—297; NICOLAS, vol. i., pp. 24, 25.

Richborough; Dubræ, now Dover; Portus Lemanus, now the present site of Hythe; and Anderida, not far from modern Hastings; and out of the privileges enjoyed by these fortresses, it has been conjectured, arose the charter which Edward the Confessor is reported to have granted to five associated ports,—Romney, in lieu of Regulbium; Sandwich, for Rutupiæ; Dover; Hythe, for Portus Lemanus; and Hastings, for Anderida. This charter, however, if ever conferred, has been lost; and all we know is that William the Conqueror found arrangements existing for the naval service just referred to, and that soon after the Norman Conquest there was organized or reorganized an association of the five towns of Dover, Sandwich, Romney, Hythe, and Hastings, helping one another doubtless in commercial enterprises and in protecting the interests of commerce, and aiding the King with a small naval force, to be prepared and maintained entirely at their own expense, and used as he chose during fifteen days of each year, exclusive of the time required for equipment, for transmission to the place appointed, and for returning home after their discharge. For any longer period that was found necessary, the ships and their crews were to be at the King's bidding, but he was to maintain them at his own cost. In this way the State had at command a fleet of fifty-seven ships, with aggregate crews of eleven hundred and ninety-seven persons, a hundred and fourteen being officers paid at the rate of 6d. per day, and the rest being entitled to a daily pay of 3d. The entire annual cost to the Cinque Ports was estimated at

983*l.* 5*s.*, which must be multiplied by nine or ten for the difference in value of currency between the twelfth and the nineteenth centuries. At a later date the number of ships was slightly augmented, and at a still later date, when much larger and costlier vessels began to be used, only two, three, or four were exacted; but the entire expense of the service in men and money was steadily kept on a par with that of the original institution. The Cinque Ports, however, in course of time, came to include a great many more than five separate towns. Partly because the original five were hardly able to bear the burthen put upon them, and partly because others were eager to share the privileges accorded for the service, several other towns were gradually incorporated with each of the principal ones. Winchelsea, Rye, Pevensey, and others, for instance, were added to Hastings; Folkestone, Faversham, and Margate to Dover; Reculver, Sarre, Storey, and Deal, to Sandwich.*

In this way the Plantagenet sovereigns were provided with a compact and well-manned fleet, strong enough by itself for their minor naval wars, and able at any time to be the nucleus of a larger gathering of fighting ships brought together, in time of need, by special imposts from all the leading ports and inland towns of England, when merchant ships were hastily adapted for warlike use. A few other vessels, known as the King's galleys, appear

---

* JEAKE, *Charters of the Cinque Ports and their Members;* HOLLOWAY, *History and Antiquities of the Ancient Town and Port of Rye, with Incidental Notices of the Cinque Ports* (1847), pp. 66—68.

to have been maintained exclusively at the cost and for the service of the Crown; and they, of course, were constructed specially for fighting purposes. But there seems to have been no very great difference between ships of war and ships of trade. The stoutest of the King's galleys had but a single mast and a single sail, and the smallest of the merchantmen, generally employed in transporting troops and stores, were large enough to carry eight or ten horses amidships, and to hold eighty or more tuns of wine. Ships of all sorts, whether built for the sovereign or prepared for private use, were held to be, in theory and fact, the property of the Crown. The King could send any wherever he chose, and, in the most summary manner, could forbid their going to any objectionable place, or even going out of port at all. "Know for certain," we read in a mandate of King John's, addressed, in 1208, to the mariners of Wales, prohibiting their departure from their homes until they were otherwise instructed, "that if ye act contrary to this, we will cause you and the masters of your vessels to be hanged, and all your goods to be seized for our use." Hundreds of similar orders were issued during the middle ages, the object being that the King's agents might choose for impressment, both the fittest vessels for transport or fighting purposes, and the ablest seamen to be employed in the royal galleys.

Thereby, of course, commerce suffered considerably; but it was chiefly by the pursuit of commerce that English shipping prospered under the Plantagenets. In each generation there was increase of the number of tough little vessels, constructed for trading round the coast or across the narrow seas, to Ireland on the one side and to France and Germany on the other; though able now and then, and under adventurous captains, to go as far northward as Denmark and even Iceland, or in a southern direction towards Spain and Italy. And if, in time of war, the merchants' ships were liable to seizure for public use, trade was helped in peaceful seasons by the employment of the King's galleys and the Cinque Ports' vessels either in actual transport of goods or in the protection of smaller craft from the native and foreign pirates who infested the seas. In peace time and in war time the English sailor of the middle ages had bold and hardy work to do, adding as much in those days as his successors have done in later times to the bold and hardy character of the whole nation of Englishmen. We may infer the rough way of life and sturdy bearing of the whole class from Chaucer's description of the typical seaman, who went on pilgrimage to Canterbury in company with priests, monks, friars, nuns, knights, yeomen, clerks, and merchants:—

> "A schipman was ther, wonyng fer by weste;
> For ought I woot he was of Dertemouthe.
> He rood upon a rouncy, as he couthe,
> All in a goune of faldyng to the kne.
> A dagger hangyng on a laas hadde he
> Aboute his nekke under his arm adoun.
> The hoote somer had maad his hew al broun,
> And certeinly he was a good felawe.
> Ful many a draught of wyn he hadde drawe
> From Burdeux-ward, whil that the chapmen sleep.
> Of nyce conscience took he no keep.

> If that he foughte, and hadde the heigher hand,
> By water he sente hem hoom to every land.
> But of his craft, to rikne wel the tydes,
> His stremes and his dangers him bisides,
> His herbergh and his mone, his lode-menage,
> Ther was non such from Hulle to Cartage.
> Hardy he was, and wys to undertake;
> With many a tempest hadde his berd ben schake.
> He knew wel alle the havenes, as thei were,
> From Gotland to the Cape of Fynestere,
> And every cryk in Bretagne and in Spayne;
> His barge yclepud was the *Magdelayne*."

England had thousands of such "good fellows" in the generations before and after the time of Chaucer, able and ready to do anything and go anywhere, working best and most to the prosperity of their country when following peaceful avocations, but adding most to its fame among the nations of Europe when summoned by their sovereigns to carry out their warlike projects.

Sailors had not much to do in the way of fighting, however, for more than a century after the Norman Conquest. Ships were used by the Anglo-Norman kings almost exclusively in transporting them and their retinues, large and small, to and from their continental possessions. Some vessels, called "piratæ," were chartered by William Rufus, in the early part of his reign, for opposing his elder brother, Duke Robert, and we are told that the English captured many of the Norman vessels, and slew most of their crews. In 1091 William also raised a fleet, with the intention of punishing Malcolm, King of Scotland, for his invasion of England; but the greater part of the ships were wrecked in passage, and the expedition was thus brought to an end; and, with the exception of preparations made by Henry I., soon after his accession in 1101, against Duke Robert, which came to nothing, there was not much other thought of sea-fighting for many years. Henry II. did a little for the extension of the English navy. Threatened, in 1167, with an invasion by the Counts of Boulogne and Flanders, supported by a fleet of six hundred vessels, he caused a sufficient force to be collected for defence of the coast, and took other measures for maintaining the honour of England: and in 1171 he went to complete the conquest of Ireland with four hundred large ships. These and some minor occupations make up the sum of our naval history till near the close of the twelfth century.

A period of more important work was inaugurated by Richard I. Of this his crusading zeal was the immediate cause. In April, 1190, in obedience to his orders, a fleet of more than a hundred vessels quitted Dartmouth for the Holy Land, a longer and more perilous voyage than appears ever before to have been undertaken by Englishmen; and the story of its progress gives interesting evidence of the character and capabilities of English shipping in those days. Four months, including the time necessary to repair the damage caused by a violent storm in the Bay of Biscay, were spent in sailing to Marseilles, and another month was required for the voyage to Messina, where King Philip of France awaited the coming of his brother crusader, Richard of England. "As soon as the people heard of his arrival," says an eye-witness, "they rushed in

crowds to the shore. In the distance they beheld the
sea covered with countless galleys, and the noise of
trumpets from afar, with the sharper and shriller clarion
blasts, resounded in their ears. Then they saw the galleys rowing in order nearer to the land, adorned and
furnished with all manner of arms, numberless pennons
and ensigns floating in the wind, and the beaks of the
vessels ornamented with various devices, while glittering shields were ranged along the prows. The sea
boiled, as it were, with the multitude of the rowers, and
the roar of their trumpets was deafening. Great indeed
was the joy of the spectators when their own magnifi-
cent King, attended by a crowd of mariners, appeared
on a prow more beautiful and higher than the others,
and, landing, showed himself, elegantly adorned, to the
multitude on the shore."* At Messina, Richard, in company with Philip, halted for the winter, the time being
considered unseasonable for further voyaging, and also
being needed for retrieving the losses incident to the
five months' tedious passage from Dartmouth. In the
interval, moreover, a smaller fleet arrived from England,
and other vessels were chartered in the Mediterranean,
so that the whole force which put to sea in April, 1191,
numbered about two hundred sail. At the end of two
months, after many delays, the fleet reached Acre, there
to wait for a year, while its crews followed Richard in
his famous crusading enterprises on land.†

* GEOFFREY DE VINSAUF, lib. ii.
† Richard was a year too late to join in the most important naval
work of this crusade; but as one of its engagements, occurring in the

The only important crusading enterprise by sea occurred just before the arrival at Acre; and then

---

spring of 1190, affords the best illustration of the sea-fights of the period, Geoffrey de Vinsauf's graphic account of it is here repeated:—
"The people of Acre ill brooked their loss of liberty upon the sea, and resolved to try what they could do in a naval battle. Therefore they brought out their galleys, two by two, and in orderly array rowed into the open sea. Then our men, preparing to receive them, hastened to the encounter. When they had advanced on both sides, our ships were arranged in a curved line, so that if the enemy attempted to break through, they might be enclosed and defeated. The ends of the line being drawn out in a sort of crescent, the stronger were placed in front, so that a sharper onset might be made by us, and the enemy be promptly checked. In the upper tiers, the shields interlaced were placed circularly; and the rowers sat close together, that those placed above might have freer scope. The sea, as if fated to receive the battle, became calm; and thus neither the blow of the warrior nor the stroke of the rower was impeded by the waves. Advancing nearer to each other, the trumpets sounded on both sides, and mingled their dread clangour. First they contended with missiles; but our men, seeking the aid of God, very earnestly plied their oars, and soon pierced the enemy's ships with the beaks of their own. Then the battle became general. The oars were entangled. The men fought hand to hand. They grappled the ships with alternate casts, and burnt the decks with the burning oil commonly called Greek fire. This fire, with a deadly stench and livid flames, consumes flint and iron, and, being unquenchable by water, can only be extinguished by sand or vinegar. What is more direful than a naval conflict? Where else does so various a fate involve the combatants? Either they are burnt or writhe in the flames, or they are wrecked and swallowed by the waves, or they are wounded and perish by arms! One galley there was that, through the rashness of its men, turned its side close to the enemy; and thus, ignited by the fire thrown on board, admitted the Turks, who rushed in on all parts. The rowers, seized with terror, leapt into the sea. None but a few soldiers, who, from the weight of their arms and their ignorance of swimming, were forced to remain, attempted to fight. By the Lord's help, however, the few overcame the many, and the half-burnt ship was retaken from the beaten foe. But another was boarded by the enemy, who had gained the upper deck, having driven off its defenders, and those could do nothing but try to escape by the aid of the rowers. A wonderful, truly, and a piteous struggle! The oars being plied partly by the

Richard's large fleet had the inglorious satisfaction of conquering a single Saracen vessel. This vessel, however, if the contemporary accounts are true, was of unparalleled size and strength: "a marvellous ship, than which, except Noah's ship, none greater was ever read of." She had three tall masts, and contained a vast number of soldiers and sailors—fifteen hundred, according to one historian; three thousand, according to another—going to the relief of Acre, with a large supply of wealth and ammunition; among the rest, a hundred camel-loads of arms, slings, darts, and arrows, a great quantity of Greek fire in bottles, and two hundred machines, known as serpents, for discharging flame and fire. King Richard, as soon as he came near enough to this sea-monster to discover her character, gave orders for her capture. But that was not easy. The English galleys sailed round and round the enemy, but could find no suitable point of attack, every part being most stoutly built, and carefully defended by fierce soldiers, whose darts, hurled from the high bulwarks, came with terrible effect upon the assailants down below. In vain

---

Turks and partly by the Christians, the galley was urged hither and thither. Yet here, also, our men prevailed; and the enemy, rowing above, were thrust off by the Christians, and made to yield. In this sea-fight the adverse side lost both a galley and a galliass, with their crews; while our men, unhurt and rejoicing, obtained a glorious success. Drawing the enemy's galley to shore, they left it to be destroyed by any who passed. Then our women seized and dragged the Turks by their hair, and beheaded them, treating them with every indignity, and savagely stabbing them; and the weaker their hands, so much the more protracted were the pains of death to the vanquished, for they cut off their heads, not with swords, but with knives."

certain skilful swimmers and divers made their way to the rudder and cables, and, by tying ropes to them, sought to make the great ship unmanageable. In vain certain brave warriors scaled the sides, and attempted to get possession of the decks by hand-to-hand combat. But at last King Richard hit upon the expedient of putting some scores of his galleys in orderly array, and causing them over and over again to row dead against the vessel, with their iron beaks pointed at her wooden sides. In that way a sufficient number of leaks were sprung to sink the clumsy enemy, and the English had just time to secure the treasures and capture as many Turks as they needed to employ in making and working the strange instruments, or were likely to turn to profit by retaining as prisoners to be ransomed, before they rowed away from the turmoil of waters that was caused by her sinking.*

Neither in sea-going nor in sea-fighting does Richard I.'s famous fleet appear in a very favourable light. But the English navy was then still in its infancy, and frequent work brought great increase of skill in the ensuing centuries. King John, praiseworthy for little else in English history, did good service by turning to account the enterprise occasioned by his brother's crusading zeal, itself necessarily short-lived, in establishing an efficient maritime force for fighting battles nearer home. He placed on an improved footing the old ar-

* GEOFFREY DE VINSAUF, lib. ii., cap. 41; RICHARD OF DEVIZES, sect. 49; ROGER OF WENDOVER (ed. 1849), vol. ii., p. 93; PETER OF LANGTOFT's *Chronicle*.

rangements for naval service from the Cinque Ports. He established a dockyard at Portsmouth, and set the fashion of using it for the construction of stout ships, exclusively the property of the Crown. He paid especial attention to the economical and satisfactory fitting-out of all ships intended for warlike purposes, saw that they were efficiently manned, and put wise and brave officers in charge of them.

The greatest of these officers was Hubert de Burgh, whom King John made Justiciary of England in 1215. He was also for many years Constable of Dover Castle. His best work was done under the ungracious rule of Henry III.'s governors. Hearing, in August, 1217, that a French fleet of eighty great ships, with a large number of galleys and smaller vessels, was on its way for the invasion of England, he promptly summoned a council to consider how the attack was to be resisted. "If these people land," he is reported to have said, "England is lost. Let us therefore boldly meet them, and God will be with us." The other members of the council were not so zealous. "We are not sea-soldiers, or pirates, or fishermen," they exclaimed; "go *thou* and die!" To do that for his country, if need were, De Burgh was resolved. Without an hour's delay he ordered out sixteen Cinque Ports' galleys, large and well manned, which happened to be then at Dover, with about twenty smaller ships, and placed himself at the head of the little armament. He met the invading fleet off the North Foreland, and, having the wind in his favour, suddenly bore down upon its rear, caused grapnels to be thrown into the ships that were first approached, and so made it impossible for them to escape. The French, disconcerted by this bold manœuvre, were soon overcome by the vigorous fighting of their opponents. The English sailors, having no arms to use, threw unslaked lime into the air, that it might be blown by the wind into the enemy's eyes, and thus might blind them. Others deftly cut the rigging and haulyards, and so caused the sails to fall down "like a net upon ensnared small birds." The cross-bowmen and archers plied their weapons with deadly effect; and before long more than half of the French ships were captured. Fifteen managed to escape, and about as many were sunk during the contest. By his promptitude and tact and valour, Hubert de Burgh secured a victory unparalleled in the previous naval history of England.*

It had many parallels, however, in the ensuing generations. The long and wasteful wars with France and Scotland, that lasted, with few intermissions, from Edward I.'s time down to Henry V.'s, afforded many opportunities for naval prowess, and resulted in the establishment, among all the European nations, of that reputation for good and brave seamanship which has been maintained by England down to the present day. The chief details of these engagements, and the general purport of the whole, are familiar matters of history, and therefore need not here be dwelt upon. So thoroughly were patriotic Englishmen, as early as

* MATTHEW PARIS, *Historia Major* (ed. 1644), p. 206; ROGER OF WENDOVER, vol. iv., p. 28.

the fifteenth century, impressed with the necessity of good seamanship to the well-being of the nation, that the prospect of naval degradation was regarded by them as the greatest of all impending evils. "Our enemies laugh at us," exclaimed one historian in 1441, when the disasters of the Wars of the Roses were beginning to be felt, "and say, 'Take the ship off from your precious money, and stamp a sheep upon it, showing thereby your own cowardice.' We, who used to be the conquerors of all nations, are now being conquered by all nations! The men of old used to call the sea 'the wall of England;' and what think you that our enemies, now that they are upon the wall, will do to the inhabitants who are not ready to meet them? Just because this matter has been so long neglected is it that our ships are already so scanty, our sailors few, and those few unskilled in seamanship from want of exercise. May the Lord take away this reproach and rouse a spirit of bravery in our nation!"*

In due time the spirit of bravery was revived, to be displayed, however, hardly any more in renewal of the ambitions projects for continental conquest in which the patriots of those times thought they saw the chief and best way of national aggrandisement, but generally in more peaceful and honourable ways. The warlike requirements of England continued to be, as they had been from the first, the leading motive to its naval advancement; but we shall see that, among the seamen of the Tudor period, fighting for fighting's sake was at any

* CAPGRAVE, *De Illustribus Henricis*.

rate only a secondary inducement, and that if fighting came it was mainly in consequence of the growth of maritime enterprise which has issued in the establishment of our vast colonial empire and the independent empires that have sprung and are springing therefrom all contributing in a very notable way to the growth in wealth and influence and character of England itself.*

* A very full and sufficient account of the earlier maritime progress of England, to which I am indebted for help in writing the foregoing pages, is to be found in the *History of the Royal Navy*, by SIR NICHOLAS HARRIS NICOLAS (1847), of which the only two volumes published treat of the period from Julius Cæsar's landing to the death of Henry V.

CHAPTER II.

The Voyages of the Cabots.

[1485—1517.]

THE traditions of English effort at maritime discovery before the time of Henry VII. are few and unimportant. For the fable about Saint Brendan, the holy Irish abbot, who in the sixth century is reported to have sailed out, with twelve chosen monks, into the unknown western sea, and, after long and tedious voyaging, to have reached a land of wondrous beauty and luxuriance, where the sun never set and winter never came;* and for the fable about Madoc, the Welsh chieftain, who in the twelfth century is said to have crossed the Atlantic and founded a Celtic colony somewhere south of the

---

* "So cler and so light hit was, that joye ther was ynough;
Treon [trees] ther wer ful of frut, wel thikke on everech bough;
Thikke hit was biset of treon, and the treon thicke bere;
Th' applen were ripe ynough, right as it harvest were.
Fourti dayes aboute this lond hi him wende [they travelled]:
Hi ne mighte fynd in non half of this lond non ende.
Hit was evere more dai; hi ne fonde nevere nyght:
Hi ne wende fynde in no stede so moch cler light.
The eir was evere in o [one] stat, nother hot ne cold.
Bote the joye that hi fonde ne mai nevere beo i told."

Saint Brendan, a Mediæval Legend of the Sea, ed. by WRIGHT (1844), for the Percy Society.

Missouri, there may have been some foundations in fact; and perhaps there is truth in the report that, near the middle of the fourteenth century, Madeira was discovered by a native of Gloucestershire named Macham.* But no authentic and persistent attempt at Atlantic voyaging and research was made until the marvellous accounts of Cathayan wealth and splendour, brought home by overland travellers in the east, stirred up the cupidity and the adventurous disposition first of Spaniards and Portuguese and then of Englishmen.

Cathay, or Khitai, is now known to have been a district to the north-east of China, peopled by an enterprising people who, alternately at feud and in alliance with the Tartars and the Chinese, were in due time the chief instruments of the Tartar conquest of the whole vast country. Some of them were Christians, and

* "About this time (1344) the island of Madeira was discovered by an Englishman, called Macham, who, sailing out of England into Spain, with a woman of his, was driven out of his direct course by a tempest, and arrived in that island, and cast his anchor in the haven which is now called Machin, after the name of Macham. And because his lover was then sea-sick, he there went on land with some of his company, and in the mean time his ship weighed and put to sea, leaving him there. Whereupon his lover, for thought, died. Macham, who greatly loved her, built in the island a chapel or hermitage to bury her in, calling it by the name of Jesus Chapel, and wrote or graved upon the stone of her tomb his name and hers, and the occasion whereupon they arrived there. After this he made himself a boat, all of a tree, the trees being there of a great compass about, and went to sea in it with those men of his company that were left with him, and fell in with the coast of Africa without sail or oar; and the Moors among whom he came took it for a miracle, and presented him unto the king of that country, and that king also admiring the accident, sent him and his company unto the king of Castille."—GALVANO, *Discoveries of the World*, ed. for the Hakluyt Society, by Vice-Admiral BETHUNE (1862), pp. 58, 59.

among them were a few Franciscan friars and missionaries, whose letters and personal reports to their friends at home, beginning about the middle of the thirteenth century, gave great incitement to the curiosity of other friars and travellers. "One day," says one them, Rubruquis, a Fleming, writing in 1255, "there sat with me a certain priest from Cathay, clothed in a crimson stuff of a splendid colour, so I asked him whence that colour was got. In reply he told me that in the eastern parts of Cathay there are lofty rocks inhabited by certain creatures which have the human form in every respect, except that they cannot bend their knees, but get along by some kind of a jumping motion. They are only a cubit high, and are hairy all over, and dwell in inaccessible holes in the rock. But the huntsmen bring beer with them, which they know how to brew very strong, and make holes in the rocks like cups, which they fill with beer. Then the huntsmen hide themselves, and the creatures come out of their holes and taste the drink that has been set for them, and call out 'Chin chin!'—and from this cry they get their name; for they are called Chinchin. Presently they gather in great numbers and drink up the beer, and get tipsy and fall asleep. So the huntsmen come and catch them sleeping, and bind them hand and foot, and open a vein in the neck of the creatures, and, after taking three or four drops of blood, let them go. And it is that blood, he assured me, that gives this most precious dye." That story, well fitted to arouse the interest of wonder-loving Europeans, the good friar evidently believed. Other tales, about which he himself was sceptical, found ready credence as they passed from mouth to ear among the people of the west. "They also used to tell as a fact, though I don't believe a word of it," he says, "that there is a certain province on the other side of Cathay, and, whatever a man's age be when he enters that province, he never gets any older."*

The friar's letter was written while Marco Polo was a young man, and it probably encouraged him to enter on his famous course of eastern travel. Marco Polo's reports about Cathay, the delight of mediæval readers and listeners, are tolerably well known. Quite as alluring were the statements of Friar Odoric, a Franciscan from Friuli, who visited Cathay and its neighbourhood near the year 1325. He was especially eloquent about Pekin, its walls and gates, its artificial lakes and gorgeous palaces. "The khan's own palace," he wrote, "is of vast size and splendour. There are four-and-twenty columns of gold, and all the walls are hung with skins of red leather, said to be the finest in the world. In the midst of the palace is a certain great jar, more than two paces in height, entirely formed of a certain precious stone, so fine that I was told its price exceeded the value of four great towns. It is all hooped round with gold, and this jar hath also fringes of network of great pearls hanging therefrom. Into this

* *Cathay and the Way Thither; being a Collection of Mediæval Notices of China*, translated and edited by Colonel HENRY YULE, C.B., for the Hakluyt Society (1866), vol. i. Every student of geographical history must be grateful to Colonel Yule for this entertaining and very learned work.

vessel drink is conveyed by certain conduits from the court of the palace, and beside it are many golden goblets from which all drink who list." Among much else, Odoric told how, in the khan's menagerie, were six horses with six legs apiece, four double-headed ostriches, giants twenty feet high, and dwarfs not two spans long, "not to mention the wild men who were in the lord's garden, and women all hairy with long grey hair, though of human form."*

The fabled marvels of Cathay were soon the talk of Europe, and many travellers were induced, as missionaries, or merchants, or pleasure-seekers, or all three combined, to follow in the steps of Marco Polo and Odoric. But these travellers went by land, until near the end of the fifteenth century, when Spain sent out its Christopher Columbus, and England its John Cabot.

Cabot, like Columbus, was an Italian by birth. He was a gold-spurred knight of Venice, who established himself, apparently while yet a young man, as a merchant in Bristol, then famous as the haunt of many of the most enterprising traders in England, with the venerable William Canynge at their head. At Bristol his youngest and most memorable son, Sebastian, was born in 1471 or 1472.† But early in 1476, John

---

* *Cathay and the Way Thither*, vol. i.

† The younger Cabot is generally said to have been a native of Venice, but this contemporary testimony appears decisive :—" Sebastian Cabott tould me that he was borne in Bristowe, and that at iiii yeare owld he was carried with his father to Venice, and so returned agayne into England with his father after certeyne yeares."—EDEN, *Decades of the New World* (1555), folio 255.

Cabot returned to Venice, and then, having been expatriated by his long absence, he was reinstated by the Senate in the rights of citizenship for a term of fifteen years.* It is probable that he spent the greater part of these fifteen years in Italy, carrying on his trading avocations, and entering heartily into the speculations which at that time were growing in the minds of bold and learned men as to the possibility of reaching the wonderful region of Cathay by sailing out into the western sea instead of travelling eastward by land. It is likely that he was personally acquainted with Columbus, who, through most of those years, was wandering about in Spain and Italy, seeking wearily for rich men's help towards fulfilment of the projects which were winning the approval of wise men too poor to give him substantial assistance.† Cabot, too, was a wanderer in the interests of science. We are told that he went to Seville and Lisbon, " asking assistance for his

* RAWDON BROWN, Calendar of State Papers and Manuscripts, relating to English Affairs, existing in the Archives and Collections of Venice and other Libraries of Northern Italy, vol. i. (1864), pp. 131, 136.

† It would be interesting to think, if the story could be relied upon, that nothing but an accident prevented England from having the glory of Columbus's, as well as of Cabot's, discoveries. It is reported that in 1489, despairing of the assistance he sought in Portugal and Spain, Columbus sent his brother Bartholomew to plead his cause before Henry VII. Bartholomew came to England, was liberally received by the King, and departed with an assurance of support, if Christopher would himself visit London and make arrangements for the work. But on his way home he was seized and robbed by pirates, and thus reduced to such poverty, that, for some years, he could do nothing but keep himself alive by chart-making. When he got back to Spain, he found that the discovery had already been made, under the auspices of Queen Isabella, and that his brother had actually embarked on a second voyage.—HAKLUYT, Voyages (1600), vol. iii., pp. 2, 3.

discoveries."* Failing in this, he returned to Bristol about the year 1490, and there his scheme for Atlantic voyaging found ready supporters. Throughout the remainder of Henry VII.'s reign Bristol was almost as famous a place of resort for English maritime adventurers as was Palos, under Ferdinand and Isabella, for Spanish seamen. " For the last seven years," wrote the Spanish ambassador in London to his sovereigns in 1498, " the people of Bristol have sent out every year two, three, or four light ships in search of the island of Brazil and the Seven Cities, according to the fancy of this Genoese,"—Genoese being written in error for Venetian.†

About the first outcome of John Cabot's fancy, occurring at least one or two years before Columbus's earliest voyage to the Indies, our only information is contained in a contemporary statement, that in 1480— clearly a wrong date—"a ship of John Jay the younger, of eight hundred tons, and another, began their voyage from King's Road to the island of Brazil, to the west of Ireland, ploughing their way through the sea, and that Thlyde, the most scientific mariner in all England, was the pilot of the ships. News came to Bristol," it is added, " that the said ships sailed about the sea during nine

---

* BERGENROTH, *Calendar of Letters, Despatches, and State Papers, relating to the Negotiations between England and Spain, preserved in the Archives of Simancas and elsewhere*, vol. i. (1862), p. 177.

† BERGENROTH, vol. i., p. 177. Brazil was one of the many names given to all or part of the vaguely-defined district generally known as Cathay, apparently from the red dye—afterwards found in the real Brazil—which, as we have seen, was one of the Cathayan marvels. The island of the Seven Cities was another of these names.

months, and did not find the island; but, driven by tempests, they returned to a port on the coast of Ireland, for the repose of themselves and their mariners."*
Of the later voyages, prior to 1497, we have no details at all, nor is it anywhere recorded that John Cabot personally shared in them. But it is clear that he was their chief instigator; and it is also clear that, though no land was reached, the Bristol explorers, by no means discouraged, only applied themselves with greater zest each year to their noble undertaking.

A chief motive to perseverance was in the report of Columbus's discoveries, "whereof," as Sebastian Cabot is said to have remarked many years later, " was great talk in all the Court of King Henry VII., insomuch that all men, with great admiration, affirmed it to be a thing more divine than human, to sail by the west into the east, by a way that was never known before."† This general interest in the subject induced John Cabot to plan a more systematic voyage of discovery than had yet been attempted. On the 5th of March, 1496, he obtained letters patent from Henry VII., empowering him and his three sons, Lewis, Sanchez, and Sebastian, with their heirs and deputies, to sail to all countries and in all seas, east, west, or north, under the banner of England, with five ships of whatever size and strength they chose, for the discovery of islands, regions, and provinces of heathens and infidels hitherto unknown to Christendom in any

* Cited by Lucas, *Secularia* (1862), p. 112.
† Hakluyt, vol. iii., p. 7.

part of the globe. This was to be done "at their own proper costs and charges;" but they were instructed to set up the English standard in all newly-found countries, and to subdue and possess them as lieutenants of the King. They were to have exclusive privileges of trade with the natives of these countries, and the King was to receive one-fifth of all their profits in return for the favours bestowed.*

This memorable expedition, second only in importance to that undertaken by Columbus four years and a half before, was not entered upon until the spring of 1497, and then it was in a more modest way than Henry's charter had sanctioned. In two stout ships, manned by three hundred of the ablest mariners that he could find, John Cabot and his sons—or, at any rate, his most famous son, Sebastian—sailed out of Bristol waters near the beginning of May. They went first to Iceland, whither Bristol merchants had been in the habit of sending ships for purposes of trade during the previous half-century or more. Sailing almost due west from Iceland, and apparently passing, without touching, the coast of Greenland, they reached the district now known as Labrador, but called by them and their successors New-found-land, on the 24th of June, 1497. It was at five o'clock in the morning that, from the prow of his ship, the *Matthew*, Cabot first saw the main land of America, just a year before Columbus, passing the West Indian islands, among which his two earlier voyages had been spent, first set eyes upon the

* RYMER, *Fœdera*, vol. xii. (1711), p. 595; HAKLUYT, vol. iii., p. 4.

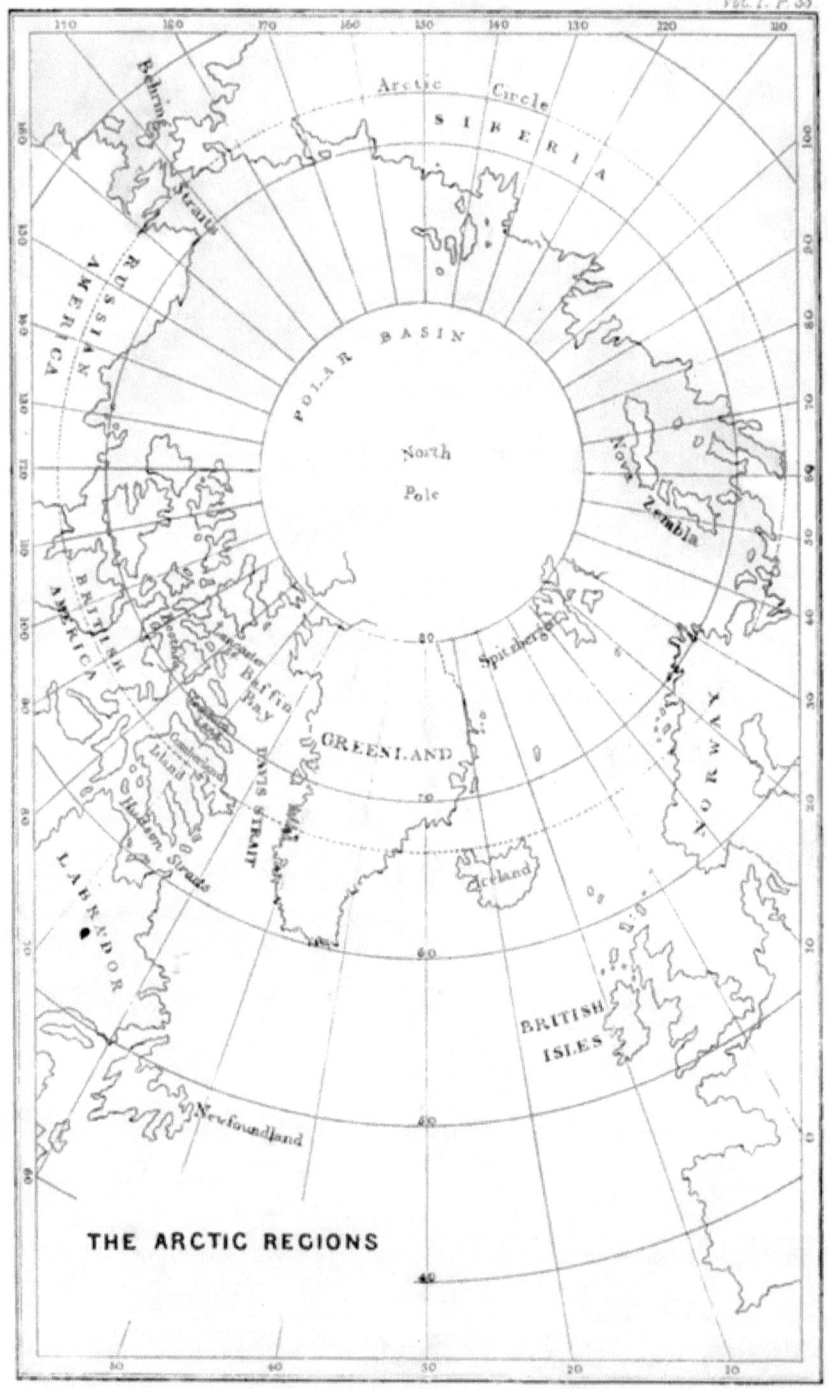

THE ARCTIC REGIONS

continent. The precise spot at which Cabot landed is not known, but it must have been very near to the Straits of Bellisle, as on the same day he also discovered the island of Newfoundland, to which he gave the name of Saint John, in honour of the saint on whose day the discovery was made.

At this island, finding it apparently more inviting than the opposite shore, which he supposed to be part of another and larger island, Cabot waited for a little while. No counterpart to the tropical beauty and wealth of gold, and pearls, and precious stones, which rewarded Columbus and his comrades for their daring enterprise, was seen by Cabot and his hardy followers. Instead, they found a bleak and rocky country, on which very few trees appeared to them to grow, and of which white bears and antelopes seemed to be the chief inhabitants. Some groups of men and women they saw, all clothed alike in the skins of beasts, and with little other furniture than the bows and arrows, pikes, darts, wooden clubs, and slings which helped them in their frequent quarrels with one another. Black hawks, black partridges, and black eagles, as they reported, were all the birds that they could find; and the place would have seemed to them altogether inhospitable but for its wonderful supply of cod and other fish. The abundance of cod, indeed, caused the island of Saint John to be also often styled by Spaniards and Portuguese the island of Baccalaos.

That is all we know of Cabot's observations in the southern portion of the lands that he discovered. We know still **less of his** impressions concerning the more northern coast of Labrador, which he skirted as he sailed onwards in search of **the** passage to Cathay. He seems nowhere else to have landed till, having passed the entrance of what is now termed Hudson's Straits, he reached a spot in Davis's Straits in $67\frac{1}{2}$ degrees of north latitude, which he called Desidea, or some English name signifying Sought-for **or** Desired, and whence, he assured himself, a little further voyaging would take him to the favoured **territory of the Great Khan.** But his sailors thought otherwise. **It was small comfort** to them that they were in a region where the clear daylight lasted eighteen hours, and the intervening six hours were twilight rather than proper night. The icebergs that they met at sea, and the snow-covered heights, which were all they could discern of the solid land, filled them with fear, and at last their discontent became so serious, that, to avoid open mutiny, Cabot was forced to abandon his project and turn towards home. He reached England early in August, having failed, as all his successors, during nearly three centuries, were to fail, in finding a northern passage to Cathay or the Indies; but having set an example, which all those successors followed with excellent effect, of the brave and hardy enterprise out of which the European peopling of the North American continent has resulted.*

* EDEN, *Decades of the New World* (translating from GOMARA), fol. 318; ANTONIO GALVANO, *Discoveries of the World*, ed. for the Hakluyt Society, by Vice-Admiral Bethune (1863), pp. 87—89; HAKLUYT, vol. iii., pp. 6—9; RAWDON BROWN, *Notices of John Cabot and his Son Sebastian* in the *Collections of the Philobiblon Society*, vol. ii. (1856);

He was received with great rejoicings. "They call him the Great Admiral," said an intelligent Venetian, resident in London, writing home to his brothers. "Vast honour is paid him, and he dresses in silk; and these English run after him like mad people, so that he can enlist as many of them as he pleases. The King has promised that in the spring he shall have ten ships, armed according to his fancy; and at his request he has conceded him all the prisoners, except such as are confined for high treason, to man them with. He has also given him money wherewith to amuse himself till then."* The amount of this money, certainly small enough, is shown in the record of Henry VII.'s privy purse expenses, where, under the date of the 10th of August, we read—"To hym that found the New Isle, 10*l*."†

King Henry, however, was generously disposed towards Cabot, and willing, for a time at any rate, to do much in furthering his enterprise. His promise of ten ships—one account says fifteen or twenty—was not fully kept; but on the 3rd of February following he granted him a tolerably liberal patent. This patent, issued in the name of John Cabot alone, without mention of his sons and their heirs, conveyed to him, as we

---

RAWDON BROWN, *Calendar*, vol. i., p. 260; BERGENROTH, vol. i., p. 177; with some other authorities cited by BIDDLE, *Memoir of Sebastian Cabot* (1831). In this learned book, Mr. Biddle has done much towards establishing a proper comprehension of Cabot history; but documents to which he had no access make it quite clear that John Cabot, and not his hero Sebastian, was the real father of North American discovery and colonization.

* *Collections of the Philobiblon Society.*
† NICOLAS, *Excerpta Historica*.

read, "sufficient authority and power that he, by him, his deputy and deputies, may take at his pleasure six English ships in any port or ports or other place within this our realm of England or obeisance, provided the said ships be of the burthen of two hundred tons or under, with their apparel requisite and necessary for the safe conduct of the said ships, and them convey and lead to the land and isles of late found by the said John, in our name and by our commandment." The document further sanctioned the employment of "all such masters, mariners, pages, and other subjects as, of their own free will, will go and pass with him in the same ships to the said land or isles, without any impediment, let, or perturbance of any of our officers, or masters, or subjects."* It is not clear whether Henry VII. did much more than lend his ships to Cabot, and give him authority for manning the five vessels of which the expedition was ultimately composed.† It is probable that most of the expense fell upon Cabot and his brother merchants of Bristol. In the enterprise we are told that "divers merchants of London adventured small stocks," and that with the larger vessels went "three or four small ships fraught with slight and gross wares,

---

* BIDDLE, pp. 76, 77. This document, found by Mr. Biddle among the National Records, is the most valuable of the contents of his volume.

† These entries are in the king's Privy Purse Book :—" March 22. To Lancelot Thirkill of London, upon a prest, for his shipp going towards the New Islands, 20l. Delivered to Launcelot Thirkill, going towards the New Isle, in prest, 20l. April 1. To Thos. Bradley and Lancelot Thirkill, going to the New Isle, 30l. To John Carter going to the Newe Isle, in rewarde, 2l."—NICOLAS, Excerpta Historica, pp. 116, 117.

as coarse cloth, caps, laces, points, and such other."*
For these commodities it was thought that a ready
market would be found in rich Cathay.

It is probable that John Cabot took no part in this
second expedition. He is supposed to have died at
Bristol early in 1498, and to have been succeeded in the
command by his son Sebastian, then about twenty-six
years old. Of the issue of the voyage we know nothing
save that the younger Cabot sailed as far north as he
was able, and then, driven back, as his father had been,
by frost and icebergs, turned southwards and explored
the coast of America as far as the neighbourhood of
what is now Chesapeake Bay, then part of Florida.†

That it was not very successful may be inferred
from the statement that though, soon after his return, Sebastian Cabot made fresh proposals " for discovering new countries," they " had no great or favourable entertainment of the King."‡ Henry seems to
have despaired of reaching Cathay by a northern route,

---

* Stow, *Annals* (1605), p. 804. The original of this statement is among the *British Museum MSS. Cotton*, Vitellius, A. xvi., fol. 173.

† Eden, fol. 318; Galvano, p. 89. One of the ships, "in which one Friar Buil went," returned to Ireland in great distress early in July. The Spanish ambassador, who gives this information in a letter to his sovereigns, Ferdinand and Isabella, adds : " I have seen, on a chart, the direction which they took and the distance they sailed, and I think that what they found, or what they are in search of, is what your Highnesses are already possessed of. I write this, because the King of England has often spoken to me on the subject, and he thinks your Highnesses will take great interest in it. I told him that, in my opinion, the land was already in possession of your Majesties; but, though I gave him my reasons, he did not like them."—Bergenroth, vol. i., p. 177.

‡ Seyer, *Memoirs of Bristol* (1821), vol. ii., p. 208—citing a contemporary record of the city.

and he had no inclination to be brought into a quarrel with the Spanish sovereigns by trespassing on the more southern territories which, by the unquestionable verdict of the Pope, were their exclusive property.

Sebastian Cabot, however, inheriting all his father's zeal for maritime research, did not abandon the work. In 1499, we are told, "with no extraordinary preparation, he set forth from Bristol, and made great discoveries."*

As to the nature of those discoveries we are altogether ignorant. It is very much to be regretted that the memoirs and descriptions of his and his father's voyages which Sebastian Cabot carefully prepared, and which existed in London nearly a hundred years later,† have all been lost. Had they survived, we might have had a record as full and interesting as that detailing the work of Columbus and his followers, of enterprises quite as daring, and eventually quite as important in their consequences as anything in the brilliant and affecting history of Spanish voyaging to the West Indies and the neighbouring districts of South and North America. As it is, all our information has to be derived from a few bald entries in state papers and official account books, a few chance letters and contemporary anecdotes, and a few meagre and often contradictory reports of statements made by the younger Cabot and his comrades

---

* SEYER, *Memoirs of Bristol* (1821), vol. ii., p. 208.

† HAKLUYT, *Divers Voyages touching the Discovery of America*, first published in 1582 (Hakluyt Society), p. 26. Much of the information before cited from Hakluyt occurs in this earlier work; but I have referred to the later publication as one more generally accessible.

many years after the occurrences to which they refer.

From these stray records it would appear that, though there was no fruitful English colonization of Labrador and its neighbourhood akin to the Spanish colonization of the West Indies and the adjoining mainland, several smaller expeditions, led by Sebastian Cabot and other adventurous merchants of Bristol, succeeded the more famous voyages of 1497 and 1498; and that in these was attempted, not only the further exploration of the districts, but also some sort of English settlement upon them. On the 19th of March, 1501, for instance, letters patent were granted by King Henry to three men of Bristol, named Richard Warde, Thomas Ashehurst, and John Thomas, and to three Portuguese associated with them, empowering them, at their own expense, to discover, take possession of, and trade with any islands, countries, regions, and provinces, in the eastern, western, northern, or southern seas, which were not yet known to Christendom;[*] and a similar patent, granted on the 9th of December, 1502, to Thomas Ashehurst, Hugh Eliot, and two of the Portuguese adventurers,[†] shows that their general authority to sail all over the world was used in furtherance of the explorations already made in the region of Labrador. Under date of the 7th of January, 1502, are two entries in the King's account book, showing that a sum of 5*l*. was given "to men of Bristol that found the Isle," and another sum of 20*l*. "to the merchants of Bristol that have been in

[*] BIDDLE, pp. 226, 227, 312.   [†] RYMER, vol. xiii., p. 37.

the New-found-land."* "This year also," says an old chronicler, "were brought unto the King three men taken in the New-found-island. These were clothed in beasts' skins, and ate raw flesh and spake such speech that no man could understand them, and in their demeanour like to brute beasts, whom the King kept a time after. Of the which, upon two years past after, I saw two, apparelled after the manner of Englishmen, in Westminster Palace, which at the time I could not discern from Englishmen, till I was learned what they were; but as for speech, I heard none of them utter one word." †

North American Indians were not the only curiosities imported by the Bristol merchants. On the 17th of November, 1503, the King's privy purse was charged with 1*l*., paid "to one that brought hawks from the New-found-island," and in August, 1505, it is recorded that "wild cats and popinjays of the New-found-islands" were conveyed to the King's palace at Richmond, at a cost of 13*s*. 4*d*.‡

---

* BIDDLE, p. 230. † STOW.
‡ BIDDLE, p. 234. In *The Four Elements*, a philosophical poem, printed in London in 1519, and lately brought to light by Mr. COLLIER, there is this allusion to the Atlantic Ocean:—

"This sea is called the Great Ocean;
So great it is that never man
Could tell it sith the world began,
 Till now within this twenty year
Westward be found new landes
That we never heard tell of before this,
By writingë nor other meanës;
 Yet many nowë have been there.

There is nothing to show that Sebastian Cabot had anything to do with these later enterprises of Henry VII.'s reign, and, if he was ever personally engaged in Bristol commerce, he appears to have abandoned it at an early age, in order that he might apply himself exclusively to geographical studies and pursuits connected with maritime discovery. We may guess something of his occupations from another account-book entry, coming after a dozen years of entire silence concerning him, to the effect that, in May, 1512, he received 20s. from Henry VIII.'s exchequer, for making a chart of Gascony and Guienne.*

That was not exactly the sort of work on which his heart was set. Therefore, having some ground for discontentment at the way in which, of late years, Henry VII. had treated him, and receiving even less sympathy in his daring projects from Henry VIII., he was willing to turn elsewhere for employment. This

> And that country is so large of room,
> Much longer than all Christendom,
>   Without fable or guile;
> For divers mariners have it tried
> And sailed straight by the coastë-side
>   Above five thousand mile . . . . .
> And also what an honourable thing
> Both to the realm and to the King
> To have had his dominion extending
>   There into so far a ground
> Which the noble King of late memory,
> The most wise prince, the Seventh Harry,
>   Caused first for to be found."

* BREWER, *Letters and Papers, Foreign and Domestic, of the Reign of Henry VIII., preserved in the Public Record Office, the British Museum, and Elsewhere in England*, vol. i. (1862), p. 1456.

was offered him, in the summer of 1512, by King Ferdinand of Spain. The Spanish monarch, more zealous than his English allies in the work of American discovery, and long before jealous of the services which Cabot had proposed to render to them, took advantage of the presence of Lord Willoughby, who went to him as ambassador from England in 1511, and asked him to send the great voyager to Seville, " which," says the sarcastic historian, " he did as a thing of little moment."*

Cabot arrived in Spain in September, 1512. He was at once made a captain and a member of the Council of the New Indies, provided with a liberal allowance, and ordered to reside in Seville, there to be in readiness for any work that might be assigned to him.† In Seville, Peter Martyr made his acquaintance. " Cabot is my very friend," he said, " whom I use familiarly, and delight to have him sometimes keep me company in my own house."‡

During this first term of Spanish service, however, Cabot was only employed as a map-maker and stay-at-home adviser in maritime affairs. After three years' waiting, he was instructed to make preparations for a voyage of discovery; but before the arrangements were completed, in January, 1516, Ferdinand died, and the jealous conduct of Cardinal Ximenes, as Regent, caused a further delay, and led to Cabot's return to England towards the close of the year. Here he repeated his

---

* CARDENAS, *Ensaio Cronologico para la Historia General de Florida*, (1723), cited by BIDDLE, p. 100.

† HERRERA, dec. i., lib. ix., cap. xiii.

‡ Dec. iii., cap. vi., translated by EDEN, fol. 119.

arguments for a voyage of north-western discovery, and with so much success that, in 1517, an expedition was fitted out by Henry VIII., and intrusted to him and Sir Thomas Spert,* with the object of "going in the back-side of the New-found-land, until they came to the back-side and south seas of the Indies Occidental, and so, continuing their voyage, to return through the Straits of Magellan."† Of the details of this bold undertaking we know even less than of its forerunners. It failed perforce, and Cabot's friends complained that "Sir Thomas Spert's faint heart was the cause that it took none effect."‡ But no one need be blamed for failure in an enterprise which, a thousand times attempted, was a thousand times unfortunate so far as the finding of a north-west passage was concerned, during nearly a dozen generations.

With the exception of one other voyage, which will be noticed hereafter, that was the only attempt made by Henry VIII. in quest of a route to Cathay or any of the real sources of wealth that became objects of pursuit after the Cathayan fable had been discarded. Cabot at once returned to Spain, and he was in Spanish service for thirty years ensuing.§ In 1518, he was

---

* He is everywhere called, by old and new historians, Sir Thomas Pert; but this is evidently an error. Spert was for some time captain of the *Great Harry*, and a useful servant of Henry VIII.

† A letter of Robert Thorne, the younger, in HAKLUYT, vol. i., p. 212.

‡ EDEN, Dedication to *A Treatyse of Newe India* (1553).

§ "Some three years ago," Cabot is reported to have said in conversation with the Venetian ambassador at Seville, on Christmas Eve, 1522, "when I was in England, Cardinal Wolsey offered me high terms if I would sail with an armada of discovery. The vessels were almost ready,

made pilot major of Spain,* and eight years were passed by him in miscellaneous employments and irksome idleness at home, from which, however, there was an excellent result in his discovery, in 1522, of the variation of the needle.† At the end of the eight years, in 1526, he was appointed to the command of an expedition, consisting of three ships and a caravel, for exploration in the southern continent of America. He visited the river and adjoining district of La Plata, and went to San Salvador, where he erected a fort; he ascended the Parana and entered Paraguay, spending more than two years in laying solid foundations for the Spanish conquest of South America. About this undertaking, unlike all the others in which Cabot was engaged, full information is on record.‡ But it had nothing to do with England or with any voyages of discovery in which England was concerned, and therefore need not here be dwelt upon.

At the time of his return to Spain, in 1531, Sebastian

---

and they had got together 30,000 ducats for their outfit. I answered him that, being in the service of Spain, I could go nowhere without the Emperor's leave; but that, if free permission were conceded to me from hence, I would serve him." He adds, "I wrote to the Emperor by no means to give me leave to serve the King of England, as he would injure himself extremely; and that, on the contrary, he should recal me forthwith."—RAWDON BROWN, *Notices of John and Sebastian Cabot*, pp. 15, 16. I can find no other allusion to this project, and think it likely that Cabot, either in vanity or in ignorance, greatly exaggerated the purport of a chance conversation with Wolsey. Nothing came of it, at any rate.

* HERRERA, dec. ii., lib. iii., cap. vii.
† RAWDON BROWN, *Notices*, p. 20.
‡ See a detailed account of it in BIDDLE, pp. 121—168.

Cabot was about fifty-five years old. He appears to have been personally employed in no later enterprise for the finding of new lands on the other side of the Atlantic. But his zeal in the work lasted for upwards of twenty years more. In 1548 he came back to England, to receive a pension from King Edward VI., and to give his sanction and encouragement to a very memorable undertaking which will have in due time to be described.

CHAPTER III.

Henry the Eighth's Navy.

[1511—1546.]

For nothing are Henry VIII. and his great counsellors, with Cardinal Wolsey at their head, more highly to be praised than for the zeal and wisdom with which they sought to augment the naval strength of England, and, by means of that naval strength, to improve the position and influence of their country among the other states of Europe. The extreme importance of an efficient navy, as we have seen, had been discovered by some of the Plantagenets, especially by Edward III. and Henry V. Henry VII., also, had done much towards laying the foundations of English maritime power. In the first year of his reign the attention of Parliament had been called to " the great minishment and decay of the navy and the idleness of the mariners," whereby it was feared that the whole nation would be ruined; and, in accordance with the rude political economy of Tudor times, a law had been straightway passed prohibiting the importation of Gascon and Guienne wines, then an important branch of English commerce, in any but English,

Welsh, and Irish ships, manned with native sailors.* This Act had been renewed and amplified four years later, and many other efforts had been made, during the four-and-twenty years in which Henry VII. was King, to promote the growth of shipping, both for warlike and for peaceful purposes. To that end the voyages of the Cabots and their associates had been encouraged, so long as there seemed a likelihood of their producing any advantage to the nation. To the same end some war ships, of famous size and strength, according to the poor standard of the times, had been constructed by the Crown; the chief of which, the *Henry Grace à Dieu*, a clumsy hulk containing five masts overloaded with rigging, so narrow and so high, especially in the rear, as to be in great danger of capsizing, and only able to move with any precision when it was following the wind, cost upwards of 14,000*l.* in the building.†

But these were only the rough beginnings of a work which was fairly inaugurated under the rule of Henry VIII. The new King saw, as clearly as his father had done, the necessity of increasing the influence of England among the nations of Europe, and he wisely held that an essential means towards this object was in the extension of English power at sea. Other states, in times when Europe still comprised nearly the whole of the known world of civilization, might do without navies; but, if England was to be anything more than

* *Acts of Parliament*, 1 Henry VII., cap. 8.
† Charnock, *History of Marine Architecture* (1801), vol. ii., pp. 28—31.

a self-contained island, was to have any considerable share in the general progress of Christendom, it must be to a great extent through the agency of a well-constructed, well-sustained, and well-manned fleet. So it appeared to Henry VIII.; and his two greatest advisers, Cardinal Wolsey and Thomas Howard, Duke of Norfolk, forgot their jealousies in furtherance of the same prudent thought. Wolsey worked chiefly in seeing to the proper building, manning, and victualling of ships. The Duke of Norfolk's principal service was in sending his two eldest sons to be the first and worthiest of the earlier Tudor admirals.

The Howards, famous for their association with every other important office of state, had already been connected with the history of English seamanship. Sir John Howard, son of the Sir William Howard who made the family illustrious by his service as Chief Justice of the Common Pleas under Edward III., was made Admiral of the King's northern fleet in 1335; and another Sir John Howard, after distinguishing himself as a land soldier in the French wars of Henry VI.'s reign, was made Captain-General of the navy by Edward IV. in 1462, and again in 1470. He had not much naval work to do, but in military and official ways he was very serviceable both to Edward IV. and to Richard III., one reward for his devotion being his elevation by the latter monarch, in 1483, to the Dukedom of Norfolk. He was slain at the battle of Bosworth, and his son, Thomas, Earl of Surrey, was, on Henry VII.'s accession, attainted for his devotion to the Yorkist party. The King, however, soon had ample evidence of the earl's ability and trustworthiness. We are told that he used to visit him and treat him as a friend even during his captivity in the Tower. The captivity was not long. In 1489 Thomas Howard was reinstated in his earldom and the possessions attached to it, and in succeeding years he was endowed with numerous important offices under the Crown. Henry VII. made him Lord Treasurer of England, and by Henry VIII. he was appointed Earl Marshal in 1510. In 1514, for his victory over James IV. of Scotland at Flodden Field he was created Duke of Norfolk.*

His eldest son was Lord Thomas Howard, born about the year 1474, who, in succession to his father, became Earl of Surrey in 1514 and third Duke of Norfolk in 1524. More famous was the second son, Sir Edward Howard, whose early death, it is probable, alone prevented him from succeeding Cardinal Wolsey to the foremost place in England during the latter half of Henry VIII.'s reign.

His public life began in 1492, when he was only sixteen or seventeen years old. In that year Henry VII. sent a little expedition of twelve ships, under the direction of Sir Edward Poynings, to punish Baron de Ravenstein and his freebooting auxiliaries, for the systematic piracies by which they did much harm, not only to the German government, whose allegiance they had thrown off, but also to all the nations trading with Flanders, and most of all to England, seeing that

* COLLINS, *Peerage*, vol. i., pp. 53, 54, 55, &c.

the English merchants then used Antwerp as a chief mart for traffic with nearly all the continental towns. Ravenstein had taken possession of the town and harbour of Sluys, fortified by two strong castles, and Poynings was sent to attack the city by sea, while the Duke of Saxony and a German army besieged it by land. For twenty days successively the ships made the best assaults in their power, and at last, though more through the accidental burning of a bridge between the two castles, than through the successful fighting of either the army or the fleet, the little nest of pirates was destroyed. For his prowess in this his first employment on naval work, young Edward Howard was highly praised.* In 1497 he was knighted for his brave deportment on land, while attending his father on an expedition to Scotland;† and in later years he was employed, and always successfully, in various minor services to Henry VII. Henry VIII., on his accession in 1509, made him Royal Standard-Bearer of England.‡

Our earliest information concerning his elder brother Thomas is that, in 1510, either in reward for some unrecorded service, or as a compliment to the famous house of Howard, he was installed as a Knight of the Garter.§ In the following year some memorable employment was found for both brothers in the capture of Andrew Barton, the great Scottish merchant and pirate, scion of

---

* HALL, *Union of the Two Noble Illustrious Families of Lancaster and York* (1548), sub *Henry* VII., fols. 17, 22b.
♦ COLLINS, vol. i., p. 80. ‡ RYMER, vol. xiii., p. 251.
§ ANSTIS, *Register of the Garter*, vol. i., p. 273.

a family which by help of merchandize and piracy attained high rank in Scotland under James IV. and James V. In 1476 a trading ship and its costly cargo, belonging to John Barton, Andrew's father, had been seized by a Portuguese squadron, and the letters of reprisal granted to him in consequence became, according to the rough usage of that period, an authority for unlimited piracy during the next thirty or forty years. The younger Bartons, Andrew, John, and Robert, prospered by it. They and Sir Andrew Wood were James IV.'s chief advisers and most zealous agents in all the maritime achievements and attempts for which this monarch's reign is memorable. The *Great Michael*, as famous for its size and worthlessness in the sixteenth century as is the *Great Eastern* in our own times, was built and sent to sea, at a cost of 30,000*l.*, under their joint direction.* It was in one of Robert Barton's ships, that, in 1497, Perkin Warbeck was sent to trouble

---

* "This ship was of so great stature and took so much timber that, except Falkland, she wasted all the woods in Fife, which were oak wood, with all timber that was gotten out of Norway; for she was so strong, and of so great length and breadth, all the wrights of Scotland, yea and many strangers, were at her device by the King's command. She was twelve score foot of length and thirty-six foot within the sides. She was ten foot thick in the walls and boards on every side, so slack and so thick that no cannon could go through her. This great ship cumbered Scotland to get her to sea. She bare many cannon, six on every side, with three great basils, two behind in her dock and one before, with three hundred shot of small artillery, to wit, falcons, slings, pestilent serpents and double dogs, with culverins, cross-bows and hand-bows. She had three hundred mariners to sail her. She had six score of gunners to use her artillery, and had a thousand men of war by her, captains, skippers, and quartermasters."—PINKERTON, *History of Scotland*, vol. ii., p. 68.

England with his pretended right of royalty; and in 1504 John Barton was despatched, at the head of a strong fleet, to bring the people of the western isles under subjection to the Crown of Scotland. Meanwhile the old Portuguese grievance was not forgotten. In 1507 fresh letters of marque were issued to the three brothers, authorizing them to scour the seas and spoil or capture any Portuguese vessels they might meet with, until they had seized property to the value of twelve thousand ducats, the supposed amount of old John Barton's loss some thirty years before. The Scottish pirates, however, were not altogether successful. Towards the end of the same year, Robert Barton was caught by the Portuguese at Campvere, in Zealand, and there detained for some years under the instructions of Margaret of Savoy. Therefrom arose much controversy between James IV. and Margaret, and so much fresh privateering on the part of the Bartons that they became pests to the ships of every nation trading along the western coast of Europe.*

In this way it happened that, in June, 1511, while Henry VIII. was keeping Court at Lincoln, formal complaint was made to him on behalf of his trading subjects, that Andrew Barton, under pretence of war with Portugal, " did rob every nation and so stopped the King's channel that no merchant almost could pass." Henry does not seem to have paid much attention to

* TYTLER, *History of Scotland* (1845), vol. iii., p. 485; vol. iv., pp. 22, 42, 51, 52. BREWER, *Letters and Papers, Foreign and Domestic, of the Reign of Henry* VIII., vol. i. (1862), pp. 128, 185, 388.

the report; but it so roused the anger of the Earl of Surrey that he vowed "the narrow seas should not be thus infested whilst he had an estate that could furnish a ship, or a son who was able to command it." And he so far kept his oath that he promptly fitted out two sturdy vessels, and, placing them under the command of his sons, Lord Thomas Howard and Sir Edward Howard, sent them in chase of the two ships, the *Lion* and the *Jenny Pirwin*, with which Andrew Barton was scouring the seas.*

The brothers sailed along the Downs together, and without finding the pirates, for some days. Then a storm arose, which separated them, and brought them into collision with the objects of their pursuit. Lord Thomas Howard fell in with the *Lion*, in which Barton was making his way with a rich load of booty to Scotland. He gave him chase and soon overtook him. "There was sore battle," says the old chronicler. "The Englishmen were fierce and the Scots defended themselves manfully, and ever Andrew blew his whistle to encourage his men, yet for all that, the Lord Howard and his men by clear force entered the main deck. Then the English entered on all sides, and the Scots fought sore on the hatches; but, in conclusion, Andrew was taken, being so sore wounded that he died there, and then all the remnant of the Scots were taken with their ship." Like good fortune attended Sir Edward Howard. Meeting with the *Jenny Pirwin*, he soon

---

* HALL, *Henry* VIII., fol. 15; CAMPBELL, *Lives of the Admirals* (1779), vol. ii., pp. 285, 286; TYTLER, vol. iv., p. 56.

boarded her, and then without delay "slew many and took all the rest."*

Independent fights with pirates were of frequent occurrence; but the fame both of Andrew Barton and of the Howards made this undertaking very memorable in its results. The ships and prisoners having been taken to Blackwall on the 2nd of August, 1511, the Scotsmen were promptly brought to trial. They acknowledged their offences, sued for mercy, and, after a few years' captivity, were sent home with an admonition to lead honester lives in future.† But James IV. was not pleased at the loss of Andrew Barton and the ships. Both he and his ally, King John of Denmark, made many angry demands for reparation; to which Henry bluntly answered that Barton had been rightly handled for his "robberies and cruel dealings," and that "it became not a prince to charge his confederates with breach of peace for doing justice upon a pirate and a thief."‡

This quarrel helped to bring about fresh war with Scotland and with Scotland's French allies; and out of it came employment both to Lord Thomas and to Sir Edward Howard, and much honour to the youngest brother at any rate.

Both were provided with important work. In May, 1512, Lord Thomas was appointed second in command, under the Marquis of Dorset, of ten thousand men, whom

* HALL, fol. 15; HOLLINSHED, vol. iii., p. 565; PINKERTON, vol. ii., pp. 69—71.
† LORD HERBERT, *Life of Henry* VIII., p. 7.
‡ BREWER, vol. i., pp. 347, 388, 467, 485; PINKERTON, vol. ii., p. 71.

Henry sent to Biscay, there to aid King Ferdinand of Spain in his war with France. The expedition was altogether unfortunate. Insubordination broke out on the voyage, when the sailors plundered the sea-sick soldiers; and the commanders were unable to establish discipline among the raw recruits, who, landing in Spain on the 7th of June, found no provision made for their maintenance. They were left to sleep in the open fields or to seek shelter from the rain by crouching under bushes.* There was no proper supply of food for them. "For the most part," it was reported, "they were victualled with garlic and drank hot wines and ate hot fruits, which procured their blood to boil in their bodies, whereby there fell sick and died more than eighteen hundred persons."† "An it please your Grace," wrote the English commissioner to Cardinal Wolsey, "the greatest lack of victuals that is here is of beer; for your subjects had liever for to drink beer than wine or cider, for the hot wines doth harm them, and the cider doth cast them in disease and sickness."‡ Those who remained alive became every day more mutinous. Had Ferdinand been willing to employ them at once in fighting against France, they would have been glad enough; but just then he was trying, in crooked ways, to gain his ends without fighting; and his English auxiliaries were left to die on the shores of Biscay.

At length the Marquis of Dorset fell ill, and Lord Thomas Howard was left in charge of the forces.

---

* BREWER, vol. i., pp. 362, 375. † STOW, p. 491.
‡ BREWER, vol. i., p. 397.

Without waiting for instructions from his master, he sent to Ferdinand to ask whether the English were to be employed upon the work for which they had been sent out. The Spanish King replied that there was no fighting then to be done, but if they would wait till next spring they should have plenty of it. To this Howard sent an indignant answer. "What report of honour," he said, "can we make of the King of Arragon? For at his desire we be come hither, and here we have lain in camp a long space, ever tarrying for the performance of his promise, and yet nothing hath he performed. Our people be dead in great number, and each one of us doth much lament that long idleness, by reason whereof many a tall man, having nothing to do but abide your master's pleasure, hath fallen into some mischief. What shall the King our master report of our slothfulness, which hath spent him innumerable treasure, and nothing gained?"* Having thus expressed himself to Ferdinand's agent, he called a council of his officers, and asked them what was to be done. For himself, he said, "in case he might have a meetly company with him, he would endeavour this winter war, and gladlier would he die for the honour of his master, the realm, and himself, than, contrary to the King's commandment, with rebuke and shame return to England."† But officers and men alike refused to stay any longer in Spain. They declared that they would return to England at all hazards, and this they did early in October, very greatly

* HALL, fol. 18. † BREWER, vol. i., p. 422.

to the anger of King Henry, and much to the amazement of all Christendom. "Englishmen have so long abstained from war," said the Emperor Maximilian and his daughter Margaret to Henry's ambassador, "that they lack experience from disuse, and are sick of it already."*

In contradiction of that taunt, and with the view of saving England from the repetition of such a sore disgrace, Henry VIII. and Cardinal Wolsey set themselves to augment and organize the warlike strength of the country; and they saw that if this was to be done by improving the art of soldiership, a much more necessary work was the advancement of its power at sea. The work, indeed, had been begun before its importance had been proved by the disaster in Spain. On the 7th of April, 1512, Sir Edward Howard, then about thirty-six years old, was appointed Admiral of the Fleet and Captain of the Army at Sea, his primary duty being the convoying of the Marquis of Dorset and his ten thousand men to the Spanish coast. The fleet comprised eighteen ships, of which the two largest were the *Regent*, of 1,000 tons burthen, and the *Mary Rose*, carrying 500 tons. The burthen of all the eighteen amounted to 4,750 tons, and there were 3,700 sailors, soldiers, and gunners on board.†

With this force, by no means inconsiderable three centuries and a half ago, though no more than a single modern man-of-war could easily disable, Sir Edward

---

* BREWER, vol. i., p. 427.

† RYMER, vol. xiii., p. 326. Sir Edward Howard's pay was 10s. a day; that of his captains, 1s. 6d. apiece; the common men had 5s. a month in wages, and an allowance of 5s. more for victuals.

Howard quitted the Solent on the 3rd of June, 1512.*
Having escorted the little army to Biscay, he proceeded
to the western coast of Brittany. There, on several
occasions, he landed and scoured the country a little to
the south of Brest. "Alas!" exclaimed the country
people, "the King of England hath ever before suc-
coured us, and now he intendeth to destroy us." At
one time, it is reported, the governors of the district
sent to beg him to desist from these sudden attacks,
and meet them in open fight. "Go say to them that
sent thee," answered Sir Edward Howard to the messenger, "that all this day they shall find me here
tarrying their coming." Accordingly, in the afternoon
about ten thousand Breton soldiers made their appearance; but no sooner were they face to face with the
two thousand five hundred Englishmen, than they
took to their heels and ran all the way to Brest; "and
when they came to their homes," adds the chronicler,
"some said the battle was great, some said the
Englishmen were forty thousand." Then the governors begged him to dictate terms of peace.
"Nay," replied Howard, "we are sent hither to make
war, not peace." And he continued his rough usage
until he thought the inhabitants were sufficiently reduced for the fame of their misfortunes to rouse the
French authorities to formidable resistance and to the
preparation of a strong fleet with which to meet him.
This being done, on his hearing that a goodly body of
ships was on its way to Brest, he returned to the Isle

* BREWER, vol. i., p. 362.

of Wight to make **ready for some bolder and more dignified fighting.***

This occurred in the following August, when **Sir Edward Howard**, with a fleet of **five-and-twenty ships**, returned to the neighbourhood of Brest, where he had heard that a French fleet of thirty-nine **sail**, commanded by an officer named Primauget or Porsmoguer, but known to the English as Pierce Morgan, **was waiting** to receive him. The enemies met on **the 11th of August** off St. Mahé. "When the **Englishmen** perceived the French navy to be **out of Brest**," says the old historian, "then the **Lord Admiral was very joyous**, then every man **prepared according** to his duty, the archers to shoot, the gunners **to loose, the men of arms to fight**. Thus, all things being provided and set in order, the **Englishmen approached towards the Frenchmen**, which came fiercely forward, some levying his anchor, some with his foresail only, to take the most advantage; and when they were in sight, they shot ordnance **so terribly together that all the sea coast sounded of it**." The battle, so eagerly desired by both parties, very soon became general. The *Sovereign*, which was the second ship in the English fleet, gave chase **to the** *Cordelier*, the largest of the French vessels, and, according to the French account, nearly twice the size **of the** *Regent*. The *Sovereign* was repulsed; and then the *Regent* took her place. Thereupon ensued a

---

* HALL, fol. 20. There is evidently some confusion in Hall's chronology, which refers this expedition to the precise time in which Sir Edward Howard was proceeding to Spain.

deadly contest. Sir Thomas Knyvet, who was in charge of the *Regent*, succeeded in grappling the French vessel, and, after much fierce struggling, in boarding her. "The archers of the English part and the cross-bows of the French part did their uttermost." Finally the French were fairly beaten; but just then, either through accident or treachery, a fire broke out in the *Cordelier*, which spread to the *Regent* before the grappling-irons could be removed; and thus both ships, the pride of England and the pride of France, were utterly destroyed, with nearly all the men on board. By this terrible mischance the fighting was stayed. The remaining French ships hurried back to Brest, and the English, we are told, "were so amazed that they followed them not." The amazement, however, soon turned to anger. "Sir Edward hath made his vow to God," wrote Wolsey to Fox, Bishop of Winchester, "that he will never see the King in the face till he hath revenged the death of the noble and valiant Sir Thomas Knyvet." He took his revenge by scouring the seas and capturing and burning a great many ships along the coasts of Brittany, Picardy, and Normandy; "and thus they kept the sea."*

While this irregular fighting continued, and during the ensuing months, Henry VIII. and his counsellors set themselves heartily to the procurement of some better way of keeping the sea. The summer of 1512, indeed, was a memorable epoch in the history of the

---

* British Museum, *Cottonian MSS.* Titus B. I., p. 99, containing Wolsey's letter to Fox; HALL, fols. 21, 22; GRAFTON, p. 970.

British navy and of English shipbuilding. The desire of prosecuting the war with France, and of repairing the injury done to the national credit by the mutinous return of the Marquis of Dorset's little army from Spain, gave a great impulse to the work. All through the year England was full of preparations for further and more zealous fighting, and most energetic of all were the plans for building, manning, and fitting out more efficient vessels of war and transports. Wolsey was supposed to be the great promoter of the contest with France; he was certainly the life and soul of the arrangements for bringing it to a successful issue. Hitherto a mere churchman who had begun to dabble in statesmanship, he suddenly appears as the foremost mover in all the administrative work of England. "He it is who determines the sums of money needful for the expedition, the line of march, the number and arrangement of the troops, even to the fashion of their armour and the barding of their horses. He it is who superintends the infinite details consequent on the shipment of a large army. He corresponds about the victualling, and is busy with beer, beef and biscuits, transports, joists and empty casks. He puts out or puts in the names of the captains and masters of the fleet, and apportions the gunners and the convoys. Ambassadors, admirals, generals, paymasters, pursers, secretaries, men of all grades, and in every sort of employment, crowd about him for advice and information."* In nearly all the voluminous State papers of the period,

* BREWER, vol. i. pp. xliv., xlv.

which illustrate this subject, he is referred to for instructions or spoken of as author of the busy work being done in England. "I pray God soon deliver you out of your outrageous charge and labour," says Bishop Fox, in one letter to him; "else ye shall have a cold stomach, little sleep, pale visage, and a thin belly, *cum pari egestione.*"*

Wolsey's work in the reconstruction of the national navy lasted over many years. But good proof of it appeared in March, 1513, when Sir Edward again put to sea for another summer's fighting with the French. His fleet then numbered four-and-twenty ships, only six more than the number with which he had been intrusted a year before, on his first appointment as Lord Admiral. In these four-and-twenty, however, there was numerically nearly twice as much strength, and actually a great deal more than twice as much, as in the eighteen of 1512. The stately *Regent* had been burnt in the action with the *Cordelier;* but there were two other ships as large as the *Regent*—the *Henry Imperial*, which seems to have been the same as the *Sovereign*, and probably was Henry VII.'s *Henry Grace à Dieu*, rechristened on Henry VIII.'s accession, and the *Trinity*, each of 1,000 tons burthen, and carrying 700 men apiece. The portage of the whole amounted to 8,460 tons, containing in all 26 captains and 4,650 soldiers, 24 masters, and 2,880 mariners, a total of 6,480 officers and men. To these twenty-four fighting ships there were attached twenty-seven smaller vessels

* BREWER, vol. i., p. 585.

as victuallers; and in addition there were some eighty or ninety other ships, barks, buoys, and other craft, mostly the property of merchants and private adventurers, chartered for purposes of transport, or retained for supplying any deficiencies that might occur in the regular fleet.*

On Saturday, the 19th of March, the King went down to Greenwich to inspect the greater number of his fighting ships, and he gave instructions to Sir Edward Howard that he was to send him a particular account of the way in which each vessel comported itself upon the sea. This account has come down to us in a mutilated state. It tells how the fleet set sail on the following Monday, a contrary wind having made it impossible for the usual sailors' luck to be courted by embarking on a Sunday, and in what order the different ships made their way along the Downs and past the Goodwin Sands. Some of the smaller craft gave very little satisfaction to the Admiral. The *Christ*, a vessel of 300 tons burthen, he says, "was one of the worst; she may bear no more sail; no more may the *Katherine*," which was of the same size. But of the larger ships he speaks very highly. The *Mary Rose*, carrying 600 tons, his own flagship, was the swiftest of them all, being inferior only in bulk to the *Sovereign* or *Henry Imperial*. "Sir," he says, "she is the noblest ship of sail, is this great ship, at this hour, that I trow be in Christendom; the flower, I trow, of all ships that ever sailed." And the conclusion of his

* BREWER, vol. i., pp. 550—554.

report is, that "such a fleet hath been never seen in Christendom." *

In that temper Sir Edward Howard led his ships to Plymouth, there to wait for victuals and reinforcements; and thence, on the 5th of April, he wrote up to Wolsey, begging him, for God's sake, to be prompt in sending him an abundance of good food, better than some of that previously supplied, as he had heard that a hundred sail of Frenchmen were coming towards him, and as he expected to have an engagement with them within five or six days. When they did meet, he added, he trusted in God and Saint George that he would have a fair day with them.† In this he was disappointed. Passing out of Plymouth Roads on Sunday, the 10th of April, with more than a hundred craft of all sorts, of which forty-two were "ships royal and others of war," he fell in on the following morning with fifteen French ships, and offered battle; but, as he reported, "they fled like cowards as soon as they spied the English," and he could do no more than pursue them as far as the mouth of Brest Harbour, where he saw them join the main body of the French fleet, numbering in all about fifty sail.‡

This fleet comprised the greater part of the navy then possessed by France, augmented, just about the time of Howard's putting to sea, by six stout Mediterranean galleys led by Pierre Jean le Bidoulx, called by

---

* Ellis, *Original Letters*, Second Series (1827), vol. i., pp. 212—217.

† *Ibid.*, Third Series, vol. i., pp. 145—151.

‡ British Museum, *Cottonian MSS.*, Caligula D. vi., p. 337; Hall, fol. 22.

the English Prester John, a knight of Rhodes, considered in his day the greatest naval commander in the world, who at once took charge of all the enemy's shipping. Unabashed by Prester John's great name, and only stimulated by it to a stronger desire for his overthrow, Howard counted on an easy victory. "Sir," he wrote to King Henry, "we have them at the greatest advantage that ever men had. Sir, God worketh in your cause and right. Sir, the first wind that ever cometh, they shall have broken heads, that all the world shall speak of it. Sir, if God thinketh good to send us any wind, the navy of France shall do your Grace little hurt."

The harbour of Brest being adapted for the passage of large vessels only at high tide, Howard considered that he would be able to keep the alien fleet in a sort of prison until he could demolish it. But the same circumstance that prevented the egress of Prester John and his ships, hindered Howard from attacking them at a convenient time. He therefore held at bay for a few days, using his leisure in sending parties of his men to land on the neighbouring coast and do as much damage as was possible. One large and four small French ships that ventured out of the harbour were burnt by him; and one of his own vessels, whose officers were ignorant of the hidden dangers of the situation, was dashed to pieces among the rocks, though not too soon for the people to be saved. This was the *Nicholas of Hampton*, under Captain Arthur. "Sir," said Howard, in another letter to his sovereign, "I have taken all Master Arthur's folks and bestowed them in the arms where I am deficient by reason of death by casualty and otherwise. And, sir, I have given him liberty to go home; for, when he was in the extreme danger, he called upon Our Lady of Walsingham for help and comfort, and made a vow that, an it pleased God and her to deliver him out of the peril, he would never eat flesh nor fish till he had seen her. Sir, I assure you he was in marvellous danger; for it was marvel that the ship, being with all her sails striking full butt a rock with her stern, brake not in pieces at the first stroke."*

In that position the rival fleets continued for a fortnight. Prester John used the interval in strengthening his defences, one of his measures being the lashing together of twenty large hulks which, in the event of an attack, he proposed to set on fire and drive, while they were burning, among the opposing vessels. But Sir Edward Howard was in no way disheartened. So confident was he of ultimate success, that he wrote to the King, begging him to come in person to lead the battle, and " have the honour of so high an enterprise." If Henry's own chivalrous disposition at all inclined him to this work, he was promptly restrained by his advisers. The King's Council wrote back to Howard, sharply reproving him for his suggestion, and bidding him, without any further delay, "accomplish that which pertained to his duty." †

---

* BRITISH MUSEUM MSS., *Cotton*, Caligula D. vi., pp. 337—339, and Caligula E. ii., pp. 141—143; HALL, fol. 22.

† HALL, fols. 22, 23; HERBERT, *Life and Reign of Henry* VIII.

That unkind message is reported to have driven Sir
Edward Howard, always over-bold, to the rash act
which cost him his life and deprived England of the
ablest sea-warrior that, up to that time, she had possessed. Stronger inducement doubtless came from the
fear, newly enforced in his mind each day, that Prester
John would find some means of making an escape, and
so thwart his project of, by one day's work, spoiling the
whole navy of France. At any rate he lost patience. On
Sunday, the 24th of April, he put all his six thousand
fighting men on shore, with the intention of attacking
the French fleet by land; but, before they had marched
far, he hastily recalled them, under the impression that
Prester John was making ready to sail out of the harbour while his gaolers were away. On the following
morning, the morning of Saint Mark's Day, he resolved
to be idle no longer. Calling together a few chosen
friends, Lord Ferrers, Sir Thomas Cheyne, Sir John
Wallop, Sir Henry Shirborne, and Sir William Sidney
—Philip Sidney's grandfather—among the number, he
told them that he was determined, at any risk, to attack
Prester John's own ship and some of his Mediterranean
galleys, which were stationed in a corner by themselves.
He asked whether they would help him to make the
attack as secretly as possible, and with the help of two
such boats as would be able to enter the harbour even
at low water. They assented, and lost no time in setting
out. Rowing quickly right up to the enemy, they made
good progress before they were discovered; but then
they were assailed with balls and arrows, which "came

together as thick as hailstones," according to the statement of Captain Edward Ichyngham. These volleys were answered by sharp firing from the boats, until Lord Ferrers, who had command of one of the two parties, had no more ammunition left. For shelter he crept under one of the great galleys, while Howard led his boat close up to the side of Prester John's vessel, and, with seventeen of his followers, succeeded in boarding it. Then ensued a desperate conflict. The English were in a fair way of capturing the galley, when the cable with which they had fastened their boat to it was severed. Those near enough jumped off and saved themselves. Sir Edward Howard, who, with the rest, was in another part of the ship, shouted, "Come aboard again! come aboard again!" But his comrades had no other cable or grappling-iron, and drifted away perforce. Then Howard took his admiral's whistle from his neck and flung it into the sea. The Frenchmen pressed round him, forced him with their morris pikes against the rails of the galley, and, when he was dead, he fell into the water to be seen no more. Presently, Sir Henry Shirborne and Sir William Sidney, with some others of Lord Ferrers' party, forced their way up the sides of the galley, hoping to rescue their master; but they could not find him. A mariner who had started in the first attack, and who stood faithfully by Howard to the last, managed to swim to one of the boats, in spite of eighteen wounds. It was from him and from a Spanish boy, who had watched the proceedings from a boat's side, that the English heard of their great misfortune. "Jesu, have mercy!" wrote one of them, not very friendly hitherto towards Howard, to Cardinal Wolsey; "for now we be bodies without a head." "There was never noble man so ill lost as he was," said another of Wolsey's correspondents, uttering the sentiments of nearly all his comrades, "that was of so great courage and had so many virtues, and that ruled so great an army so well as he did, and kept so great order and true justice." Even James IV. of Scotland, though at war with Henry, wrote in condolence to him. "Surely, dearest brother," he said, "we think more loss is to you of the late Admiral, who deceased to his great honour, than the advantage might have been in winning all the French galleys."*

Henry was well aware of the extent of his loss; but he was not disposed to give up hope of capturing all the French galleys. Without delay he appointed Lord Thomas Howard to succeed his younger brother as Admiral of England, and bade him lose no time in avenging the brave man's death.† This, however, was more than Lord Thomas Howard could do. The sailors were so depressed by the misfortune, so badly off for food, and so troubled with sickness, that the fleet had returned to Plymouth before the new Admiral had received his patent; and before fresh supplies of men and victuals could be procured, the Frenchmen had moved out of Brest Harbour. Six weeks were wasted in

---

* *Cottonian MSS.*, Caligula E. i., p. 11, and D. vi., p. 107; ELLIS, First Series, vol. i., p. 76; HALL, fol. 23; HOLLINSHED, vol. iii., p. 574.

† BREWER, vol i., p. 557; GRAFTON, p. 962.

making good the deficiencies. Bishop **Fox** wrote to Wolsey, saying that the pursers of the ships deserved hanging for their negligence. Wolsey wrote to Howard, saying that the stores he had ordered for the fleet had been kept back " by some lewd persons that would not have the King's navy continue any longer on the sea."* The "lewd persons" attained their object. The English fleet did little more that summer or for some years after. Henry crossed over to Calais to take command of the land forces with which alone the war with France was carried on, while Lord Thomas Howard followed his father to Scotland, there to take part in the victory at Flodden Field. The father, having been made Duke of Norfolk for his conduct of that business, the son succeeded him as Earl of Surrey, and, as Earl of Surrey, during the time of peace with France, he was Lord Deputy of Ireland.

In these years, however, ship-building and the improvement of the navy were not forgotten. The trivial events of 1513 had shown that if the English were stronger than the French at sea, they were still very weak indeed. Therefore Henry VIII. and Wolsey continued their efforts in the direction of naval reform. They devised better ways of enlisting sailors and training them for zealous service. They sought out the best ways of fitting out ships for war, and paid great attention to the manufacture of guns and other fighting implements. They improved the old ships, and fashioned

* Brewer, vol. i., pp. 585, 590.

new ones upon the best models that could at that time be procured.

The building, between 1512 and 1514, of the *Henry Grace à Dieu* or *Great Harry*, namesake and successor of Henry VII.'s great ship, marks an epoch in the history of naval architecture. It was begun on the 3rd of October, 1512, and during the next twenty months, a hundred and forty-one of the cleverest shipwrights that could be procured were busy at its construction. Their wages amounted to 2,378*l*. 2*s*. 10*d*., besides the cost of their clothing, bedding, and food,* and the expense of other occasional labour. They made use of 1,752 tons of timber, which cost 437*l*. 17*s*. 7¾*d*.; 408*l*. 19*s*. 7¾*d*.'s worth of iron wrought and unwrought; 243*l*. 6*s*. 3½*d*.'s worth of brass, and 133*l*. 12*s*. 6*d*.'s worth of coal. The expense of cordage amounted to 969*l*. 2*s*. 11*d*.; in ox-hair, lime, and rosin, were expended 100*l*. 13*s*. 10*d*.; in blocks and pulleys, 63*l*. 10*s*. 9*d*. The entire cost of building, including three small galleys to attend on the great ship, amounted to 7,708*l*. 5*s*. 3*d*. The burthen of the great ship herself was 1,500 tons, so that she was half as large again as the largest vessel hitherto known in the English navy. She was arranged in seven tiers, one above another, and, as the Emperor Maximilian's ambassador reported, had "an incredible array of guns,

---

* They consumed 7,498 dozen loaves of bread, worth 370*l*. 7*s*. 8*d*.; 1,543 pipes of beer, 526*l*. 19*s*. 11*d*.; 557 beeves, 706*l*. 17*s*. 9*d*.; 205 score of sheep, 32*l*. 5*s*. 8*d*.; 4,522 codfish, 87*l*. 2*s*. 10*d*.; a goodly quantity of other flesh and fish, with a number of other articles, including only 7 barrels of butter, worth 4*l*. 6*s*., and 30 weys of cheese, worth 19*l*. 4*s*.; the cost of the whole being 1,969*l*. 18*s*. 2*d*.

with a scuttle on the top of the mainmast, eighty serpentines and hackbuts." Four hundred men were at work four days in dragging her from the building yard at Erith to Barking Creek.*

On the 13th of June, 1514, the King, with a stately company, including the Queen, the Princess Mary, the foreign ambassadors, several bishops, and a large number of noblemen, went down to christen this famous ship.

On the 25th of October, 1515, King Henry was again at Greenwich, christening another great vessel. "Those who were in the galley, dining with the King of England," wrote the French envoy to his sovereign, "have told me for certain that there are in the said galley two hundred and seven pieces of artillery, large as well as small, of which seventy are of copper and cast, and the rest of iron, with four or five thousand bullets and four or five hundred barrels of powder. The galley is propelled by six score oars, and is so large that it will hold eight hundred or a thousand fighting men. The King of England acted as master of the galley, wearing a sailor's coat and trousers of frieze cloth of gold. He had on a thick chain, in which were five links, and amongst the same there were three plates of gold, on which was written as a device, 'Dieu et mon droit;' and at the bottom of the said chain was a large whistle, with which he whistled almost as loud as a trumpet or clarionet. Mass was sung on board by the Bishop of Durham, and the galley was named by Queen Mary *The Virgin Mary*."

* BREWER, vol. i., pp. 828, 839 ; CHARNOCK, vol. ii., p. 28.

The Frenchman was not well pleased with this show of warlike strength and grandeur. "I went immediately," he says, "to my lord the Duke of Suffolk. He told me that it was true that the King of England had made an appearance of preparing himself for war, and for this cause had got ready a small number of ships: but this he had done solely to content his subjects, who desired in my master's absence that England should go to war with him; but the King of England had no such inclination." Then the agent went to Wolsey, who was at Westminster. "I told him," he proceeds, "that if he and the King of England thought that the King my master, at his departure into Italy, had not left his kingdom strong and powerful, they had been greatly deceived; yet, at the same time, the King had never thought to invade his country, and make war upon him in his absence. On this he laid his hand on his breast, and swore to me that the King his master had never thought of such a thing, nor his Council; and as for the ships which he had prepared during this time, and chiefly his great galley, that was done solely to give pleasure and pastime to the Queen and the Queen Mary his sister."*

Wolsey might swear and Suffolk protest that Henry's ship-building meant no harm to France; but it was clear to all the world that these preparations were meant for much more than the pleasure and pastime of queens and courtiers. The preparations continued, and year by year the English navy grew in strength.

* Brewer, vol. ii., pp. xlvii—l.

Better vessels were built, and better furniture was put in them. Improvements were steadily made in naval tactics, and full advantage was taken of the lessons taught by experience as to the training and employment of seamen and sea-going soldiers. The result was great credit to England, and great advancement of English influence over the politics of Europe.

But in actual warfare very little was done that is worth recording. Down to the close of Henry's reign the attitude of the navy was chiefly passive: for the most part it was only a deterrent power, and a warning against invasion. Its principal occupation was in the punishment of pirates, and in damaging the enemy's trading operations, which in those days were held akin to piracy, and often were hardly distinguishable from it. During Lord Thomas Howard's long service as High Admiral there were numerous actions similar to the capture of Andrew Barton's ships, by which he and his brother Edward had made themselves famous. Often, too, the fleets were employed in scouring the seas and devastating the alien coast, after the fashion of Sir Edward's achievements on the shores and in the adjoining districts of Brittany. But till near the close of Henry's reign, there was no sea fight at all comparable to that in which the *Regent* and the *Cordelier* were destroyed in 1512. Even in 1522, when Thomas Howard, then Earl of Surrey, bearing an admiral's commission from the Emperor Charles V. as well as from Henry VIII., commanded a fleet of nearly two hundred vessels, his chief work was in landing troops in Normandy, and thus aiding the land warfare with France.

The navy was still in its infancy, consisting of a few royal ships, built especially for fighting, and of numerous smaller craft, designed for merchandize, and only turned into war ships as occasion required. The men employed in these vessels also had little save bravery in common with the servants in modern ships of war. The sailors and their masters were fishermen, merchants' apprentices, and often merchants themselves. The fighting men were land-soldiers, rarely at their ease in naval warfare, and always much more useful in the sort of fighting for which they had been trained, if indeed they also were not raw recruits, practised only in such use of weapons as was in those days common with every Englishman. Even the superior officers were generally landsmen. Lord Thomas Howard, as we saw, varied his employment as admiral with service at the battle of Flodden and civil government in Ireland; and in later years, succeeding his father as Duke of Norfolk, he succeeded him also as Lord Treasurer, to which he added other work as a military commander, an ambassador, and a domestic statesman.

Howard outlived his master and his master's son, Edward VI. He died in the first year of Queen Mary's reign, seventy-six years old. A crowd of men acquired under him their share of fame, about which posterity need not trouble itself, as sea-captains. The most notable of them was Sir William Fitzwilliams, who was wounded in the battle with the French off Brest in

1513, who succeeded Howard as High Admiral, became Earl of Southampton in 1536, and died in 1542, while on his way to fight the Scots.

The last of Henry VIII.'s High Admirals, then gaining influence in the State as Viscount Lisle, was the great Duke of Northumberland, who became virtually King of England during Edward VI.'s sovereignty. He was first mover in the sea-fighting with which, after thirty years of trifling work, the naval history of Henry's reign was brought to a close.

After Wolsey's disgrace and death, in spite of the zealous efforts of Lord Thomas Cromwell, the navy had fallen into some decay. Peace having been made with France in 1527, there was little even of desultory fighting for ten years.*

In 1537 began preparations for another war. There was fresh energy in ship-building and fortifying. New

---

* Evidence of the way in which, during these years, other nations brought their warfare into English seas is in a letter which John Arundel wrote to Cromwell in 1536:—"There came into Falmouth Haven a fleet of Spaniards," he says, "and the day after came four ships of Dieppe, men-of-war, and the Spaniards shot into the Frenchmen, and the Frenchmen into the Spaniards, and during three hours great guns shot between them, and the Frenchmen were glad to come higher up the haven; and the morrow after, Saint Paul's Day, the Spaniards came up to assault the Frenchmen, and the Frenchmen came up almost to the town of Truro, and went aground there. I went to the admiral of the Spaniards and commanded him to keep the King's peace, and not follow further; but the Spaniard would not, but said, 'I will have them, or I will die for it.' And then the Spaniards put their ordnance in their boats and shot the French admiral forty or sixty shot during a long hour, the gentlemen of that city taking pleasure at it. Then I went to the Spaniards and told them to leave their shooting or I would raise the country upon them. And so the Spaniards left."—*State Paper MS.*, cited by FROUDE, *History of England*, vol. iii., p. 248.

batteries were set up at St. Michael's Mount, at Falmouth, at Fowey, at Plymouth, at Dartmouth, at Torbay, at Portland, at Cowes, and at Portsmouth;* and castles were built or strengthened at Dover, Deal, Sandwich, Hull, Scarborough, Newcastle, and Berwick. Having hitherto shrewdly increased the importance of England by keeping up the feud between France and Scotland on the one hand and Spain and Germany on the other, Henry now found himself in danger of attack by the united forces of Catholic Europe. "I have heard," wrote the English ambassador in Flanders to Cromwell, " that the French King, the Bishop of Rome, and the King of the Scots be in league to invade us this summer, and how the Emperor will send to their aid certain Spaniards."† Great preparations were made to withstand this invasion, in the course of which, we are told, King Henry himself " made very laborious and painful journeys towards the sea-coast;" and enough was done to frighten away a fleet of about two hundred and seventy sail, which left Antwerp in April, and made warlike show off Dover.

There was no real fighting till 1545. Then, another French invasion being expected, a formidable fleet

---

* "The town of Portsmouth," said LELAND in 1548, "is walled from the east tower a furlong's length, with a mud wall armed with brass ordnance, and this piece of the wall, having a ditch without it, runs so far flat south south-east, and is the place most apt to defend the town, there open on the haven. There runs a ditch almost flat east for a space, and within it is a wall of mud like to the other, and then goes on round about the town for the circuit of a mile. There is a gate of timber at the north-east end of the town, and by it there is cast up a hill of earth ditched, whereon be guns to defend the entry into the town by land."—*Itinerary.*

† *State Papers, Henry* VIII., edited by LEMON, vol. viii., p. 167.

was prepared under the guidance of Lord Lisle, and with much personal supervision from the King himself. The French fleet, under the command of Admiral D'Annebault, comprised twenty-five galleys, a hundred and fifty large ships, and fifty smaller vessels and transports. In the English fleet there were a hundred and four vessels of war and merchantmen fitted up for warlike use, with 12,738 men of all sorts on board.*

Lord Lisle put to sea on the 15th of June, intending to anticipate the invasion by sailing boldly up to the mouth of the Seine, and there attacking the French shipping in its moorings. But a tempest drove him back, and he was waiting in Portsmouth Harbour, when, on the 18th of July, while the King was reviewing the forces, balefires on the cliff above Ventnor gave warning that the Frenchmen were in sight. D'Annebault anchored in Brading Harbour, and along the coast towards Ryde. Lisle arranged his ships in warlike order, almost within gunshot, at Spithead. Next morning anchors were weighed and the guns were put to use. For an hour the French had the advantage. There was no wind to fill the English sails, and the French galleys made great havoc. The *Great Harry* was almost sunk, and many others of the English vessels were partially disabled. The threatened defeat

* *State Papers, Henry* VIII., edited by LEMON, vol. i., p. 810. The English fleet was manned in great part by the bold fishermen of the neighbourhood, whose customary work had therefore to be undertaken by their wives. "The women of the fishers' towns," wrote Lord Russell, "eight or nine of them, with but one boy or one man with them, adventure to sail a-fishing, sixteen or twenty miles to sea, and are sometimes chased home by the Frenchmen."—*State Papers*, vol. i., p. 828.

was averted, however, by a kindly breeze from the west, which enabled Lord Lisle to advance against the enemy, to disperse their ships, and while he damaged many of them, to drive many others within reach of the guns that surmounted the earthworks around Portsmouth. The Frenchmen retreated before very much mischief had been done to them, and Lord Lisle, satisfied with his easy victory, returned to his anchorage at Spithead.

The victory was marred by one heavy disaster. The *Mary Rose*—the same vessel of six hundred tons burthen which, when it was newly built two-and-thirty years before, Sir Edward Howard declared to be "the noblest ship of sail in Christendom, the flower of all ships that ever sailed"—had done good service during the early part of the action. That its guns might be worked more efficiently, they had been removed from their fastenings and pointed full upon the attacking galleys of France. When the west wind suddenly arose, the *Mary Rose* tilted to the leeward, all the guns rolled together on one side, and so overbalanced the vessel that the sea poured in at her open portholes and sunk her, with four hundred men on board. It was an accident precisely similar to that which, two hundred and thirty-seven years later, befel the *Royal George* in the same waters. A like mischance also happened to a French treasure-ship, *La Maitresse*, though so near to Brading Haven that the wrecked vessel, its crew, and its money-chest were brought on shore.

The French and English fleets met again on the 15th

of August, when D'Annebault having returned to the English coast, and done some damage to Brighton and the adjoining towns, was met by Lisle off Shoreham and forced to retire, after some desultory and unimportant fighting. After that, the war was suspended for the summer, and the peace that was concluded in June, 1546, put a stop to any further contest during the short remainder of Henry's reign, and for many years ensuing. Save in the loss of the *Mary Rose*, great credit was brought to English seamanship at a very trifling cost of life. The expenditure in money, judged by modern standards, was also tolerably insignificant. Of the 1,300,000*l.*, however, which Henry spent during two years in preparation for this naval war, only 300,000*l.* were met by the subsidy and benevolence which Parliament granted for the purpose. The rest had to be obtained with not a little difficulty, by pawning some of the crown lands, melting down much of the royal plate and turning it into coin, procuring loans from Flemish merchants at exorbitant interest, and other ignoble devices.*

Yet it was by such devices, and in succession to such trivial fightings as we have noticed, that Henry VIII. prepared the way for the greatness of England as a maritime power.

* *State Papers*, vol. i., pp. 789, 790, 814—830 ; vol. x., p. 468. It is worth noting that, during this brief war, the watchword used, for the first time apparently, was "God save King Henry !" with " Long to reign over us" for its answer—words that were afterwards incorporated in the national anthem.

CHAPTER IV.

SEBASTIAN CABOT'S LATER WORK.

[1527—1557.]

WHILE Henry VIII., in his devotion to maritime affairs, paid almost exclusive attention to the development of shipping as a means of war and to the encouragement of military seamanship, the more adventurous of his subjects were not unmindful of those projects for distant voyaging and discovery which John Cabot and his friends had first made popular, and to which fresh interest came with every new report of the brilliant progress of Spanish colonization. By Papal mandate and the consent of nations, the more accessible parts of America were reserved to the people who, under Columbus's leadership, had gone westward to possess the Indies. Englishmen, if they would share in the fabled riches of Cathay, or in the substantial treasures to be found on the way to it, must seek some other channel; and this they were resolved to do in spite of the unproductive nature of the elder Cabot's labours. While Sebastian Cabot gave himself up, for a time and to a great extent at any rate, to the service of Spain, they continued their endeavours in the course he had at first pursued, and were led by those endeavours to embark in other enterprises very helpful to the maritime advancement of their nation.

The first of these endeavours, in Henry's reign, was made by Robert Thorne, a native of Bristol and a merchant of London. His father had been connected with John Cabot in his schemes for reaching Cathay. He himself, when carrying on his trade in Seville during some time previous to 1527, had made or renewed acquaintance with Sebastian Cabot, and out of that arose in him fresh interest in the projects that had been the delight of his boyhood. To the La Plata expedition which Cabot headed, in the interests of Spain, in 1526, he contributed fourteen hundred ducats, " principally," as he said, " for that two English friends of mine, which are somewhat learned in cosmography, should go in the same ships, to bring me certain relation of the country and to be expert in the navigation of those seas."* Early in 1527, having been written to by Dr. Lee, Henry VIII.'s ambassador at the Court of Charles V., for information about Cathayan exploration, he replied in a learned treatise, discussing the various efforts made by the nations of Europe in the way of American colonization and discovery, and strongly urging a revival of English participation in the work. This treatise was followed by a letter from Thorne to King Henry himself, and by Thorne's return to England, in company with Dr. Lee, with the avowed object of further setting forth his recommendations.

* HAKLUYT, *Divers Voyages*, p. 215.

"It is my bounden duty," said the merchant, in bold satire, in his letter to the King, "to reveal this secret to your Grace, which hitherto, I suppose, hath been hid; which is, that with a small number of ships there may be discovered new lands and kingdoms, in the which, without doubt, your Grace shall win perpetual glory and your subjects infinite profit." As peace had just been made with France, Thorne urged that the present time was especially convenient for Henry to fulfil the natural desire and bounden duty of all wise monarchs in respect of increasing their dominions. "The world knows," he said, "that the desires of princes have been so fervent that, to obtain their purpose, they have in a manner turned the world up and down." But rarely had any prince such an easy opportunity of doing his share in turning the world up and down as was now offered to King Henry. The southern, eastern, and western quarters of the world were already occupied, and any interference with them must be attended with great bloodshed and great waste of treasure; but the northern parts still waited for a possessor. They would certainly bring to their fortunate owner immense wealth and vast increase of power, and it was clear that, by the goodness of God, they had been reserved for England. If there had been failure in the previous undertakings, conducted by the Cabots, the experience of thirty years had suggested remedies. "Concerning the mariners, ships and provision, an order may be taken much better than heretofore: the labour is much less, the danger and the way shorter, to us than to Spain and Portugal. Concerning the navigation, it is very clear and evident that the seas that commonly men say that, without very great danger, difficulty and peril, it is impossible to pass, those same seas be navigable, and without any such danger but that ships may pass, and have in them perpetual clearness of the day, without any darkness of the night; which thing is a great commodity for the navigants to see at all times round about, as well the safeguards as the dangers." In that region of perpetual daylight, about the North Pole, there would be ice and coldness, it was true; but Thorne urged that those obstacles would soon be overpassed, and then the voyagers would have open sea and temperate climate for all the rest of their way. Dangers and darkness had not hindered the Spaniards and Portuguese from discovering strange realms to their great advantage; and if Englishmen were deterred on these accounts, said the merchant, "it will seem your Grace's subjects to be without activity or courage, in leaving to do this glorious and noble enterprise."

Thorne proposed that an expedition should sail from England in a north-westerly direction till it reached the shores visited by John Cabot just thirty years before, and then proceed northwards till it had passed out of the icy region into the warmer climate which he believed to be in the neighbourhood of the North Pole. "Then," he proceeded, "it may be at the will and pleasure of the mariners to choose whether they will sail by the coasts that be cold, temperate, or hot. If they will go towards the orient, they shall enjoy the regions of all the Tartarians that extend towards the mid-day, and from thence they may go and proceed towards the land of the Chinese, and from thence to the land of Cathay Oriental; and if from thence they do continue their navigation, following the coast that returns towards the occident, they shall fall in Malacca and so in all the Indies we call Oriental; and following that way they may return hither by the Cape of Good Hope, and thus they shall compass the whole world. And if they shall take their course, after they be passed the Pole, towards the occident, they shall go in the back-side and south seas of the Indies Occidental, and so they may return through the Straits of Magellan to this country, and so compass the world that way. And if they go right towards the Pole Antarctic, and then decline towards the lands and islands situated between the Tropics and under the Equinoctial, without doubt they shall find there the richest lands and islands in the world, of gold, precious stones, balms, spices, and other things that we here most esteem." Thus by each of the three routes which it was possible to take—the three routes which Thorne was the first to describe and which all later Arctic voyagers have attempted to follow or to improve upon only in detail—sure success was promised. " By this it appeareth," said Thorne in the conclusion of his argument, "that your Grace shall have not only a great advantage of riches, but also your subjects shall not travel half of the way that others do which go round about as aforesaid."*

* HAKLUYT, *Divers Voyages*, pp. 212—219.

These fair promises—broken a hundred times as generation after generation of Arctic adventurers was tempted by them to embark upon an enterprise whose history is without a parallel for its constant course of failure and for the excellent benefit that resulted, in spite of and even in consequence of the failure, to the English character for pluck and perseverance—were broken for the first time in the very year in which they were uttered. Henry VIII. listened to them, and in the summer of 1527 sent out "two fair ships, having in them divers cunning men, to seek strange regions;" and among the cunning men was a Canon of Saint Paul's, "a wealthy man and a great mathematician," whose name has not come down to us. The ships were the *Mary of Guildford*, of which John Rut was captain, and the *Sampson*. They left Plymouth on the 10th of June, and sailed bravely up to old John Cabot's New-found-land, which they reached on the 21st of July. Thence they proceeded a little further north; but they soon lost heart. "We found many great islands of ice and deep water," as Captain Rut said in a letter to Cardinal Wolsey, "but we found no sounding, and then we durst go no further to the northward for fear of more ice." While seeking for some place of safety, the ships were parted by a storm, and the *Sampson* was never heard of afterwards. The *Mary of Guildford* sought her for ten days, and then her mariners, believing that she was wrecked, and fearing that they also would be lost if they waited any longer in the region of ice, turned back and put into a harbour of the New-found-land, and thence, after making some further search for their missing comrades, came back to England in October.*

That, as far as we know, was the last experiment in Arctic voyaging made by Henry VIII. Of the private enterprises conducted during his reign very little is recorded. There is only one about which any details at all have come down to us, and many of these details are hardly credible. The chief promoter of this expedition was one Master Hore, of London, a lawyer who dabbled in cosmography, and, with more zeal than wisdom, sought to emulate the projects of the Cabots. In 1536 he so far interested others in his views that, with the assistance of several gentlemen of the Inns of Court and other people of substance, and with King Henry's sanction, he managed to leave Gravesend at the end of April in charge of two ships, the *Trinity*, of 140 tons burthen, and the *Minion*, which was somewhat smaller. His crew comprised thirty gentlemen "of good worship," and seventy persons of meaner sort. This company sailed westward, with a curve to the south, and after two months' voyaging, touched land for the first time near Cape Breton Isle. Passing thence towards the north-east they arrived at an island which they called the Isle of Penguins, because it was well stocked with great fowls, apparently our Newfoundland, which earlier voyagers, delighted with its store of fish, had called the Isle of Cod or Baccalaos, and different

* PURCHAS, *His Pilgrims*, vol. iii., p. 809; HAKLUYT, *Voyages* (copying from Hall and Grafton), vol. iii., p. 129. The accounts are contradictory and both extremely meagre.

from the mainland of Labrador, which was John Cabot's New-found-land. They had great enjoyment from the birds and birds' eggs which they found upon this island. They also saw and killed a number of black and white bears, and "took them for no bad food." It is likely that they idled here too long, and wasted the provisions that should have been husbanded for the time when they had really entered on their Arctic voyaging. At any rate, in leaving Newfoundland, they left all their good fortune behind them.

They sailed northwards along the coast of Labrador, and gave chase to a few natives who came out in a boat to look at them. But when their stores were exhausted, and they were forced to land in search of food, they found nothing to eat. Ice-covered rocks and huge pine-forests were before them and around them, but no food, and no natives of whom food, by fair means or foul, could be procured. At last they were reduced to such straits, that, according to the testimony of one of the party, when they wandered about in the woods, two and two together, in search of anything that could satisfy their hunger, it often happened that "one fellow killed his mate while he stooped to take up a root for his relief, and, cutting out pieces of his body, whom he had murdered, broiled the same on the coals and greedily devoured them." Once one of the party, discovering a smell of cooked flesh about a comrade, reproved him for having food and not sharing it with his friends. "If thou would needs know," answered the man, "the broiled meat that I had was a piece of such a man's buttock." The captain exhorted his comrades to abstain from such foul practices, to have patience, and to trust in God. But even he had to give way to the cravings of hunger and agree to a plan for deciding by lot who of the party should be eaten, when a way of escape was opened. "Such was the mercy of God," says the survivor who told the tale, "that, the same night, arrived a French vessel, well victualled; and such was the policy of the English, that they became masters of the same." With the stolen vessel those who were left of the party made their way back to England in October. The Frenchmen followed them in the vessels that Hore's company had deserted, and claimed restitution of their goods; whereupon King Henry, we are told, "was so moved with pity for his subjects' distress, that he punished them not, but with his own purse made full and royal recompense to the French."*

That is the story of Hore's expedition as it has come down to us from the report of one of the mariners. It is clearly exaggerated in parts, and we may fairly hope that the account of cannibalism is a traveller's apocryphal tale. It is evident, however, that the expedition failed utterly, and it seems to have been followed by no other attempts at Arctic voyaging during Henry's reign.

Very soon after Edward VI.'s accession there was famous renewal of the work. Fresh energy came with Sebastian Cabot's return to England in 1548. Six-and-thirty years before, not liking Henry's treatment of him, he had gone to Spain, and, with the exception of the

* HAKLUYT, vol. iii., pp. 129—131.

enterprise in which, in 1517, he had embarked with
Sir Thomas Spert, he had been a servant of Ferdinand
the Catholic and Charles the Great all through that
time. King Henry's death induced him, at the age of
seventy-seven, to come back to the land of his birth,
and he was honourably received by Edward VI. and his
subjects. The young King made him Grand Pilot of
England, with a salary of 166*l*. a year and general
supervision of the maritime affairs of the country;* and
important work was at once found for him in settlement
of the disputes, long growing, that had just then reached
their height, between the German merchants of the
Steelyard, a colony of foreign traders existing during a
dozen generations in the heart of London, and the
company of the Merchant Adventurers of England.
For his good offices in this matter he received a reward
of 200*l*. from the Crown in 1551.† There are records of
other services performed by him, throughout King
Edward VI.'s brief reign, in the interests of commerce
and navigation. ‡

But, though an old man of fourscore years, he was as
young as ever in devotion to the projects that had
occupied his youth. In 1552 he took advantage of the
great stagnation of trade which just then was resulting
from the disturbed condition and warlike attitude of
Europe. "Our merchants," says one of his friends,
" perceived the commodities and wares of England to be

---

* HAKLUYT, vol. iii., p. 10; RYMER, vol. xv., p. 427.
† STRYPE, *Historical Memorials*, vol. ii , p. 495.
‡ BIDDLE, *Memoirs of Sebastian Cabot*, p. 176, &c.

in small request with the countries and people about us and near unto us, and that those merchandizes which strangers in the time and memory of our ancestors did earnestly seek and desire were now neglected and the price thereof abated, although by us carried to their own ports." Accordingly, "certain grave citizens of London and men of great wisdom and careful for the good of their country, began to think with themselves how this mischief might be remedied." In their trouble they took counsel with Cabot, and, "after much speech and conference together," were induced by him to make another effort "for the search and discovery of the northern part of the world, to open a way and passage to our men for travel to new and unknown kingdoms."*

The notion at once obtained great favour in England. A "Mystery and Company of Merchant Adventurers for the discovery of regions, dominions, islands, and places unknown," was straightway formed, with two hundred and forty subscribers of 25*l.* apiece, and Sebastian Cabot for its Governor; and immediate steps were taken for putting to good use the 6,000*l.* thus collected. Skilful shipwrights were employed in constructing, out of the best seasoned oak that could be procured, three vessels as strong as in those days it was possible to make them. These vessels were sheeted with lead, at that time a novel expedient for protection from worms, well supplied with every kind of necessary furniture, and stocked with an abundant store of suitable

* CLEMENT ADAMS, cited by EDEN, *Decades of the New World*, fol. 256.

provisions, enough to last through eighteen months of voyaging.*

The next care was to bring together a competent crew, and place it under the charge of efficient captains. Many ignorant persons, we are told, clamoured for the leadership. But Cabot and his merchant-counsellors wisely chose men fitted for the work. Among the common sailors were some who afterwards distinguished themselves in maritime history,—William Burrows, who wrote a work on navigation, and became Comptroller of the Navy, and Arthur Pet, in especial. Stephen Burrough, who in due time rose to fill the place then held by Cabot as Chief Pilot of England, after engaging in several later voyages of discovery, was master of the largest vessel. The supreme command was given to Sir Hugh Willoughby, whose previous career is unknown to us, but who commended himself to his contemporaries as "a most valiant gentleman and wellborn," of excellent stature, and famous for "his singular skill in the services of war."† In courage and generous bearing, at any rate, he proved worthy of the trust placed in him; but a yet better man, as it seems, was Richard Chancelor, the second in command. He had been brought up in the household of Sir Henry Sidney, Edward VI.'s dearest friend, the father of Sir Philip Sidney, and the son of that Sir William Sidney who was associated with Sir Edward Howard in his naval fighting in 1513.

* CLEMENT ADAMS, cited by EDEN, *Decades of the New World*, fol. 256.
† *Ibid.*

Chancelor had already distinguished himself in seafaring, having in 1550 gone with one Roger Bodenham on a trading expedition to the Levant.* Cabot had discerned his worth, and helped him in his studies of cosmography.† He was chosen to his present post at the recommendation of Sidney, who made a speech before the council of merchants which is worth listening to.

"My very worshipful friends," he said, "I cannot but greatly commend your present godly and virtuous intention in the serious enterprising, for the singular love you bear to your country, in a matter which, I hope, will prove profitable for this nation, and honourable to this our land. Which intention of yours we also of the nobility are ready, to our power, to help and further; neither do we hold anything so dear and precious unto us, which we will not willingly forego and lay out in so commendable a cause. But principally I rejoice in myself, that I have nourished and maintained that wit which is like, by some means and in some measure, to profit and speed you in this worthy action. But yet I would not have you ignorant of this one thing, that I do now part with Chancelor, not because I make little reckoning of the man, or that his maintenance is burdensome and chargeable unto me, but that you may conceive and understand my goodwill and promptitude for the furtherance of this business, and that the authority and estimation which he deserveth may be given him. You know the man by report, I by experience; you by

* HAKLUYT, vol. ii., p. 99.   † EDEN, fol. 357.

words, I by deeds; you by speech and company, but I by the daily trial of his life have a full and perfect knowledge of him. And you are also to remember into how many perils, for your sakes and his country's love, he has now to run; whereof it is requisite that we be not unmindful, if it please God to send him good success. We commit a little money to the chance and hazard of fortune; he commits his life, a blessing to a man of all things the most dear, to the raging sea and the uncertainties of many dangers. We shall here live and rest at home quietly with our friends and acquaintances; but he in the meantime, labouring to keep the ignorant and unruly mariners in good order and obedience, with how many cares shall he trouble and vex himself? with how many troubles shall he break himself? and how many disquietings shall he be forced to sustain? We shall keep our own coasts and country; he shall seek strange and unknown kingdoms. He shall commit his safety to barbarous and cruel people, and shall hazard his life amongst the monstrous and terrible beasts of the sea. Wherefore, in respect of the greatness of the dangers and the excellency of his charge, you are to favour and love the man thus departing from us, and, if it fall so happily out that he return again, it is your part and duty also liberally to reward him."*

What Sir Henry Sidney thought of Richard Chancelor, all England thought of the expedition of which Willoughby and Chancelor were the leaders. After nearly

* EDEN, fol. 256.

a year spent in preparations, all things were ready for its departure in May, 1553. The little fleet consisted of three vessels, the *Bona Esperanza*, Willoughby's ship, of 120 tons burthen, the *Edward Bonaventure*, with Richard Chancelor for its captain, of 160 tons, and the *Bona Confidentia*, of 90 tons, each with a pinnace and boat attached to it. The company comprised a hundred and fifteen officers and men of all grades, including eleven merchants and one parson.* Willoughby was provided with several copies of a curious letter written by Edward VI. to "the kings, princes, and other potentates inhabiting the north-east part of the world, towards the mighty empire of Cathay," written in Latin, Greek, and other languages, proposing alliance with them, and asking permission for the passage of his servants through their dominions.† He was also furnished with an elaborate series of instructions, which were to be read aloud in each ship once a week for the guidance of both officers and seamen. In these strict obedience was enjoined, and absolute authority in enforcing it was given to the superior officers. It was especially ordered, "that no blaspheming of God or detestable swearing be used in any ship, nor communication of ribaldry, filthy tales, or ungodly talk;" and "that neither dicing, carding, tabling, nor other devilish games be frequented, whereby ensueth not only poverty to the players, but also strife, variance, brawling, fighting, and oftentimes murder, to the utter destruction of the parties, and provoking of God's most just wrath and

* HAKLUYT, vol. i., p. 258.   † *Ibid.*, pp. 257, 258.

sword of vengeance." Morning and evening prayers, with other services, were to be used by the crew; but, in dealing with any strangers they might meet, they were "not to disclose the state of our religion, but to pass it over in silence, without any declaration of it, seeming to bear with such laws and rights as the place hath." The mariners were to make every effort to understand the natures and dispositions of the people, and men and women were to be tempted, "without violence or force," to visit the English ships; "the persons so taken to be well entertained, used and apparelled, to the intent that he or she may allure others to draw nigh to show the commodities; and if the person taken be made drunk with your beer or wine," it was slily added, "you may know the secrets of his heart." On the whole, however, a very high morality was enjoined, and very worthy objects were enforced.*

The little fleet sailed from Deptford on the 10th of May. On the 11th it passed Greenwich, where the Court was staying. Edward VI. could not come out to honour it with his further sanction, as he then lay on his death-bed; but the courtiers ran out and crowded with the common people to cheer it as it passed, and the ships sent forth a peal of ordnance, with the noise of which was joined the merry shouting of the sailors. Hardly had they passed Harwich, however, before Chancelor discovered that part of the victuals provided for their use were already rotten, and that many of the hogsheads of wine were leaking, and he feared that the

* HAKLUYT, vol. i., pp. 251-255.

food would not last out the voyage. "His natural and fatherly affection also somewhat troubled him," we are told; "for he left behind him his two little sons, which were in the case of orphans if he sped not well."* But that thought was not allowed to hinder him, and it was feared that, if they turned back for fresh provisions, the summer would be too far gone for them to do anything that year. So they hastened on.

The plan appointed by Cabot was for Willoughby and his company to sail northward past the coast of Norway, and thence to proceed as nearly due east as they could until they had passed the whole northern coast of Asia and were able to turn southward and make their way to what was supposed to be the empire of Cathay, really the north-eastern part of China. This was thought to be a better route than that attempted long before by Cabot and his father, or the new one specially recommended by Robert Thorne, in 1527, which was to take the voyagers straight across the North Pole and bring them out on the other side of the globe.

Willoughby followed his directions as far as he was able. He reached the Luffoden Isles on the 2nd of August, and sailed on past the North Cape, intending to enter a harbour on the borders of Lapland, and there wait for a pilot who, the people of the district told him, would be able to help him on his way. "But when we would have entered the harbour," he said, in his journal, "there came such flaws of wind and terrible whirl-

* EDEN, fol. 257.

winds, that we were not able to bear in, but by violence were constrained to take the sea again. And that night, by violence of wind and thickness of mists, we were not able to keep together within sight, and then about midnight we lost our pinnace, which was a discomfort to us." Next morning, the fog being dispersed, Willoughby discovered the *Bona Confidentia;* but the *Edward Bonaventure,* which was Chancelor's ship, was nowhere to be seen. The Admiral therefore, after making a vain search, determined to proceed with the two smaller vessels.

He sailed due east, and on the 14th of August reached the coast of Nova Zembla.* Thence he proceeded northwards for three days. But, on the 18th, finding no harbour in which he could repair some damage that had been done to the *Bona Confidentia,* and being prevented from further voyaging in the same direction by a heavy wind that set in from the north-east, he turned back and sailed southwards and then westward. He seems to have lost heart, or at any rate to have concluded that it was impossible to proceed further on the route to Cathay without repairing his ships and obtaining fresh supplies of food. He sailed slowly back, keeping as near to the main land as he could, vainly looking for a suitable harbour at which to put in, until, on the

---

* Mr. Rundall, in his *Narratives of Voyages towards the North-West* (Hakluyt Society, 1849), pp. iv—xii, has clearly shown that the point here reached by Willoughby was Nova Zembla, and not Spitzbergen, as has been generally asserted. Dr. Beke has given further proof of this in his *Three Voyages by the North-East towards Cathay and China, undertaken by the Dutch* (Hakluyt Society, 1853).

18th of September, he reached the same point at which he had been separated from Chancelor six weeks before. This was a small haven on the coast of Lapland, near the mouth of the Warsina. "This haven," we read on the last page of Willoughby's journal, "runneth in the main about two leagues, and is in breadth half a league, wherein were very many seal fishes and other great fishes, and upon the main we saw bears, great deer, foxes, with divers strange beasts, as guloines" —apparently elks—"and such other which were to us unknown and also wonderful. Thus remaining in this haven the space of a week, seeing the year far spent, and also very evil weather, as frost, snow, and hail, we thought best to winter there." He and the sixty men who were with him never left it. Two years afterwards, later travellers found their bones, their papers, and other remains, with evidence that some of them at any rate, Willoughby among the number, were alive in January, 1554. It would seem that they died of cold and hunger.*

Thus miserably perished the main hope of Sebastian Cabot's north-eastern expedition. Richard Chancelor was more fortunate. His ship having been separated from the other two during the storm of the 2nd of August, he went, according to the instructions that had been issued in anticipation of such a mischance, to Wardhus, the easternmost point of Norway. There he waited for seven days, and then, believing that the others had been lost, set out alone upon the projected voyage. Some

* HAKLUYT, vol. i., pp. 258—263; PURCHAS, vol. iii., p. 463.

Scotch traders whom he met at Wardhus, it is recorded by the friend to whom he described his adventures, "began earnestly to dissuade him from the further prosecution of the discovery, by amplifying the dangers which he was to fall into, and omitted no reason that might serve to that purpose; but he, holding nothing so ignominious and reproachful as inconstancy and levity of mind, and persuading himself that a man of valour could not commit a more dishonourable part than for fear of danger to avoid and shun great attempts, was nothing at all changed or discouraged with the speeches and words of the Scots." Most of his crew desired to go home, but all agreed to submit to his orders. Therefore they sailed on, in what precise direction we are not informed, until they came to "a place where they found no night at all, but a continual light and brightness of the sun shining clearly upon the huge and mighty sea." If that report be true, they must have gone far north and entered the region of the long arctic day. But in that case, they turned back again. The first place which we know them to have visited was in the neighbourhood of the White Sea. They entered it and made friends with the natives. These natives treated them kindly, and sent a messenger to their Emperor to inform him of "the arrival of a strange nation." Without delay, the Emperor of Muscovy sent to invite Chancelor to Moscow. He went thither, was courteously entertained, made close observation of the habits of the people, and effected a commercial treaty with the Emperor. The prospects of new trade thus opened, and the long delay consequent on his visit to Moscow, induced him to abandon for the present any further voyaging to the east, and to go home at once with the letter of friendship to Edward VI. that had been entrusted to him by the Emperor, and with many substantial proofs of the good work he had done.*

The loss of Willoughby and two of the three ships sent with him, and Chancelor's success in Russia, induced the Merchant Adventurers who had fitted out the expedition to alter their purposes. "The discovery of regions, dominions, islands, and places unknown," was given up, and the association became, by a charter of Queen Mary, dated February, 1555, "The Fellowship of English Merchants for Discovery of New Trades," afterwards better known as The Muscovy or Russia Company. Nearly every year one or more expeditions, important from a commercial point of view, were despatched, and work of geographical importance was done in exploration of the northern coast of Russia. The most memorable of these was a voyage made by Stephen Burrough, who had been master of the *Edward Bonaventure* under Willoughby, and who was now captain of the *Searchthrift*, for discovery in the direction of the river Oby. He examined the southern parts of Nova Zembla, and went very near to the mouth of the Oby, when the impenetrable ice drove him back. In 1580, Arthur Pet, another of Willoughby's followers, visited the same regions, and was driven back by the

* CLEMENT ADAMS, cited by EDEN; also in HAKLUYT.

same cause. After that, no noteworthy attempt at finding a north-eastern passage to the Indies was attempted by Englishmen under the Tudors.

Richard Chancelor made one other journey to Russia. Returning to England in November, 1556, with the first Russian ambassador to the English court for his passenger, his ship, the same *Edward Bonaventure* in which he had made his first voyage, was driven ashore by a storm at Pitsligo, in the north of Scotland, and there dashed in pieces among the rocks. Chancelor, "using all carefulness for the safety of the body of the ambassador and his train," placed the foreigners in the ship's boat as soon as the wreck appeared imminent, and sought to convey them at once to land. But, says the chronicler, "the same boat, by rigorous waves of the seas, was by dark night overwhelmed and drowned, wherein perished not only the body of the said Grand Pilot, with seven Russes, but also divers of the mariners of the ship; the noble personage of the ambassador, with a few others, by God's preservation and special favour, only with much difficulty saved."* So that, after all, Chancelor's "two little sons" were "in the case of orphans."

Sebastian Cabot did not long survive his young disciple. At the institution of the Muscovy Company, he was appointed its Governor for life, as being "the chiefest setter forth of the enterprise;" and Stephen Burrough, in his account of his voyage in the *Search-thrift*, tells how "the good old gentleman, Master

* HAKLUYT, vol. i., p. 286.

Cabot, accompanied with divers gentlemen and gentlewomen," went to Gravesend to inspect the ship previous to its departure. "Master Cabot," adds Burrough, "gave to the poor most liberal alms, wishing them to pray for the good fortune and prosperous success of the *Searchthrift;* and then, at the sign of the Christopher, he and his friends banqueted, and made me and them hat were in the company great cheer; and, for very joy that he had to see the towardness of our intended discovery, he entered into the dance himself among the rest of the young and lusty company; which being ended, he and his friends departed, most gently commending us to the governance of Almighty God." *

With that pleasant view of Cabot giving alms and dancing, at the age of eighty-four, to show his sympathy with the adventurers in that work of arctic discovery to which his long life had been devoted, we almost lose sight of him. He appears never to have been in favour with Queen Mary and her Spanish husband, who owed him an old grudge for withdrawing himself from the service of Spain; and it is supposed to have been in an outburst of royal spite that he was forced, on the 27th of May, 1557, to resign his appointment as Grand Pilot of England,† and only allowed two days afterwards to resume it in partnership with a William Worthington.‡ Cabot's old age may have been sufficient reason for this change; but friends of English enterprise declared that in Worthington's ap-

* HAKLUYT, vol. i., p. 274.
† RYMER, *Fœdera*, vol. xv., p. 427.   ‡ *Ibid.*, p. 466.

pointment the office of Grand Pilot, "to the great hindrance of the commonwealth, was miserably turned to private uses."* Posterity, at any rate, owes no gratitude to William Worthington. He seems to have done nothing in the interests of commerce and navigation; and by him, or those to whom he confided them, were lost all the charts and documents, in illustration of his own and other men's voyages of discovery which Cabot had been collecting for sixty years. †

Our last view of Cabot, eminently characteristic of the man, is on his death-bed. During his last hours, we are told, the thoughts and wishes that had been with him all through life were as strong as ever. He talked flightily to his friend Richard Eden about a divine revelation made to him as to an infallible way of finding the longitude of any place, which he was not allowed to disclose to the world;‡ and then he died, certainly not less than eighty-five years old. Concerning the date and place of his death we have no information. In the turmoil of religious persecution he and his cherished projects were almost forgotten. But the projects were revived under the better rule of Queen Elizabeth, and suggested a field for the exercise of that adventurous spirit for which, above all others, her reign is famous.

* HAKLUYT, vol. i., *Dedication.* † BIDDLE, p. 221.
‡ EDEN, *Epistle Dedicatory* to his translation of *A Very Necessary and Profitable Book concerning Navigation* by JOANNES TAISNERUS, cited by BIDDLE.

CHAPTER V.

The Promoters of Cathayan Enterprise under Queen Elizabeth.

[1558—1575.]

WITHIN the limits of Sebastian Cabot's lifetime is comprised all the first period of American discovery. As a young man he heard of the memorable voyage by which Columbus, going out in search of the fabled riches of Cathay, opened the way to a new world of substantial wealth. Five years later he himself took part in the hardly less memorable voyage conducted by his father, also in quest of Cathay, which issued in the first landing of civilized Europeans upon the solid continent of America. In many later enterprises, moreover, he was personally engaged, and in every one of the hundreds of others that were led by other adventurers he took a lively interest. Those which had for their object or their consequence the discovery and colonization, by Spaniards, Germans, and Portuguese, of the central and southern districts of America do not here concern us. Those in which Englishmen attempted a passage to the Indies through the seas north of America we have already reviewed. But there were a few foreign enterprises in the direction indicated by the

Cabots which must be glanced at if we would understand the condition of geographical knowledge touching the districts sought and found by Frobisher and Davis when they embarked upon their work, and the precise extent to which thereby they served the cause they had at heart.

The first of these was conducted by Gaspar de Cortereal, a Portuguese gentleman, who in 1500, and again in 1502, visited the coast of North America, near the mouth of the Saint Lawrence, and tracked that river for a little way under the impression that it was a channel to the Eastern Ocean. It resulted in the establishment of a small Portuguese fishing colony in Newfoundland, and the extension, little by little, of discovery in those parts visited each summer-time by the fishing-smacks.

The French soon followed in the steps of the Portuguese, and for some years previous to 1523 they appear to have conducted annual trading expeditions to the neighbourhood of the Saint Lawrence. In 1523 they entered upon bolder work, at the instigation of their first great voyager, Juan de Verrazano, a Florentine by birth, but a Frenchman by adoption. Provided by Francis I. with four vessels, Verrazano lost two of them in a storm off the coast of Brittany, and from another he was separated near the Azores. In the fourth, the *Dolphin*, he left Madeira on the 17th of January, 1524. His object was to find a passage north of America towards Cathay. He only succeeded, however, in exploring the North American coast between what is now called Hudson's River, at which he first saw land, and the Saint Lawrence, whence he returned to France.

In the same year the Spaniards, not satisfied with their triumphs in the central parts of the continent and the islands adjacent to it, sent a Portuguese pilot in their employ, named Estevan Gomez, partly, as it seems, at the instigation of Sebastian Cabot, then Pilot Major of Spain, to seek a short route to the Spice Islands. His fancy was that such a route was to be found in a channel between all those northern districts to which the Spaniards gave the vague name of Baccalaos, and the more southern parts as vaguely indicated by the name of Florida. He therefore sailed up to the mouth of the Saint Lawrence, and thence searched the coast, in an opposite direction to that followed a few months before by Verrazano, down to Hudson's River, and to some distance further south. Cathay was not reached by it, but the Spaniards were thus led to take their part in the trade of fishing for cod, north and south of Newfoundland, in which the Portuguese and the French were already profitably engaged.

In these ways Europe was made tolerably familiar, before the middle of the sixteenth century, with the entire eastern coast-line of North America; and it was clearly proved that, if the Indies were anyhow to be reached by sailing out into the west, the sailing must be through those icy regions first approached by the Cabots in 1497. In proof that such a route was possible, and in earnest entreaty that it might be attempted, a number of learned arguments were put forward by a crowd of enterprising Englishmen, almost immediately after the staying of domestic troubles consequent on the succession of Queen Elizabeth to the throne.

The man who did more than any other to bring about a revival of the search for Cathay by voyaging to the north of America was Sir Humphrey Gilbert. But he appears to have been himself much encouraged thereto by earlier arguments adduced by Anthony Jenkinson in favour of further enterprise among the icy seas to the north of Asia.

Jenkinson was a traveller by profession. We first meet with him in the year 1553, when he went with John Lock, who appears to have been a brother of the famous merchant of London, Sir William Lock, on a trading voyage to the Levant, and thence to Jerusalem.* In 1557 he went as agent of the Muscovy Company to Russia; and from Moscow he proceeded, in the following year, upon a long and important journey to Bokhara and the districts around the Caspian Sea. There he collected itineraries of the overland route to Cathay, but was himself unable to pursue it.† In 1561 he was sent on a second journey to Russia, and there he resided for about three years.‡ On the 30th of May, 1565, soon after his return, he addressed a letter to Queen Elizabeth, urging her to advance her fame and increase her realm and riches by despatching an expedition to Cathay. He told how, when

---

* HAKLUYT, vol. ii., part i., pp. 101—126.
† Ibid., vol. i., pp. 310, 314, 324.
‡ Ibid., vol. i., pp. 343, 382, 395.

in Moscow, he had seen a unicorn's head, which had been brought from Cathay by sea to Vaigats, and thence overland; and represented that as Englishmen had already sailed as far as Vaigats, it must be as easy for them, aided by their wit and prowess, as it could be for rude barbarians, to perform the rest of the voyage. He himself, he said, had been in districts so far north that he had been in daylight ten weeks long, and he was assured, by the reports of other travellers and native merchants, that during those long arctic days the seas and land were temperate enough for residence and passage. He added that it was now well known that Cathay far surpassed in wealth all the parts of the Indies visited by the Spaniards and the Portuguese, and that near it were vast islands with boundless stores of gold, silver, and precious jewels, and other excellent treasures; and he represented that, if her Majesty would embark in this enterprise, she would insure for herself infinite wealth, and become " the famous princess of the world."*

At about the same time, though the precise date of the document is not recorded, a petition to the same effect was addressed to the Queen by Master Humphrey Gilbert, of whose previous history all we know is, that he was born in or near the year 1539, and the second son of Otho Gilbert, of Greenway, in Devonshire; so that he was then about twenty-five years old. In his petition Gilbert represented that nothing had been

* RECORD OFFICE MSS., *Reign of Elizabeth, Domestic Series*, vol. xxxvi., No. 60.

publicly said or done, for a long time past, touching the discovery of a north-eastern passage to Cathay. He therefore asked permission to fit out an expedition with this object, at his own expense, and with the assistance of certain friends who were willing to aid him in the project. In recompense for this he proposed that the exclusive use of the passage, if he found it, should be reserved to him, his two brothers, and their heirs, or to any one to whom they might transfer their privileges, and that all the profits of the enterprise should go to those who embarked upon it, with the exception of the fifths which, according to the usage in all such cases, belonged to the Crown.*

Almost immediately after this, we find Jenkinson and Gilbert holding conference together on the subject of this projected expedition, and Jenkinson writing to Sir William Cecil, the Principal Secretary of State, begging for an answer to their previous proposals, and again urging the advantages that would result from the enterprise if they were allowed to embark upon it on the terms already proposed.† Queen Elizabeth, however, does not seem to have listened very readily to the project. Without actually refusing it she sent Jenkinson‡ back to Russia as her ambassador, and found employment for Gilbert near home.

* BRITISH MUSEUM MSS., *Birch*, No. 4159, fol. 176, described by Mr. SAINSBURY in his *Calendar of State Papers, Colonial Series, East Indies, China, and Japan*, vol. i.—a work to which I am very largely indebted.
† RECORD OFFICE MSS., *Domestic Series*, vol. xlii., No. 23 a.
‡ HAKLUYT, vol. i., p. 372.

He was ordered to Ireland, in July, 1566, there to take employment under the Lord Deputy, Sir Henry Sidney. He was made a captain in the little army with which Sidney resisted the forces of the treacherous rebel, Shane O'Neill, if patriotic resistance of invasion can at any time be called treachery or rebellion. He took an active part in the fighting that ensued in September and October,* and he was busy in Ireland during the greater part of the next four years.

His Cathayan project, however, was not forgotten. Having been sent to England with despatches by Sir Henry Sidney, in November, 1566, he took the opportunity of again petitioning Queen Elizabeth. He reminded her that he was a member of the Corporation for the Discovery of New Trades to which she had just given a charter, and that therefore he had good reason, in the interest of trade, to undertake the discovery of a route to Cathay "and all other the rich parts of the world not found." On this occasion he asked for use of two of the Queen's ships, provided he supplied two others, requiring only as his recompenses the life government of any countries he might conquer in the Queen's name, a tenth part of all the land they might contain, and diminution of customs duties upon any goods he might export or import during the first forty years. This petition differed essentially from the previous one, in that it proposed to reach the Indies by sailing to the north-west instead of to the north-east, and to this

---

* RECORD OFFICE MSS., *Reign of Elizabeth, Irish Correspondence*, vol. xix., Nos. 43, 44.

change of plan Gilbert steadily adhered in all his later proposals for Cathayan enterprise.* Queen Elizabeth and Sir William Cecil appear to have favourably entertained the project. But the Company of Merchant Adventurers stoutly protested against it as an infringement of the charter lately accorded to them, and therefore it was abandoned.†

Early in 1567 Gilbert was sent back to Ireland. He was there in March, and in June the Queen wrote to Sidney bidding him see how far the Irish rebels could be restrained by the establishment of a colony of obedient subjects in Ulster, and in this work to use the assistance of Captain Gilbert. These colonists were to come chiefly from the West of England. Gilbert was to help in selecting them, to conduct them to the neighbourhood of Lough Foyle, and there to be their president.‡ The undertaking fell to the ground, however, and Gilbert returned to his former work of soldiering. Through 1568 and 1569 Gilbert's band of horsemen was Sir Henry Sidney's main stay. Having been sent to England in the summer of 1568 he there fell dangerously ill, whereupon the Queen took occasion to write to Sidney, saying he was to have his full pay during his absence, and that some better place was to be found for him on his return. The better place was a colonelcy, and as a colonel, Gilbert defeated the celebrated McCarthy More in September, 1569. In October Sidney

* RECORD OFFICE MSS., *Domestic*, vol. xlii., No. 23.
† *Ibid.*, vol. xlii., No. 5.
‡ *Ibid.*, Ireland, vol. xx., No. 56; vol. xxi., Nos. 10, 49, 56, 64.

placed him in entire charge of the province of Munster, where he had to keep McCarthy More and his friends in subjection. Therein he acted as harshly as Queen Elizabeth could wish. In December he wrote to the Lord Deputy saying that he was determined to have neither parley nor peace with any rebel; that he had put many to the sword; and that he should leave no malefactor who came into his hands unexecuted, as he was convinced that no conquered nation could be ruled with gentleness. Thereupon Sidney sent to the Queen special praise of Gilbert's "discretion, judgment, and lusty courage;" and on the 1st of January, 1570, he knighted him for the same at Drogheda. His stern conduct brought temporary peace to Ireland, and early in 1571, when Sir Henry Sidney resigned his Lord Deputyship, he also was allowed to return to England.*

He was not in England long. His fighting experience in Ireland led him to join, as a volunteer soldier, in the more nobler contest then beginning in Holland. In the summer of 1572, while Gilbert's band, as it was still called, kept Ireland in awe, he went to Flanders with fourteen hundred Englishmen, and there took some part in the brave struggle for independence which the Protestants of Flanders were maintaining against the forces of Philip of Spain and his deputy the Duke of Alva. He helped to besiege Sluys, and when induced by his new friends to abandon that work, he took part in two assaults on Tergoes. But his hot-headed mode of fighting, acquired in Ireland, did not agree with the

* RECORD OFFICE MSS., *Ireland*, vols. xxiii.—xxxii., *passim*.

more prudent tactics of the Dutchmen. He had hoped to take Tergoes before it was relieved by the Spaniards; and when that relief was effected by Mondragon's famous march of five hours' length, through country under water, on the 20th of October, he came to the strange conclusion that the Flemings were not bold enough to make useful any further fighting on their behalf. Therefore he returned to England.*

For the next few years he lived quietly at Limehouse, where also he had resided during the twelve months previous to his Flemish enterprise. In the summer of 1571 he had been employed by Queen Elizabeth in preparing statutes for the maintenance of artillery, and for the suitable provision of horses and armour to be used in the Queen's service.† During the first few months following his return, he was busy negotiating for the establishment of some alum, copperas, and copper works in the neighbourhood of London. In February, 1572, he offered to pay to Lady Katherine Mountjoy 400*l*. or 500*l*. a year for the use of her house and grounds in this way. But others with whom he was associated in this project wished to add alchemy to their chemistry, and to attempt the transmutation of iron into copper. Gilbert was wise enough to object to this, and therefore in May he withdrew from the concern, earning thereby the abuse of his partners.‡

Amid these and other occupations, however, he

* Sir ROGER WILLIAMS, *Actions of the Low Countries*, in SCOTT's edition of the *Somers Tracts* (1809), vol. i., pp. 359—365.
† RECORD OFFICE MSS., *Domestic*, vol. lxxxviii., No. 46.
‡ *Ibid.*, vol. lxxxv., Nos. 45, 46; vol. lxxxvi., Nos. 14, 44.

retained all his interest in the schemes for Cathayan voyaging and discovery about which we saw him petitioning the Queen a few years before. George Gascoigne, the poet, tells how, in the winter of 1574, he visited him at Limehouse and asked him "how he spent his time in this loitering vacation from martial stratagems." By way of answer Gilbert took his friend into his study and there showed him "sundry profitable and very commendable exercises which he had perfected plainly with his own pen." The chief of these "exercises" was a learned 'Discourse to prove a Passage by the North-West to Cathay and the East Indies,' which Gascoigne borrowed, and, either with or without permission, lost no time in publishing.* This 'Discourse' so clearly and completely sets forth the arguments on the subject that were in force during Elizabeth's reign that we shall best understand the state of opinion thereupon, if we look at it in some detail.

Gilbert began with reference to Plato's Atlantis, which he identified with America, considering the America of his day to be so much of the old Atlantis as was not swamped by floods in ancient times; and Plato's speculations he supported by the opinion of later writers and cosmographers. "All which learned men and painful travellers," he said, "have affirmed with one consent and voice that America is an island, and that there lieth a great sea between it, Cathay, and Greenland, by

---

* Preface to the *Discourse*, printed by EDEN in his *Decades*; and afterwards, without the preface, by HAKLUYT, in his *Voyages*, vol. iii., pp. 11—24.

the which any man of our country that will give the attempt may, with small danger, pass to Cathay, the Moluccas, India, and all other places in the east, in much shorter time than either the Spaniard or Portuguese doth or may do, from the nearest part of any of their countries within Europe."

That America is a great island, Gilbert thought to be proved by the testimony of various travellers both in the east and in the west, and by the fact that none of its natives had ever wandered into Europe or Asia, and that no Tartars, Scythians, or other migratory tribes of the Old World had ever found their way to it, or, if they had done so, ever returned to tell their comrades of its treasures. "It also appears to be an island," he said, "because the sea runneth by nature circularly from east to west, which motion of the water is most evidently seen in the sea which lieth on the south side of Africa, where the current that runneth from the east to the west is so strong that the Portuguese, in their voyages eastward to Calicut in passing by the Cape of Good Hope, are enforced to make divers courses, the current there being so swift as it striketh from thence all along westward upon the Frith of Magellan." Gilbert urged that as this current passed northward, from Magellan's Straits, along the whole coast of America, and there met another current, almost as strong, which came from the north-east, they must necessarily proceed together past the northern coast of America till they entered the Pacific Ocean. "The current of the great ocean could not have been maintained to run continually one way from the beginning of the world unto this day had there not been some through passage; so that this perpetual current cannot be maintained but by continual re-access of the same water which passes through the frith and is brought thither again by the circular motion." And if water took this course, thought Gilbert, ships could certainly sail upon its surface in the same direction. He did not take account of the treacherous icebergs and the frozen crust, far less easily to be traversed than solid land.

Having proved to his satisfaction the existence of a north-western passage, Sir Humphrey Gilbert brought together all the reports of voyagers, from Cabot downwards, who had attempted it at its eastern entrance, or visited the neighbourhood of its termination in Behring's Straits. Though Europeans had not yet succeeded, he made much of a story, believed in his day, that it had been accomplished by some natives of Asia who came to Germany in 1160; and what barbarous red men had done he urged that civilized white men could certainly accomplish. He next adduced many weighty arguments against Anthony Jenkinson's project, in which he himself had believed a few years previously, in favour of a north-eastern passage to Cathay, without perceiving that they weighed quite as strongly against his present plan for sailing round the northern shore of America. He concluded his 'Discourse' with enumeration of the advantages that must result to England from the successful carrying through of his project. By this and by this only, he said, could we hope to take a share of the rich trade carried on with the east by Portugal and with the west by Spain. In this direction, and in no other, could we pursue our traffic without opposition from either nation, and the facilities of the route, when once made clear, would enable us to undersell them in all the markets of the world. "Also we might sail to divers very rich countries, both civil and others, out of both their jurisdictions, where there is to be found great abundance of gold, silver, and precious stones, cloth of gold, silks, all manner of spices, grocery-wares, and other kinds of merchandize of an inestimable price, which both the Spaniard and the Portuguese, through the length of their journey, cannot well attain unto." Gilbert speculated that the finding of this north-west passage would result in the establishment of rich English colonies in distant parts, which would provide a comfortable home for the people now starving or toiling painfully in the overcrowded mother-country, and furnish unspeakable wealth to those who remained in the land of their birth. "These things considered," he said, "I must needs conclude that this discovery has been reserved for some noble prince or worthy man, thereby to make himself rich and the world happy."

This treatise of Sir Humphrey Gilbert's was the prelude to a general revival of interest among Englishmen in the project that it advocated. Though not printed, apparently, till 1576, it was handed about in manuscript during at least a year and a half previous to that date,* and seems to have been the chief incentive to a letter which, near the close of 1574, Queen Elizabeth addressed to the governor and directors of the Muscovy Company, reminding them that twenty years had passed since they had last despatched an expedition in search of Cathay, and telling them that as they had been incorporated with the chief object of pursuing that search, it was right that they should continue it or else transfer their privileges to other adventurers who were eager to possess them.† The bearer of that letter was Martin Frobisher, and the chief adviser of the Company at the time of its coming was Michael Lock. These two men, in different degrees, share with Gilbert the merit of reviving the Cathayan project.

Michael Lock was the son of Sir William Lock, a rich London merchant, who was associated with Sir Thomas Gresham in many commercial undertakings. The son was born in 1532. "My late father," he said, in a short memoir of himself, written in 1577, "kept me at schools of grammar in England till I was thirteen years old, and, he being sworn servant to King Henry VIII., his mercer and also his agent beyond the seas in divers affairs, he then sent me over seas to Flanders and France to learn these languages and to know the world. Since which time I have continued these thirty-two years in travail of body and study of mind, following my vocation in the trade of merchan-

---

* British Museum MSS., *Cotton*, Otho E. viii., fol. 43.
† *Ibid.*

dize; whereof I have spent the first fifteen years in continued travail of body, passing through almost all the countries of Christianity, both by land and by sea, not without great labours, cares, dangers, and expenses of money incident; having had the charge, as captain of a great ship of burthen, by the space of more than three years." After that he settled in London as a merchant. While applying himself to commerce, however, as he said, " by a certain inclination of mind, I have been drawn continually as my vocation and care of my family would permit, to the study of cosmography." " By divers conferences with men of divers nations, travellers and merchants," he acquired all the information that he could about all parts of the world; and, as he studied, the conviction grew upon him, he tells us, that by opening a north-west passage to the Indies great advantages might be brought, not only to himself and his family, but also to England and the whole commercial world.*

Martin Frobisher arrived at a similar conviction in a kindred way. Of his early history we know very little. He was a native of Normanton, in Yorkshire, and was about as old as Gilbert. Lock, in the memoir just cited, says that " he was born of honest parentage, a gentleman of a good house and antiquity, who, in his youth, for lack of schools thereabout, sent him to London, where he was put to Sir John York, knight, being his kinsman, who, perceiving him to be of great spirit and bold courage and natural hardness

* *Cotton MSS.*, Otho E. viii., fols. 41, 42.

of body, sent him in a ship to the Gold Country of
Guinea, in company of other ships set out by divers
merchants of London." That was in the autumn of
1554. The expedition in which young Frobisher was
put to learn seamanship was the first, with the exception of a short tentative voyage undertaken in the
previous year, in which Englishmen explored the
western coast of Africa, and followed in the track of
Portuguese voyagers past the Cape of Good Hope to
India. Its commander was John Lock, either the uncle
or the brother of Michael Lock, and the adventurers,
after traversing the Gold Coast, landed and made a
beginning of a prosperous trade in elephants' teeth and
African gold. They returned to London in the summer
of 1555.* For the next eleven years we hear nothing
of Frobisher; but it is pretty certain that he continued
the occupation in which his rich kinsman had started
him, and shared in some of the expeditions which were
every year despatched either to the west coast of Africa
or to its northern shores and the district of the Levant.
By the summer of 1566, at any rate, he had risen to
the rank of captain. On the 30th of May, and again
on the 11th of June, in that year, he was examined by
order of the Queen's Council on suspicion of having
fitted out a ship with the intention of using it in piratical ways.† Of the issue of that examination we are
ignorant, and we lose sight of him for five other years.
We can only infer that he continued to make way as

* HAKLUYT, vol. ii., part ii., pp. 14—23.
† RECORD OFFICE MSS., *Domestic Series*, vol. xl., Nos. 2—7.

sailor, trader, and pirate—piracy being an employment which in those times was either praised or punished according to its value or inconvenience to the State. In August, 1571, we find that a hulk was being built for him at Portsmouth, with the sanction, if not under the direction, of Lord Burghley, to be used in furtherance of Elizabeth's plans for the subjugation of Ireland and the annoyance of Irishmen, and he appears to have been frequently employed upon Irish work during the next two or three years.* This employment brought him into close relationship with the State and under the immediate notice of Queen Elizabeth. It probably also secured for him the friendship of Sir Henry Sidney and of Sidney's brother-in-law, the Earl of Warwick, as well as of Sidney's favourite, Sir Humphrey Gilbert.

One result of these associations was the Queen's letter conveyed, as we have seen, in December, 1574, by Frobisher to the Muscovy Company. The Company found Russian trade so profitable that it demurred to Queen Elizabeth's suggestion of a voyage in quest of Cathay. Thereupon without delay the Queen sent a second message, ordering that, if the Company refused itself to take the matter in hand, it was to grant a licence for the enterprise to certain adventurers who desired to embark upon it. A licence was accordingly granted, in February, 1575, to Master Martin Frobisher and divers gentlemen associated with him; and out of

* RECORD OFFICE MSS., *Domestic Series*, vol. lxxx., Nos. 31, 54; *Irish Series*, vol. xxxviii., No. 48.

that grew Frobisher's three voyages in search of a north-west passage to the Indies.*

The chief promoter of the work was Sir Humphrey Gilbert; but his pupils appear to have soon grown jealous of him, and while they zealously pursued their quest his services were well-nigh forgotten.

* Lock's *Memoir*, in *Cotton MSS.*, Otho E. viii., fols. 41—43.

CHAPTER VI.

Martin Frobisher's Three Voyages in the Direction of Cathay.

[1575—1579.]

THE licence granted to Martin Frobisher and his partners in the enterprise for finding a north-west passage to Cathay was dated the 3rd of February, 1575. During the next sixteen months the friends were busily preparing for the work. Sir Humphrey Gilbert, no great traveller, brought the results of long study and much scientific observation, but, having little money with which to second his arguments, and meeting with much opposition from richer and less learned men, soon turned aside from it in chagrin, or only watched its progress from a distance. Michael Lock was the richest of the group, and his influence with City people secured promises of assistance from others richer than himself, and helped to bring into the little company of schemers some men of large experience and scientific observation. Science was represented by Dr. Dee, the astrologer. The advisers of most practical experience in northern voyaging were Stephen Burrough, the old associate of Willoughby and Chancelor, and Anthony Jenkinson, the famous Russian traveller and early advocate of a

north-eastern voyage to the Indies. Frobisher himself
brought great experience in seamanship, acquired in
more temperate regions, and the favour of Queen Elizabeth and Lord Burghley; but, as Lock alleged four
years afterwards, when the friends had quarrelled, very
little liking from some supporters of the project.

The first thing to be done was to collect money
enough for the enterprise. Lock himself subscribed
100*l.*; and Sir Thomas Gresham, then fifty-six years old,
and at the height of his commercial greatness, William
Bird, then Customer—that is, chief collector of customs
—of London, and Alderman William Bond, also contributed 100*l.* a piece; Lord Burghley, the Earl of
Sussex, the famous Earl of Leicester, and his brother
the Earl of Warwick, each subscribed 50*l.*; and promises of 25*l.* a piece were given by Leicester's nephew,
Philip Sidney, by Secretary Walsingham, by Anthony
Jenkinson, by Lionel Duckett, the great merchant of
London, and by four other gentlemen. Thus a fund of
875*l.* was secured; but this, though the amount must
be multiplied by six or seven, to get its equivalent in
modern currency, was quite insufficient for carrying
out the project, and no more could be collected in time
for action during the summer of 1575. At that, says
Lock, Frobisher was "a sad man." In a very boastful
account of his services in the work, which must be read
with some distrust, however, Lock represents that he
pledged himself to secure its accomplishment in the following year; and then Frobisher was "alive again." In
default of other assistance, Lock reports that he him-

self, in addition to his previous subscription of 100*l.*, supplied as much money as from time to time was needed, making in all 738*l.* 19*s.* 3*d.* He tells us that he helped Frobisher in all sorts of other ways. He lent him all the books, charts, maps, and instruments that he had been collecting during twenty years. He introduced him to men of influence and wisdom. "I made my house his home, my purse his purse, and my credit his credit," he says, "when he was utterly destitute both of money, and credit, and of friends."

The autumn of 1575, and the ensuing winter and spring were spent in zealous consultations and preparations. That he might be nearer to Lock's residence and to the docks in which the vessels were being fitted out, Frobisher left his lodgings in Fleet Street, and went to live at Widow Hancock's house in Mark Lane. Frequent conferences were held in the house of Alderman Bond, close by; yet more frequent were the meetings under Lock's roof, where charts were examined, plans propounded and considered, and arrangements made for the choice and fitting out of vessels, selecting of mariners and officers, and the like. Meetings were held also at Court, where Frobisher's best friend appears to have been the Earl of Warwick, who advanced him in the favour of Queen Elizabeth and the more cautious support of the great Earl of Burghley. The Court being generally held at Greenwich, statesmen and courtiers took their share in personal inspection of the arrangements for the voyage. Thus, with help from divers sources, and a good deal of advice that was by no means

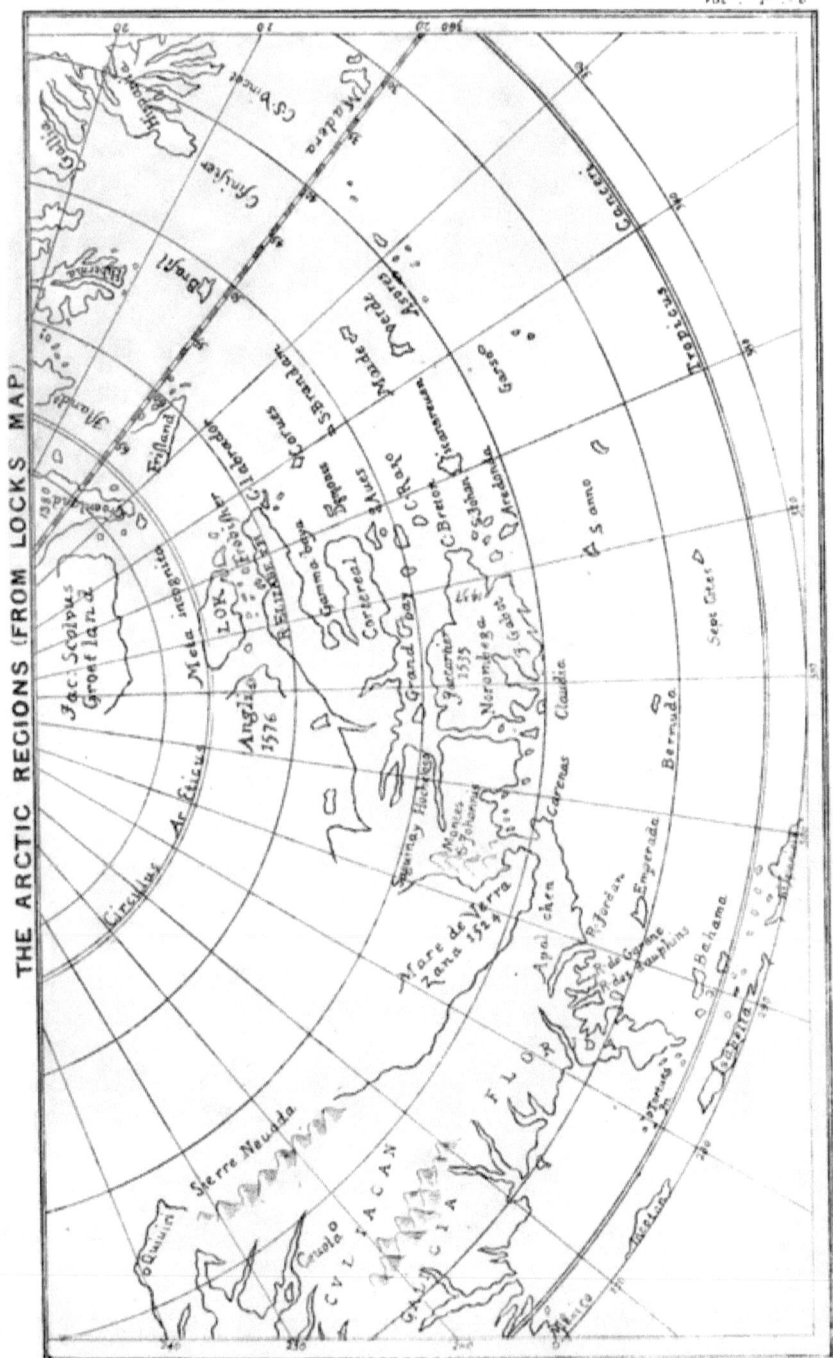

helpful, the arrangements were completed by the end of May, 1576, and two stout little barks, the *Gabriel* and the *Michael*, each of twenty-five tons' burthen, with a small pinnace, carrying ten tons, attached to them, lay in the Thames, near to old London Bridge, ready for departure. Frobisher received his commission as admiral or captain of the expedition; Christopher Hall and Owen Griffin were appointed masters of the ships, and Nicholas Chancelor was made purser of the voyage.*

The little company, numbering not more than thirty-five or forty officers and men, started on the morning of Thursday, the 7th of June. Off Deptford, the pinnace was run down by a ship coming into port, which broke her bowsprit and foremast, and that caused a day's delay. At mid-day on Friday, the vessels passed Greenwich with a volley of ordnance and other parting show of honour to the Court. Queen Elizabeth watched them and waved her hand from a window, and then sent a messenger in a rowing boat to tell the adventurers that she had good liking of their doings and thanked them for it, and that she desired Frobisher to come next day and take his leave of her. This he did while the vessels lay at anchor, and while another messenger went on board and bade the crews, in her Majesty's name, to please her by being diligent

---

* RECORD OFFICE MSS., *Domestic*, vol. cxix., No. 32; vol. cxxix., No. 44; *Cotton MSS.*, Otho E. viii., fols. 42, 43, 46; HAKLUYT, vol. iii., pp. 29, 57. The following details of the voyage are taken from the two accounts by Captain Hall and Captain Best in HAKLUYT, and from LOCK'S *Memoir*, already cited—Otho E. viii, fols. 46—53.

and faithful servants to Master Frobisher and his deputies. The final leave-taking was not over till the 12th of June, and on that day Frobisher really set out on his enterprise. He sailed round the western coast of England and Scotland, and on the 25th of the month passed the Shetlands, where he halted to stop a leak in the *Gabriel*, and to take in fresh supplies of water. Bearing round Faroe Islands, and sailing thence due west, he had sight, on the 11th of June, of some " high and ragged land rising like pinnacles of steeples," which seems to have been the southernmost part of Greenland, then known as Friesland. There he wished to land, but was deterred from seeking a harbour by " the great store of ice that lay along the coast and the great mists that troubled them not a little."

Worse trouble befel him as he passed on towards the broken mainland and islands lying west of Greenland and north of Labrador. A great storm arose, in the course of which his pinnace disappeared, never to be heard of afterwards. Thereby he lost three men; and next day he experienced a much greater loss in the disappearance of the *Michael*, which was carried away by the storm. After vainly searching for their comrades, its crew sailed westward till they reached land, apparently a part of Labrador; but, we are told, " they found it so compassed with monstrous high islands of ice, that they durst not approach." Thereupon, supposing that Frobisher and the others were wrecked, they returned to England and arrived at Bristol on the 1st of September.

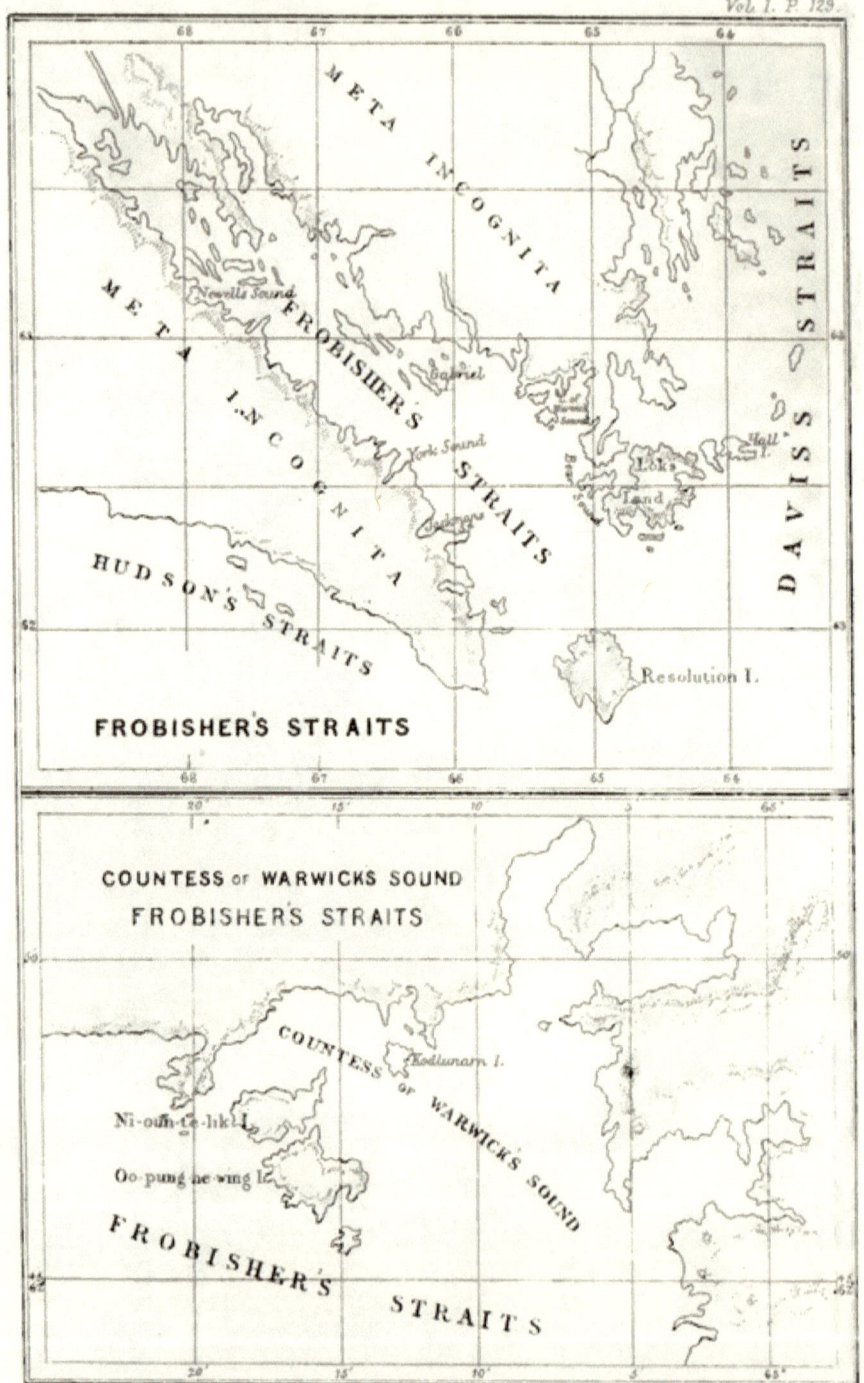

Thus Frobisher was left alone with the *Gabriel*, with eighteen mariners and gentlemen on board. In no way daunted, though his own little ship had been seriously injured, he continued his voyage. On the 21st of July he reached the group of islands lying westward of what is now called Davis's Straits. These he supposed to be a part of Labrador, and he named the one which he first saw Queen Elizabeth's Foreland. Deterred by fogs and snow-covered rocks from landing, he sailed up and down the coast, hoping to meet with a suitable harbour in which to land and repair his ship. At last, after several days' searching, he found a resting-place on an island which he called Hall's Island, in honour of the master of the *Gabriel*, who, in a rowing-boat, with four sailors, first made a landing on it on the 1st of August. Thence he sailed into the more southern of the two bays in Cumberland Island. To this bay he gave the name, still borne by it, of Frobisher's Straits. Through it he supposed that he could easily proceed to the other side of America. On his first voyage, however, he only explored some of the islands and part of the northern coast-line near the entrance to the Straits. All this neighbourhood was afterwards called Meta Incognita.

One of the voyagers has given a lively description of Frobisher's experiences. "He saw mighty deer which seemed to be man-kind, which ran at him, and hardly he escaped with his life in a narrow way, where he was fain to use defence and policy to save his life. In this place he saw and perceived sundry tokens of the people's resorting thither. And being ashore upon the top of a hill, he perceived a number of small things fleeting in the sea afar off, which he supposed to be porpoises or seals, or some kind of strange fish; but coming nearer, he discovered them to be men in small boats made of leather. And before he could descend from the hill, certain of those people had almost cut off his boat from him, having stolen secretly behind the rocks for that purpose: whereupon he speedily hasted to his boat, and went himself to his halberd, and narrowly escaped the danger and saved his boat. Afterwards he had sundry conferences with them, and they came aboard his ship, and brought him salmon and raw flesh and fish, and greedily devoured the same before our men's faces. And to show their agility, they tried many masteries upon the ropes of the ship after our mariners' fashion, and appeared to be very strong of their arms and nimble of their bodies. They exchanged coats of seals and bear-skins and such like with our men, and received bells, looking-glasses, and other toys, in recompense thereof again."

Chiefly in hopes of finding the passage to Cathay, which he believed to be within his reach, and partly also that he might fully explore the district at which he had arrived, Frobisher made several little expeditions in the neighbourhood, sometimes in the *Gabriel*, sometimes in a rowing-boat. He observed many small islands, and landed upon a few of them. In some places he saw huts and signs of human life, but no actual residents. In others he met with men "of a nature given to fierceness and rapine." In others the natives treated him kindly, and seemed anxious to have intercourse with him and to understand the wonderful circumstances of civilization that he brought within their reach. But concerning all of them it was reported that "their manner of life and food is very beastly." "They be like to Tartars, with long black hair, broad faces and flat noses, and tawny in colour, wearing seal-skins; and so do the women, not differing in fashion; but the women are marked in the face with blue streaks down the cheeks, and round about the eyes. Their boats are made all of seal-skins, with a keel of wood within the skin. The proportion of them is like a Spanish shallop, save only they be flat in the bottom and sharp at both ends."

In these investigations three weeks were profitably spent. But on the 20th of August occurred a terrible disaster. One of the Esquimaux having been brought on board the *Gabriel*, Frobisher gave him a bell and a knife, and then sent him ashore in the ship's boat, with five men to manage it. These five men, anxious to make a little exploration on their own account, disobeyed orders and rowed out of sight. They never returned. After waiting for them all that day, Frobisher spent the four following days in coasting the shore in the direction which they were supposed to have taken, blowing a trumpet and firing guns to let them know he was in search of them. Then, feeling persuaded that they had been murdered by the natives, and being convinced that it would be impossible for him to pursue his voyage with only the thirteen men and boys that were left to him and without any ship's boat to aid him in his researches, he resolved, much against his hopes and wishes, that he must abandon the work for that year and return to England.

His last act was only excusable on the plea that it accorded with the universal practice of those times—a practice which he had hitherto honourably abstained from following, and that he only did it now under the impression that his plans had been ruined by the treachery of the natives. "The captain," reports one of the crew, "being desirous to bring some token from thence of his being there, was greatly discontented that he had not before apprehended some of the people. Therefore, to deceive the deceivers, he wrought a pretty policy; for, knowing well how they greatly delighted in our toys, and especially in bells, he rang a pretty low bell, making signs that he would give him the same that would come and fetch it. And because they would not come within his danger for fear, he flung one bell unto them, which of purpose he threw short, that it might fall into the sea and be lost. And to make them more greedy of the matter, he rang a louder bell, so that in the end one of them came near the ship's side to receive the bell, which when he thought to take at the captain's hand, he was thereby taken himself; for the captain, being readily provided, let the bell fall and caught the man fast, and plucked him with main force, boat and all, into his bark out of the sea. Whereupon, when he found himself in captivity, for very choler and disdain he bit his tongue in twain with his mouth.

Notwithstanding he died not thereof, but lived until he came in England, and then he died of cold which he had taken at sea."

With this poor Esquimau on board, Frobisher weighed anchor on the 26th of August. He followed the same track that he had taken on his outward voyage, passing Greenland on the 1st of September and Iceland on the 6th, with no memorable incident on the way, save that a man who had been blown overboard by a violent gust of wind having caught hold of the foresail sheet, Frobisher was able to pick him up with the same strong arm that he had used in capturing the Esquimau. The *Gabriel* sailed into Harwich water on the 2nd of October, having been absent from England rather less than four months, and having in the interval explored a district considerably further north than the northernmost point reached by any previous travellers, with the exception of John Cabot, but having done very little towards finding the much-coveted passage to Cathay.

The voyagers were received with great honour. The report brought home just a month before by the master and crew of the *Michael* had led to a general belief that they had all been lost. That made their welcome all the heartier. In London, where they arrived on the 9th of October, says Michael Lock, " they were joyfully received with the great admiration of the people, bringing with them their strange man and his boat, which was such a wonder unto the whole city and to the rest of the realm that heard of it, as seemed never to have happened the like great matter to any man's knowledge."

When the "strange man" was dead, a yet greater theme of wondering interest arose. Let young Philip Sidney, writing in 1577 to his good friend and tutor, Hubert Languet, tell the story. Referring to an earlier letter which is lost, he says: "I wrote to you about a certain Frobisher, who, in rivalry of Magellan, has explored the sea which, as he thinks, washes the north part of America. It is a marvellous history. After having made slow progress in the past year, he touched at a certain island in order to rest both himself and his crew. And there by chance a young man, one of the ship's company, picked up a piece of earth which he saw glittering on the ground, and showed it to Frobisher; but he, being busy with other matters, and not believing that precious metals were produced in a region so far to the north, considered it of no value. But the young man kept the earth by him, as a memorial of his labour, till his return to London. And there, when one of his friends saw it shining in an extraordinary manner, he tested it and found that it was the purest gold, unalloyed with any other metal."* According to another report, this fancied treasure, which in its natural condition was "black stone, much like to sea-coal in colour," was preserved and brought to England by Frobisher himself, not as a thing of any value in itself, but as a curious relic of his arctic experiences, and, on his return, was broken up and distributed among his friends. "And it fortuned a gentlewoman, one of the

* Cited from the *Zurich Letters* in my *Memoir of Sir Philip Sidney* (1862), p. 177.

adventurers' wives, to have a piece thereof, which by chance she threw and burnt in the fire so long that at length, being taken forth and quenched in a little vinegar, it glittered with a bright marcasite of gold. Whereupon the matter being called in some question, it was brought to certain gold-finers in London to make an assay thereof, who gave out that it held gold, and that very richly for the quantity."*

Very great was the stir made in England by this report of Frobisher's gold-finding. Courtiers and merchants, men of science and hardy seamen, clamoured for a renewal of the enterprise, urging that it was of little matter whether Cathay were reached, if treasures equal to those of Cathay could be procured from nearer regions. Queen Elizabeth herself and Lord Burghley entered heartily into the project; and accordingly, in answer to petitions tendered by Frobisher and his leading friends, a charter of incorporation was issued, on unusually liberal terms, to a Company formed in furtherance of the work. This was the Company of Cathay, endowed with privileges equal to those of the Muscovy Company, which it was meant to supersede, as far as the original purposes of its formation were concerned.

The new association was composed of all the contributors to Frobisher's first expedition and of such new adventurers as chose to take shares in it. Michael Lock was appointed its governor for six years,

* HAKLUYT, vol. iii., p. 58. Detailed reports on the subject from Michael Lock, and the goldsmith whom he employed to make the assay, are among the RECORD OFFICE MSS., *Domestic*, vol. cxii., No. 25.

in consideration of his "industry, good direction, and great travail in the first voyage;" and in recompense for the great outlay of money which he had made therein he was to receive " to his own use for ever " one per cent. of the proceeds of all goods exported from the districts newly found or yet to be discovered. A similar provision was made for Martin Frobisher, to whom also was promised a fixed yearly stipend—the amount of which, however, is not mentioned—in return for his services as " Captain General by sea and Admiral of the ships and navy of the Company." The Company was directed, without delay, to make arrangements for a second voyage, and with this object to put its stock to use. This stock, it appears, amounted to 4,313*l.* 19s. 3d., of which 813*l.* 19s. 3d. were obtained by sale of the ships and goods employed in the first voyage, and 3,500*l.* consisted of new subscriptions. The Queen subscribed 1,000*l.*; Michael Lock and two others, 200*l.* a-piece; Secretary Walsingham, 175*l.*; and the rest was collected from thirty-five other contributors of smaller amounts. Among these the more notable were, Lord Burghley and Sir Thomas Gresham, Sir Philip Sidney, his sister the Countess of Pembroke, and his uncles the Earls of Leicester and Warwick. Sir Humphrey Gilbert promised 25*l.*, but does not seem to have paid it until the expedition had returned.[*]

The formal charter of the Cathay Company was issued on the 17th of March, 1577. But preparations

[*] RECORD OFFICE MSS., *Domestic*, vol. cxi., Nos. 48, 49; vol. cxix., Nos. 31, 34, 36, 40, 41, 44, 45.

for Frobisher's second voyage were begun some months before. By the 30th of March it was decided that he should be provided with three ships, his old *Gabriel* and *Michael*, each of 25 tons' burthen, and having between them twenty mariners and five soldiers on board, and one much larger vessel lent by the Queen, the *Aid*, of 200 tons' burthen, furnished with sixty-five sailors and twenty-five soldiers. Among the crews were ten convicts, most of them imprisoned for highway robbery, taken out of prison, and, in accordance with a very foolish custom of the times, handed over to Frobisher, in the expectation that he would be able to turn them into honest men.* It was by such as these that mutinies were encouraged, and lawless actions, bringing dishonour to the name of Englishmen, were done. Frobisher wisely got rid of his criminals before he had parted from the English coast.†

His ships weighed anchor at Blackwall on Whit Monday, the 26th of May. Nine days before a code of instructions for his guidance during the voyage had been addressed to him, as her "loving friend," by the Queen. In these it openly appeared that the discovery of a passage to Cathay was regarded, by merchants and statesmen at any rate, as quite subordinate to the finding of a gold district in the northern parts of America, and its conversion into an English colony. Frobisher was to go at once to Hall's Island, there to leave his large ship in

---

* RECORD OFFICE MSS., *Domestic*, vol. cxi., No. 48; vol. cxix., No. 40.
† HAKLUYT, vol. iii., p. 58.

safe harbour, and with the two smaller ones to visit the place whence he had brought the ore last year, and to search for other gold-producing districts. If he succeeded, he was to plant a colony and leave the *Aid* and its soldiers to protect it; if he failed he was at once to send the *Aid* back to England. In either case, he was only to pursue his Cathayan search in the *Gabriel* and *Michael*; if, indeed, it seemed desirable that he should do even that. In the course of the expedition he was to capture eight or ten people of the country, both young and old; " whom we mind shall not return again thither," it was said, " and therefore you shall have great care how ye do take them, for avoiding of offence towards them and the country."*

After one day's halt at Gravesend, where the sacrament was administered and the crews were, according to the report of one of them, "prepared as good Christians towards God and resolute men for all fortunes," and three days' waiting at Harwich, where additional provisions were taken in, and some who were found to be neither good Christians nor resolute men were weeded out of the company, Frobisher proceeded in the track of his previous voyage. He stopped at Orkney and found its inhabitants almost as barbarous as the Esquimaux. " At our landing," we read, " the people fled from their poor cottages, with shrieks and alarms to warn their neighbours of enemies; but, by gentle persuasions, we

---

* RECORD OFFICE MSS., *Domestic*, vol. cxiii., No. 13. The details of Frobisher's second voyage, like the first, are chiefly taken from the two eye-witnesses' reports, printed by HAKLUYT.

reclaimed them to their houses. It seemeth they are often frighted with pirates, or some other enemies, that move them with such sudden fear. Their houses are very simply built with pebble stone, without any chimneys, the fire being made in the midst thereof. They are destitute of wood; their fire is turfs and cowshards. The goodman, wife, children, and other of the family, eat and sleep on the one side of the house; and the cattle on the other; very beastly and rudely, in respect of civility. They have corn, bigg, and oats, with which they pay their king's rents, to the maintenance of his house. They take great quantities of fish, which they dry in the wind and sun. They dress their meat very filthily, and eat it without salt. Their apparel is after the rudest sort of Scotland. Their money is all base. Their Church and religion is performed according to the Scots."

Leaving these wild people on the 8th of June, Frobisher and his crew sailed on for six-and-twenty days, meeting on their way a fishing smack which had come from Iceland, but seeing no land and suffering much from contrary winds and boisterous seas. Through these they were able to pass more safely by reason of the continual day, or alternation of daylight and twilight, in which they found themselves. Great trees, torn up by the roots and brought by the currents from the coast of America, and some icebergs, came in their way, and on the 4th of July there was great firing of guns and rejoicing because the men of the *Michael*, which was in advance of the other vessels, mistook a group of larger icebergs for the northern shore of Greenland. Greenland was close by, however, and they came within sight of it in the evening of the same day. They were unable to land. During three days Frobisher wandered up and down in a rowing-boat, seeking some safe harbour; but he saw nothing but a ragged coast-line of high mountains and desolate table lands covered with snow and snow-wrapped rocks, hardly to be distinguished from the huge lumps of ice jutting out of the stormy and mist-enveloped sea.

Leaving this region on the 8th of July, Frobisher sailed on to the north-west and made for the islands which he had visited the year before. On the way the *Michael* was nearly wrecked, her steerage being broken and her topmast blown overboard, so that she was beaten out of sight and given up for lost until the morning of the 17th, when all the ships came together in the neighbourhood of Hall's Island. Frobisher tried to enter the Straits that bore his name, but they were blocked up with ice; and therefore, after some search for a better harbouring, he put into the little bay in Hall's Island, at which he had previously anchored. Then he entered upon five weeks' careful examination of the adjacent islands and waters, made sometimes with the whole fleet, sometimes in the *Gabriel* and *Michael*, and oftenest in one or more of the ships' boats.

Concerning the results of this examination we have many curious details. Frobisher's first work, and the work to which all through this expedition he seems, in accordance with his instructions, to have chiefly applied himself, was in searching for the gold ore which was supposed to abound in the district. On the 18th of July, immediately after his little fleet had cast anchor, he proceeded with his gold refiners to the island from which the deceptive mineral had been procured the year before. He found none there; but in some other little islands he met with ore enough to make him believe that there was plenty waiting to be found.

On the following day he started on a more important searching expedition. Taking with him forty of his followers, he proceeded in a couple of boats as far into Frobisher's Straits as the ice would allow. Then he landed upon its northern shore, and marched inland for two or three miles. Ascending a high hill, he caused his men to make a column of stones, and after sounding a trumpet and offering up suitable prayers, he named the hill Mount Warwick, in honour of his patron, the Earl of Warwick. On his way down he met a party of natives, who made great show of friendship, and skipped, danced, laughed, and cried for joy at the sound of the English trumpets. Englishmen and Esquimaux conversed in dumb show and seemed to have arrived at a good understanding with one another. Pins and other trifles were gladly taken by the natives in exchange for bow-cases and whatever other articles they had about them. "Their manner of traffic," says the narrator of the voyage, "is thus: they do use to lay down of their merchandize upon the ground so much as they mean to part withal, and so looking that the other party with whom they make trade should do the like, they themselves do depart, and then, if they do lke of their part, they come again and take in exchange the other's merchandize; otherwise, if they like not, they take their own and depart." In this way Frobisher's company spent most of the day. In the afternoon they hurried back to the shore, intending to return to the ships before nightfall. The Esquimaux followed them to the shore, making all possible signs of friendship, and beckoning them to stay with or return to them. Frobisher on his part was anxious to take some of them back to the ships, and this induced him to a very foolish and unjustifiable measure. Having coaxed two of his new friends to the water's edge, he caught hold of them and tried, with Captain Hall's assistance, to force them into a boat. The natives slipped away, ran for their bows and arrows, which they had left on the road, and then made such a desperate attack upon Frobisher and Hall that they, having no weapons with which to defend themselves, nearly lost their lives. Thereupon both Englishmen and Esquimaux crowded up, and a general scuffle ensued, which resulted in the capture of one native and in the turning of all his comrades, who had shown their willingness to be friends, into dangerous enemies.

That same night Frobisher had another narrow escape. Having rowed from the larger island to a small one at a little distance off, he was compelled to stay there all night by a violent storm which sprang up and nearly wrecked the ships that were waiting for him out at sea. During the day the wind had changed, and before evening it brought down upon the little fleet a whole army of icebergs, great and small. The mariners thought that they exceeded a thousand in number, and that the smallest of them by itself would certainly destroy the ships if it came into collision with them. The night-long twilight they spent in evading the pursuit of these formidable enemies, sailing now in one direction, now in another, as one iceberg after another approached and threatened to overwhelm them. "Some scraped us, and some happily escaped us," says the sailor historian. But in the end they were saved by careful seamanship, he adds, "God being our best steersman." In the morning, Frobisher rejoined them with his comrades and his captive; and all united, of course excepting the captive, in hearty thanksgiving to God for his protection of them in the time of danger.

The storm being overpassed, it proved very serviceable to the voyagers. Frobisher's Straits were thereby sufficiently cleared of ice to be navigable. Therefore they, for the first time, fairly entered them, and proceeded by degrees, halting often on the way, for a distance of about a hundred miles into the channel. Frobisher's first anchoring was in a little bay, on the southern side of the Straits, which in honour of his chief mate, an expert sailor, he called Jackman's Sound. This, which seemed to him a safe resting-place, was rendered dangerous by numerous great blocks of ice which, breaking off from the frozen covering of the remoter part of the Straits, rode through it with a curve on their way to the open sea. But the ships remained in it without injury, while Frobisher investigated some adjoining islands, and then proceeded to explore the southern coastland, which was really a promontory dividing Hudson's Straits from Frobisher's Straits, but which he supposed was a portion of the American continent.

Upon the island he gathered large quantities of what he took for gold ore, and his wonder was aroused by "a great dead fish, which," we are told, "as it should seem, had been embayed with ice, and was, in proportion, round like to a porpoise, being about twelve feet long and in bigness answerable, having a horn of two yards long growing out of the snout or nostrils." This horn, "wreathed and straight, like in fashion to a taper made of wax," was taken home and presented to Queen Elizabeth, who kept it among her treasures.

On the 23rd of July, Frobisher and all the men who could be spared from the ships landed on the promontory, and made some research into the characteristics of this part of Meta Incognita, though deterred from doing as much as they desired by the strict orders given to them to make it their great business to search for the coveted gold ore. "At our first arrival," says one of the sailor historians, "our general, with his company in marching order, entered the land, having special care by exhortations that, at our entrance thereunto, we should all with one voice, kneeling upon our knees, chiefly thank God for our arrival; secondly, beseech Him that it would please His Divine Majesty long to continue our Queen, for whom he and all the rest of our company took possession of the country; and, thirdly, that by our Christian study and endeavour these barbarous people, trained up in paganism and infidelity, might be reduced to the knowledge of true religion and to the hope of salvation in Christ our Redeemer. After this we all marched through the country with ensign displayed, so far as was thought needful, and now and then heaped up stones on high mountains and other places, in token of possession."

Satisfied with that, the voyagers crossed the straits and paid a similar visit to the northern shore, which they thought was either Asia itself or one of its insular appendages. Thence they sailed further west, visiting both the northern and the southern barriers of Frobisher's Straits, and halting finally in a little bay which they called the Countess of Warwick's Sound, with an islet in its midst, to which they gave the name of the Countess of Warwick's Island. There they found plenty of the fancied gold of which they were in search, but being prevented by the ice from going further, prepared for returning to England.

Let the two sharers in this voyaging, whose narratives are our only sources of information thereupon, tell us some of their experiences in their own quaint words. "Upon the mainland, over against the Countess's Island," says one of them, "we discovered and beheld, to our great marvel, the poor caves and houses of those country people, which serve them, as it should seem, for their winter dwellings, and are made two fathoms under ground, in compass round like to an oven, being joined fast one to another, having holes like a fox or coney, to keep and come together. They undertrench these places with gutters, so that the water filling from the hills above them may slide away without their annoyance; and are seated commonly in the foot of a hill to shield them better from the cold winds, having their door and entrance ever open towards the south. From the ground upwards they build with whales' bones for lack of timber, which, bending one over another, are handsomely compacted in the top together and are covered over with seals' skins, which, instead of tiles, fence them from the rain. In which house they have only one room, having the one half of the floor raised with broad staves a foot higher than the other, whereon, strewing moss, they make their nests to sleep in. They defile these dens most filthily with their beastly feeding, and dwell so long in a place, as we think, until, their sluttishness loathing them, they are forced to seek a sweeter air and a new seat. They are, no doubt, a dispersed and wandering nation, as the Tartarians, and live in hordes and troops, without any certain abode."

" They are of the colour of a ripe olive," says another of the voyagers. " They are men very active and nimble. They are a strong people and very warlike, for, in our sight, upon the tops of the hills they would often muster themselves after the manner of a skirmish, trace their ground very nimbly, and manage their bows and darts with great dexterity. They go clad in coats made of the skins of beasts, as of seals, deer, bears, foxes, and hares. They have also some garments of feathers, being made of the cases of fowls, finely sewed and compacted together. In summer they use to wear the hair side of their coats outward, and sometimes go naked for too much heat, and in winter, as by signs they have declared, they wear four or five fold upon their bodies with the hair for warmth turned inward. These people are by nature very subtle and sharp-witted, ready to conceive our meaning by signs, and to make answer well to be understood again ; and if they have not seen the thing whereof you ask them, they will wink and cover their eyes with their hand as who would say, it hath been hid from their sight. If they understand you not whereof you asked them, they will stop their ears. They will teach us the name of each thing in their language which we desire to learn, and are apt to learn anything of us. They delight in music above measure, and will keep time and stroke to any tune you shall sing, both with their voice, head, hand, and foot, and will sing the same tune aptly after you. They will row with our oars in our boats, and keep a true stroke with our mariners, and seem to take great delight therein. For their weapons to offend their enemies or kill their prey withal, they have darts, slings, bows and arrows headed with sharp stones, bones, and some with iron. They are exceeding friendly and kindhearted one to the other, and mourn greatly at the loss or harm of their fellows, and express their grief of mind with a mournful song and dirges. They are very choice in the manner of their living. They are good fishermen, and in their small boats, being disguised in their coats of sealskins, they deceive the fish, who take them rather for their fellow seals than for deceiving men. They are good marksmen. With their dart or arrow they will commonly kill a duck or any other fowl in the head, and commonly in the eye. When they shoot at a great fish with any of their darts, they use to tie a bladder thereunto, whereby they may the better find them again, and the fish, not being able to carry it so easily away—for that the bladder doth buoy the dart—will at length be weary and die therewith. They have nothing in use among them to make fire withal, saving a kind of heath and moss which groweth there, and they kindle their fire with continual rubbing and fretting one stick against another, as we do with flints. They draw with dogs in sledges upon the ice, and remove their huts therewithal, wherein they dwell in summer, wherein they go a hunting for their prey and provision against winter. They do sometimes parboil their meat a little and seethe the same in kettles made of seals' skins. They have also pans, cut and made of stone very artificially. They use putting gins wherewith they take fowl. They use to traffic and exchange their commodities with some other people, of whom they have such thing as their miserable country, and ignorance of art to make, deemeth them to have, as bars of iron, heads of iron for their darts, needles made foursquare, certain buttons made of copper, which they use to wear upon their foreheads for ornament, as our ladies in the Court of England do use great pearl.

The women carry their sucking children at their backs, and do feed them with raw flesh, which first they do a little chew in their own mouths. The women have their faces marked or painted over with small blue spots. They have black and long hair on their heads and trim the same in a decent order. The men have but little hair on their faces and very thin beards. These people are great enchanters, and use many charms of witchcraft; for when their heads do ache, they tie a great stone with a string upon a stick, and with certain prayers and words done to the stick, they lift up the stone from the ground, which sometimes with all a man's force they cannot stir, and sometimes again they lift as easily as a feather, and hope thereby, with certain ceremonious words, to have ease and health. And they made us by signs to understand, lying grovelling with their faces upon the ground and making a noise downward, that they worship the devil under them."

These descriptions, very correct in the main, and only in error where the voyagers, unacquainted with the language of the people, were likely to make false inferences, show that Frobisher and his comrades made careful observation of all that came in their way. Their treatment of the natives seems for the most part to have been very kind and conciliatory. On only one occasion did they exercise their soldiership upon them, and this was not until having landed at a new place with friendly intentions, they were assailed with darts and arrows.

It was not in the nature of Tudor Englishmen to understand that they had no right to enter the territory of people who resented their coming.

But in this case they fought no more than seemed to them absolutely necessary. Being attacked by the Esquimaux, they startled them with a volley of ordnance and arrows, hoping thus to frighten them away. In this they were mistaken. "Desperately returning upon our men," says one of the number, "they resisted them manfully, so long as their arrows and darts lasted, and after gathering up those arrows which our men shot at them, yea, and plucking our arrows out of their bodies, encountered afresh again and maintained their cause until both weapons and life failed them. And when they found they were mortally wounded, being ignorant of what mercy meaneth, with deadly fury they cast themselves headlong from off the rocks into the sea, lest perhaps their enemies should receive glory or prey of their dead carcases; for they supposed us belike to be cannibals. In this conflict one of our men was dangerously hurt in the belly with one of their arrows, and of them were slain five or six, the rest by flight escaping among the rocks, saving two women, whereof the one being old and ugly, our men thought she had been a devil or some witch, and therefore let her go. The other being young, and cumbered with a suckling child at her back, hiding herself behind the rocks, was espied by one of our men, who, supposing she had been a man, shot through the hair of her head and pierced through the child's arm; whereupon she cried out, and our surgeon, meaning to heal her child's arm, applied salves thereunto. But she, not acquainted with such kind of surgery, plucked those salves away, and by continual licking with her own tongue, not much unlike our dogs, healed up the child's arm."

This captive was retained, and taken back to the ships with a kindly purpose. "Having now got a woman-captive for the comfort of our man," our quaint chronicler proceeds, " we brought them both together, and every man with silence desired to behold the manner of their meeting and entertainment. At their first encountering, they beheld each other very wistly a good space, without speech or word uttered, with great change of colour and countenance, as though it seemed the grief and disdain of their captivity had taken away the use of their tongues and utterance. The woman at the first very suddenly, as though she disdained or regarded not the man, turned away, and began to sing as though she minded another matter. But being again brought together, the man broke up the silence first, and with stern and staid countenance, began to tell a long solemn tale to the woman, whereunto she gave good heeding, and interrupted him nothing till he had finished. And afterwards, being grown into more familiar acquaintance by speech, they were turned together, so that, I think, the one would hardly have lived without the comfort of the other; and for so much as we could perceive, although they lived continually together, yet did they never use as man and wife, though the woman spared not to do all necessary things that appertain to a good housewife indifferently for them both, as in making clean their cabin, and every other thing that appertained to his ease; for when he was seasick she would make him clean; she would kill and flay the dogs for their eating and dress his meat."

While studying the habits of the Esquimaux, and noticing the features of their country, Frobisher made it his chief business to collect the mineral which was supposed to be richly freighted with gold. By the middle of August he had loaded his ships with about two hundred tons of it; and then, being warned by the approach of colder weather, which gave hard work to many of his people in breaking the ice that threatened to block up the vessels and make the whole party fast prisoners for the winter, he resolved to go home. By his instructions he was authorised, sending home the *Aid*, to pursue his quest of Cathay in the *Gabriel* and the *Michael*. But he saw that it was impossible to make much further voyaging that autumn, and he himself seems to have partly shared the opinion of his employers, that, if Cathayan wealth could be found near at hand, it was better to amass it than to endure fresh perils in a more distant search. At any rate, he decided to postpone the search till the next year. Accordingly, on the 22nd of August, having prepared the ships for departure, he lit a great bonfire on the highest point in the Countess of Warwick's Island, and, marching round it, with ensigns flying and trumpets sounding, discharged a farewell volley of ordnance. On the morning of the 23rd he weighed anchor, but was becalmed. On the 24th he set sail in earnest, and, in the course of eighteen hours, made the entire passage of so much of the Straits as he had discovered, and entered the open sea.

The homeward voyage was easily performed, in spite of a succession of heavy storms. On the 30th of August one of the company was washed overboard and drowned. This, however, was the only loss incurred during the whole enterprise, excepting the death of one sailor who was ill at the time of starting from England, but who insisted upon accompanying the expedition because "he rather chose to die therein than not to be one to attempt so notable a voyage." On the 1st of September the greatest of the storms separated the ships. The *Aid*, taking a different route from that previously followed, arrived at Milford Haven on the 23rd of September, whence she proceeded leisurely to Bristol, where Frobisher found that the *Gabriel* had already entered that port, and that the *Michael* had reached Yarmouth in safety.

The welcome accorded to Frobisher far exceeded that with which he had been greeted on his return in the autumn of 1576. He was at once summoned to the Court at Windsor, and there heartily thanked and graciously entertained by Queen Elizabeth. The report that he had brought with him two hundred tons of gold ore filled England with rejoicing. A large part of the treasure was deposited in Bristol Castle; the rest was conveyed to the Tower of London, Queen Elizabeth sending down a special message that four locks were to be placed upon the door of the treasury, and that the keys were to be handed over to Martin Frobisher, Michael Lock, the Warden of the Tower, and the Master of the Mint. Thence it was doled out to the best gold refiners that could be found. Similar experiments were carried on at Bristol under the instructions of Sir William Winter. A crowd of new adventurers hurried up with money to be applied in the carrying on of these experiments, and it was long before people could be brought to believe that the ore did not really contain any gold worth speaking of. When one mode of smelting proved disastrous, it was thought that another sort of manipulation would bring the gold to light. Before long the truth oozed out. On the 30th of November Michael Lock had to inform Secretary Walsingham that a schism had grown up, as he said, "among us commissioners through unbelief, or I cannot tell what worse, in some of us, which the time must open." On the 6th of December Sir William Winter wrote to say that they could not get a furnace hot enough "to bring the work to the desired perfection." At length it was admitted that the ore was "poor in respect of that brought last year, and of that which we know may be brought the next year."[*]

With that opinion, the adventurers in the Cathay Company, the English Court, and the English people comforted themselves. Already great preparations had

---

[*] RECORD OFFICE MSS., *Domestic*, vol. cxvi., No. 25; vol. cxviii., Nos. 36, 39, 41—43, 54; vol. cxix., Nos. 8—10, &c.

been begun for sending out another and much larger expedition early in 1578, and it was resolved that these should not be stayed. The old subscribers to the Company increased their shares, and new men were allowed to join in the venture. It was planned that a sufficient expedition should be despatched for the bringing home of two thousand tons of ore—one memorandum of Lord Burghley's suggests five thousand tons—and for the planting in Meta Incognita of a colony of a hundred men; and with this end, a fleet of fifteen ships was fitted out, and suitable preparations of all sorts were made. Among the latter was "a strong fort or house of timber, artificially framed and cunningly devised, whereby those men that were appointed to stay there the whole winter might as well be defended from the danger of the snow and cold air as also fortified from the force or offence of those country people which perhaps otherwise, with too great multitude, might oppress them."*

With these preparations the last two months of 1577 and the first four months of 1578 were fully occupied. In the spring a copious series of instructions were delivered to Frobisher. Therein he was directed to do his best towards acquiring the fancied treasures of Meta Incognita and "the north-west parts." Cathay was forgotten; and he was only to pursue his discoveries some fifty or a hundred leagues, or at the outside two

---

* RECORD OFFICE MSS., *Domestic*, vol. cxix., Nos. 35. 37, 39, 12, 46; vol. cxxiii., Nos. 5, 7, 50, 51; vol. cxxiv., No. 1; HAKLUYT, vol. iii., p. 65.

hundred leagues, further westward than the Countess of Warwick's Island. He was, of course, to be Admiral or Captain-general of the whole fleet, consisting of his old ships the *Aid*, the *Gabriel*, and the *Michael*, and of a dozen new ones—the *Thomas Allen*, the *Judith*, the *Anne Francis*, the *Hope-well*, the *Bear*, the *Thomas of Ipswich*, the *Emanuel of Exeter*, the *Francis of Foy*, the *Moon*, the *Emanuel of Bridgwater*, the *Solomon of Weymouth*, and the *Denis*. For these he was to select a hundred and thirty able seamen, a hundred and sixty pioneers, and sixty soldiers, besides a suitable number of gunners, shipwrights, carpenters, and surgeons, with "a minister or two, to administer divine service and the sacraments according to the Church of England." Captain Edward Fenton, who had gone in the expedition of 1577 and apparently done nothing, but who was a favourite at Court, was to be Vice-admiral of the voyage and Captain of the colony appointed to settle in the new country. He, Captain Yorke, Captain Richard Philpott, Captain George Best, and Captain Henry Carew were to be Frobisher's chief advisers in the expedition; and for additional advice, if needed, he was to look to his trusty master mariners, Christopher Hall, Charles Jackman, James Bear, and Andrew Dyer. He was to proceed at once to the Countess of Warwick's Island, and there, in the first place, look for the eight hundred tons of ore, that being the quantity ultimately resolved upon, which he was to send home in the autumn; then to find a suitable place in which to erect a fort and plant his colony; and finally to pursue such general explorations as he deemed advisable. He was also, if possible, either on the outward or on the homeward voyage, to examine "the new land of Friesland,"—that is, the southern part of Greenland; and he was to see that, in the whole enterprise, strict order was observed, and every man did his duty, or was sternly punished for neglect of it.*

Thus instructed, Frobisher assembled his ships at Harwich, on the 27th of May, where eight that had been fitted out in the Thames were joined by the *Aid*, the *Gabriel*, and five others which had left Bristol about three weeks before, and had called at Plymouth to take on board part of their crews. On the 28th Frobisher and his fourteen captains repaired to the Court at Greenwich, and there received fresh thanks and kindly treatment from Queen Elizabeth. "Her Highness," we are told, "besides other good gifts and greater promises, bestowed on the General a fair chain of gold, and the rest of the captains kissed her hand, took their leave, and departed every man towards their charge."

From Harwich the fleet sailed on the 31st of May. Taking a new route, it passed round the southern coasts of England and Ireland. Cape Clear was skirted on the 6th of June, and on the same day Frobisher fell in with some Bristol traders who had been assailed by

* RECORD OFFICE MSS., *Domestic*, Conway Papers. The authorities for the following description of Frobisher's third voyage are the two narratives printed by HAKLUYT, vol. iii., pp. 65–70, 107–129, by Thomas Ellis and Captain Best, and two others, by Christopher Hall and Edward Sellman, among the BRITISH MUSEUM MSS., *Harleian*, clxvii., fols. 165–180, and clxix., fols. 183–200, which contain many interesting details that are not in the printed records.

French pirates, and left "so sore wounded that they were like to perish in the sea, having neither hand nor foot whole to help themselves with, nor victuals to sustain their hungry bodies, some of them having neither eaten nor drunk more than olives and stinking water in many days before." Frobisher had their wounds dressed, gave them a good supply of food, and put them in the way of returning to England.

Then he struck out in a north-westerly direction, and on the 20th reached the south of Greenland. Here, in his second voyage, he had tried, without success, to effect a landing. On this occasion he was more fortunate. He discovered a good harbour, with some of the native boats in it; and on shore he met with tents, whose furniture, including nails and articles of clothing, gave evidence of a certain measure of civilization. But, according to the report of Captain Best, "the savage and simple people, so soon as they perceived our men coming towards them, supposing there had been no other world but theirs, fled fearfully away, as men much amazed at so strange a sight, and creatures of human shape so far, in apparel, complexion, and other things, different from themselves." Frobisher respected their innocence, and took none of their property—chiefly, perhaps, because it was not worth taking—except a couple of white dogs, for which he left payment in the shape of knives and pins. He took formal possession of the district on the Queen's behalf, calling it West England, and, "for a certain similitude," giving the name of Charing Cross to the last cliff of which he had sight as he sailed past on the 22nd of June.

One of the next incidents of the voyage is quaintly described. "The *Solomon*, being under both her courses and bonnets, happened to strike a great whale with her full stem with such a blow that the ship stood still, and stirred neither forward nor backward. The whale thereat made a great and ugly noise, and cast up his body and tail, and so went under water; and within two days after there was found a great whale dead, swimming above water, which we supposed was that which the *Solomon* struck."

Nine more days of sailing brought the fleet within sight of Meta Incognita and the opposite islands. On the morning of the 2nd of July orders were issued for its stately entrance into Frobisher's Straits, and it was expected that another day or two would bring the voyagers in safety to the Countess of Warwick's Island. Therein they were grievously disappointed. The mouth of the bay was so choked up with ice that Christopher Hall, the experienced master of the *Aid*, advised waiting for a few days, in hopes of a clearer passage. Frobisher persisted, however, and the ships pushed on as best they could. "We were forced many times," says Captain Best, "to stem and strike great blocks of ice, and so, as it were, make way through mighty mountains. All these fleeting ice are not only so dangerous in that they wind and gather so near together that a man may pass sometimes ten or twelve miles, as it were, upon one firm island of ice, but also for that they open and shut together in such sort with the tides and sea-gate that, whilst one ship followeth the other with full sails, the ice which was open to the foremost will join and close again before the latter can follow the first. Thereby many times our ships were brought into great danger, as being not able so suddenly to take in our sails or stay the swift way of our ships. By such means some of the fleet, where they found the ice open, entered in, and passed so far within the danger thereof, with continual desire to recover their port, that it was the greatest wonder of the world that they ever escaped or were heard of again."

The *Michael* and the *Judith* fared best in this battle with the ice. Pressing on as well as they could, avoiding the huge masses that were driven towards them, hurrying through clefts in the frozen surface, and often taking shelter in the tiny bays that occurred in the rugged edges of the ice, they slowly worked their way up to the Countess of Warwick's Sound, and there anchored in safety.

Another ship, the *Denis*, of 100 tons, was struck down by an iceberg and lost, with its cargo, comprising a great part of the moveable fort which was to be erected against winter, though fortunately not before its crew was saved by boats sent from some of the other ships. "This," says Captain Best, whose vivid sentences will best help us to understand the situation of the voyagers, "was a more fearful spectacle for the fleet to behold, for that the outrageous storm that presently followed threatened them the like fortune and danger.

For, the fleet being thus compassed on every side with ice, having left much behind them through which they passed, and finding more before them through which it was not possible to pass, there arose a sudden and terrible tempest, which, blowing from the main sea directly upon the place of the straits, brought together all the ice a-seaboard of us upon our backs, and thereby debarred us of returning back to recover sea room again; so that, being thus compassed with danger on every side, sundry men with sundry devices sought the best way to save themselves. Some of the ships, where they could find a place more clear of ice, and get a little berth of sea room, did take in their sails and there lay adrift. Other some fastened and moored anchor upon a great island of ice, and rode under the lee thereof, supposing to be better guarded thereby from the outrageous winds and the danger of the lesser fleeting ice. And, again, some were so fast shut up and compassed in among an infinite number of great countries and islands of ice that they were fain to commit themselves and their ships to the mercy of the unmerciful ice, and strengthened the sides of their ships with junks of cable, beds, masts, planks, and such-like, which, being hanged overboard on the sides of their ships, might the better defend them from the outrageous sway and strokes of the said ice. But as in greatest distress men of best valour are best to be discerned, so it is greatly worthy commendation and noting with what invincible mind every captain encouraged his company, and with what incredible labour the painful mariners and poor miners unacquainted with such extremities, to the everlasting renown of our nation, did overcome the brunt of these great and extreme dangers. For some even without board upon the ice, and some within board upon the sides of their ships, having poles, pikes, pieces of timber, and oars in their hands, stood almost day and night, without any rest, bearing off the force and breaking the sway of the ice with such incredible pain and peril that it was wonderful to behold; which otherwise no doubt had stricken quite through and through the sides of their ships, notwithstanding our former provision; for planks of timber of more than three inches thick, and other things of greater force and bigness, by the surging of the sea and billows with the ice, were shivered and cut in sunder at the sides of our ships. And amidst these extremes, whilst some laboured for the defence of the ships and sought to save their bodies, other some, of more mild spirit, sought to save their souls by devout prayer and meditation to the Almighty, thinking, indeed, by no other means possible than by a divine miracle to have their deliverance; so that there was none that were either idle or not well occupied; and he that held himself in best security had, God knoweth, but only bare hope remaining for his safety."

This grievous peril lasted for a day and a night. At length the storm abated, but hardly had the sea grown calm enough for Frobisher to muster his ships in the open sea, and there, during one pleasant day, within sight of a far greater iceberg than they had ever seen before, to cause special thanksgivings to be offered up for their deliverance and to do something towards repairing the damage that had been done, than a heavy fog set in which lasted, with slight intermission, for twenty days.

The mariners tried to find their old resting-place at Hall's Island. But in the darkness they could not say whether the solid masses that they saw were land or rocks, or ice or denser lumps of fog. Keeping together with great difficulty, they wandered about until the 10th of July. On that day, the mist being partly removed, they found themselves opposite an opening in the coast, which Frobisher declared to be the straits named after him. Christopher Hall averred that it was not. Thereupon ensued a serious quarrel, in the course of which, says Hall himself, Frobisher fell into "a great rage, and sware, by God's wounds, that it was it, or else take his life." Hall held to his opinion, which proved to be the correct one, and, in mutinous mood, quitted the *Aid*, and, in the *Thomas Allen*, whose officer, Captain Yorke, the Vice-Admiral, sided with him, put out to sea again. Two other ships accompanied him, and he was soon joined by a third, the *Francis of Foy*, which, either by the fog or by the choice of its captain, had also been separated from the rest of the fleet. With these vessels he examined the coast as well as the mists would allow, reached the real Frobisher's Straits on the 18th of the month, and waited in the neighbourhood for a week, hoping to fall in with the other ships. He succeeded in rescuing two or three from the confusion in which they were sailing up and down, quite ignorant of their position and not knowing where to go, and with these he ultimately made his way up the straits, now tolerably clear of ice, as far as the Countess of Warwick's Sound, where, on the 2nd of August, he found that Frobisher and the main body of the fleet were already at anchor.

Frobisher in the meanwhile had discovered the great inlet afterwards known as Hudson's Straits. The opening which he had mistaken for Frobisher's Straits was really the passage between Resolution Island and the south-eastern corner of Meta Incognita. This he traversed, soon to find himself in a broad and inviting channel, out of which, with proper navigation, he might have made his way into the much-coveted passage to Cathay.* He saw at once that he had been at fault in his dispute with Hall, but the new waters in which he found himself were too tempting for him readily to turn back. He therefore pursued this route for about three hundred miles, using subterfuges to persuade his doubting followers that "they were in the right course and known straits."

This falsehood did not work its purpose. As Frobisher proceeded further through the wide and inviting chan-

* This would not, of course, have been the route, through Lancaster Sound and so into Barrow's Straits, followed by Sir John Franklin, and finally marked out by Captain M'Clintock, but a passage through Hudson's Straits and Fox's Channel into the Gulf of Boothia, leaving the group of islands which Frobisher had explored and all Cockburn Land to the right, and thus, by way of Regent's Inlet, making another entrance into Barrow's Strait. The great ice-blockings, increased by frequent windings of the passage, would have made this passage especially difficult; but Frobisher rightly inferred that it was possible.

nel, with ever-growing hope that here he was at last in the way of realizing his long-cherished project for reaching Cathay, the discontent of his companions increased in like proportion. It was nothing to them that the southern parts of Meta Incognita, along which they coasted, were found to be "more fruitful and better stored of grass, deer, wild fowl, bears, hares, foxes, and other things than any other part they had yet discovered, and more populous," or that, in occasional intercourse with the natives, they exchanged their bells and other trinkets for better commodities than they had hitherto procured, and saw the country people possessed of great boats large enough to hold twenty persons a-piece. At first in individual and temperate discourse, and then in general clamour, they requested to be taken to their appointed destination in the Countess of Warwick's Sound, and Frobisher was, in the end, forced to give way to them. He himself also felt that, in compliance with his instructions from England, and on behalf of the seven or eight ships of which he had lost sight and which he supposed had already made their way up Frobisher's Straits, it was right that, though sorely against his wishes, he should turn back.

This accordingly he did. He again entered the region of fog, and—with imminent risk of shipwreck, during which, we are told, the constant cry of the mariners was, " Lord, now help or never! now, Lord, look down from Heaven and save us sinners, or else our safety cometh too late!"—cleared the corner of Meta Incognita on the 23rd of July. There many of the mariners, who believed that they had only just been saved from death by a special miracle wrought on their behalf, were unwilling to trust themselves any more to the mercies of God. They proposed at once to go home, leaving their missing comrades to their fate. There was fresh danger of a mutiny. "The remembrance of the perils past and those present to their face," says Captain Best, "brought no small fear and terror into the hearts of many considerate men. Some began privily to murmur against the general for his wilful manner of proceeding. Other some, forgetting themselves, spake more undutifully in this behalf, saying that they had as lief be hanged when they came home as, without hope of safety, to seek to pass and so to perish in the ice." But Frobisher mastered them, and, amid other storms and dangers, conveyed his fleet to the Countess of Warwick's Sound, which he reached on the 31st of July. There he was welcomed by the crews of the *Judith* and the *Michael*, which had been waiting ten days for him, and two days afterwards the rest of the fleet, led by Christopher Hall, arrived.

Special thanksgivings were offered up for this happy meeting; a godly sermon was preached; and the mutinous conduct of Hall and more than half of the crews, countenanced by many of the officers, was freely forgiven. But the mutinous spirit was by no means quenched. Christopher Hall openly declared that he had lost all the General's confidence, and could be of no further use in the enterprise; and his sullenness was shared by a great many others. Many of the crew, too, were made ill by the serious pains and privations through which they had passed. Nearly all the ships were seriously damaged by the storms they had weathered and the icebergs and ice-rocks with which they had come in collision. A month had been wasted in reaching the Sound, and the best part of another month had to be spent in making good the injuries received. All these circumstances were, perforce, discouraging to Frobisher as well as to his followers. Moreover, he could not forget the new straits which he had discovered, and the hope thus quickened in the direction of fresh Cathayan enterprise. He therefore resolved that he would soon return to England, which, indeed, it was necessary for him to do, unless he chose to stay in the Arctic district all through the fast approaching winter.

During August, however, as much as possible was done both in further exploration of Frobisher's Straits and in collection of the ore which the ships were specially sent out to gather. The soundest vessels and the best crews were despatched in various directions, and thus some fresh though unimportant discoveries were made and a good deal of worthless mineral was brought together. In particular, Captain Best, with his own ship, the *Anne Francis*, and two others, went far up the inlet, though not far enough to find that Frobisher's Straits were really only a narrow bay, and collected much store of fancied treasure. Frobisher himself led another expedition, though of it we know little, as none of the chroniclers of the voyage seem to have been in his party.

Thus the month was passed, and, as it drew to a close, preparations were made for returning home. Most of the material for the intended winter fort had been lost in the *Denis*, and the intending colonists were not willing to stay longer in so inhospitable a region. Therefore all the materials that remained were put together in a great heap and cased in lime and stone, there to be available for use by the fresh expedition which, it was supposed, would be fitted out next year.*

---

* Tudor Englishmen never returned to Meta Incognita; but many traces of their visit were discovered by Captain C. F. Hall, the enterprising American explorer, in 1861 and 1862, nearly three centuries after the time to which they belong. In his journal of April 9, 1861, he says: "Among the traditions handed down from one generation to another there is this, that many, very many years ago some white men built a ship on one of the islands of Frobisher Bay and went away." While at Rescue Harbour he reports: "I had several conversations with an intelligent Esquimau, who spoke of a time long, long ago, when white men built a vessel on an island in the bay lower down 'Frobisher Bay); spoke also of brick, timber, chips, &c., as having been left there" (*Life with the Esquimaux*, 1864, vol. i., pp. 271, 272). Passing up the bay, one of his native friends pointed out to him an island where "white men a long time ago had masted a ship" (vol. i., p. 278). In May he met an old woman, who told him that "the white men of the ships landed in Niountelik, an island near Oopungnewing," which Captain Hall identifies with the Countess of Warwick's Island. "She then proceeded to say, that upon Niountelik she had seen bricks and coal, and pieces of timber of various sizes. She had also heard from old Innuits that, many years before, ships had landed there with a great number of people. I asked her if she knew how many ships had come there? Her reply was, 'They came every year; first two, then three, then many—a great many ships.' The old lady further informed me that frequently, in her lifetime, she had seen wood, chips, coal, and bricks, and large pieces of very heavy stone, on the island of Niountelik. I asked her what kind of stone it was, and to this she replied, ' It was black and very heavy. No Innuits had ever seen such kind of stones before.'" Captain Hall adds, that this old woman told him also, "that further down the white people took away two Innuits women, who never came back again;

Then the fleet set out, leaving the Countess of Warwick's Sound in detachments, and meeting lower down,

---

that five white men were captured by Innuit people at the time of the appearance of the ships a great many years ago; that these men wintered on shore; that they lived among the Innuits; that they afterwards built a large boat, and put a mast into her, and had sails; that early in the season, before much water appeared, they endeavoured to depart; that, in the effort, some froze their hands; but that finally they succeeded in getting into open water, and away they went, which was the last seen or heard of them" (vol. i., pp. 302—304). On another day Captain Hall says that, while conversing with two Esquimaux, one of them showed him a piece of bright-coloured brick. "I then asked whence they got it; and both Innuits pointed to the island Niountelik, which was less than half a mile from where we stood." Another Esquimau, to whom he showed it, said, "Many of my acquaintances up the inlet have pieces of the same kind that came from that island" (vol. i., pp. 315, 316). In August Captain Hall carefully explored this island in search of Frobisher remains. There he found large quantities of coal, covered with moss and grass, but no other relics (vol. ii., pp. 77—80). In September he explored a neighbouring island, called by the natives Kodlunarn, and supposed by him to be the Countess of Warwick's Island. There he found "an excavation eighty-eight feet long and six feet deep," which he supposed to be one of Frobisher's fancied gold mines; also "coal, flint-stone, fragments of tile, glass and pottery; a trench made by the shore on an inclined plane, such as is used in building a ship on the stocks; the ruins of three stone houses, one of which was twelve feet in diameter, with palpable evidence of its having been erected on a foundation of stone, cemented together with lime and stone; and some chips of wood found on digging at the base of the ship's trench." On the same island he discovered "iron time-eaten, with ragged teeth, weighing from fifteen to twenty pounds, on the top of a granite rock, just within reach of high tide at full change of moon." "This island," he says, "is generally called Kodlunarn, because *white men* lived on it, and built stone houses and also a ship. From what I saw that day I was fully convinced that many, very many years ago, men of civilization did live upon the island, and that they did build a vessel, probably a schooner, there" (vol. ii., pp. 150—153). On another island in the same bay he found more coal, as much, he thought, as about five tons, "also a little pile of flint-stones, similar to those discovered in the coal at Niountelik, and in the cement of the stone-house ruins at Kodlunarn;" and nearly fifteen inches below the

on the 1st of September, at a harbour known as Bear's Sound. There the suppressed flame of discontent, that had been increasing during the last two months, rose to such a height, that it was even proposed by some of the mariners to follow the frequent example of Spanish voyagers and leave Frobisher behind. That evil thought, however, was not acted upon, and the company, robbed by death of about forty men, embarked on the 2nd of January.

They had hardly entered the open sea when they were harassed by renewal of the storms that had all along been so disastrous. The ships were dispersed,

---

surface of the ground, "a large chip, imbedded in the coal, which had the appearance of having been chopped out of a large piece of oak timber with an axe" (vol. iii., p. 157). On another visit to Kodlunarn, "a piece of iron, semi-spherical in shape, weighing twenty pounds, was discovered under the stone that had been excavated for the 'ship's way,' and many other small pieces were found at the head of the trench: fragments of tile were found all over the island, and numerous other relics, indicating that civilized men had visited the place very many years ago" (vol. ii., p. 161). In June, 1862, Captain Hall received two other relics from Kodlunarn, a piece of very old brick or tile, two inches long, one inch thick, and one and a half wide, and a musket ball. "The ball had several small indentations upon its surface, and the whole of it was covered with a white coat (oxide of lead), in consequence of long exposure. It is $\frac{11}{16}$ths of an inch in diameter" (vol. ii., p. 283). In July he went again to Kodlunarn, and there saw "very clear evidences of the existence of a blacksmith forge or a furnace" (vol. ii. p. 293).

I have quoted, for the most part, in Captain Hall's own words, and in chronological order, his account of his discoveries of Frobisher relics, which are now lodged in the Greenwich Hospital Museum. He also gives some further traditions received from natives in various parts, from which and from the relics he considers it to be unquestionable that these are really all of them relics of Frobisher's three voyages, and that the site of Frobisher's intended colony, or the Countess of Warwick's Island, was the native Kodlunarn. These highly interesting conclusions can hardly be controverted.

and several of them were in great danger of destruction. The *Aid*, with Frobisher on board, was nearly wrecked and its pinnace was lost. The *Emmanuel of Bridgewater* was in yet greater danger, and only saved by careful steering through rocks that had not hitherto been seen, and coming out at the mouth of Hudson's Straits. This ship, quite separated from the others, passed a huge iceberg on the 12th of September, which was supposed to be an island somewhere to the south of Greenland, and which became a cause of great confusion to later map-makers and navigators.

Contrary winds and heavy storms befel the voyagers nearly all through their homeward way; and we have no distinct account of its various incidents. All the ships reached England, however, arriving, one or two at a time, at various ports, near the beginning of October.

They were heartily welcomed, and at first there was great expectation of profit from the large supplies of mineral that they brought home. But the mineral was soon declared to be inferior to that previously collected, and, as the gold refiners, who in the interval had been working at the previous importation, had been able to get no gold out of it, the rejoicings were soon exchanged for open expressions of discontent among courtiers, merchants, and common folk alike.

Thereupon ensued a complication of quarrels and vituperation very discreditable to all the parties concerned. The officers and mariners whom Frobisher had found it very hard to keep from open mutiny during the expedition now uttered their abuses without restraint, and those who had risked their money upon the project, glad enough to find an object for their wrath, readily listened to and adopted the complaints. Michael Lock, Frobisher's fast friend in time of prosperity, now led the opposition to him. Frobisher, always an impetuous man, quite lost his temper, and seems to have given back abuse for all the abuse that was heaped upon him. Lock having, as treasurer of the Cathay Company, refused to pay Frobisher the salary that was due to him, and this in spite of special orders from the Privy Council, Frobisher publicly complained that he was "a false accountant to the Company, a cozener to my Lord of Oxford, no venturer at all in the voyages, a bankrupt knave." Lock, in a long memorial to Sir Francis Walsingham, complained that Frobisher had "entered into great storms and rages with him like a mad beast, and raised on him such shameful reports and false slanders as the whole Court and City was full of." Many others made like complaints. Thomas Allen, deputy-treasurer, begged that he might be discharged "rather than be thus railed at for his pains." An anonymous memorialist, probably Lock, indulged in forty pages of slander, going over nearly the whole of Frobisher's career, all to the effect that Frobisher was an arrogant, obstinate, insolent, and prodigal knave, "full of lying talk, impudent of tongue, and perchance the most unprofitable of all that have served the Company." Before starting on his third voyage, we are here told, Frobisher had indulged in "no small raging and outrageous speaking." Even then, it was said, being thwarted on some point, "he flung out of the doors, and swore, by God's wounds, that he would hip my masters the adventurers for it;" and it was alleged that all the mischances of the expedition had resulted from his wilful neglect of duty. Not having the wit to make discoveries for himself, "his vain-glorious mind would not suffer any discovery to be made without his own presence," and therefore the whole enterprise had fallen to the ground. Coming home, and finding that he met with less favour than he expected, it was said, there were no bounds to his fury. On one occasion he had gone to a gold refiner on Tower Hill, and finding him "naked at his works and very sick, almost to death, of infection of the smoke of the minerals," he had in the course of a dispute drawn his dagger on him. At another time, when Edward Sellman was taking an inventory of the stores brought home, Frobisher was said to have beaten him, and nearly cloven his head with a dagger.*

There was plenty more of such libelling. If a tithe of the accusations brought against Frobisher are to be believed, he was a man utterly contemptible, and quite unfit for the work confided to him. His skilful management of his business, his wise care of all the people under him, and his generous bearing towards the natives of the districts that he visited, are sufficient refutations of them. At the same time, we can easily

---

* RECORD OFFICE MSS., *Domestic*, vol. cxxvi., Nos. 20, 22, 34 ; vol. cxxvii., Nos. 8, 20 ; vol. cxxix., Nos. 9, 44 ; vol. cxxx., No. 17. &c.; BRITISH MUSEUM MSS., *Lansdowne*, c., No. 1.

understand—and this conclusion is borne out by some circumstances in his later history—that finding himself blamed both for things that were not blameworthy, and for matters in which others were quite as much at fault as he was, he, too, got angry, and showed his anger in undignified ways.

It is not necessary to follow this ugly quarrel through all its tedious details, or to describe the numerous experiments that were made upon the worthless stone that had been brought home before people were convinced that it would be utter waste of money, energy, and life to carry on the search for gold in Meta Incognita, or any of the districts visited by Frobisher. This hope of gold was altogether unfortunate. By it the Cathay Company and Frobisher himself were prevented from carrying on the search for a passage round the northern part of America during the expeditions of 1577 and 1578; and by it, the real nature of the ore being discovered, Frobisher was prevented from prosecuting the search and from following up the great discovery of the channel, afterwards known as Hudson's Straits, which he had made during his third voyage.

There was much talk, however, of a fourth voyage to be undertaken by Frobisher. The Cathay Company had fallen to pieces upon the failure of the efforts to extract gold from the mineral on which the hopes of its members had been chiefly set; and Michael Lock, its treasurer and chief promoter, concerning whom it is impossible to decide whether he really deserved all the blame that was heaped upon him for his management

of the accounts, but who certainly was a great sufferer
from the failure, had been thrown into the Fleet Prison
at the suit of William Burrough, of whom a ship had
been bought for 200*l.* but never paid for.* But while
the City men refused to have any more to do with
Cathayan projects, the idea continued in favour with
many influential courtiers. Among them its chief
friend seems to have been the great Earl of Leicester.
In September, 1581, he wrote to the Earl of Shrewsbury, saying that he proposed to embark 3,000*l.* upon a
new adventure if others would join with him. The
Earl of Shrewsbury promised to fit out his bark, the
Talbot, which, including the furniture, would represent
1,000*l.*† Sir Francis Drake, lately returned from his
voyage round the world, offered, besides the best
advice he could bestow, to give the equivalent of
another 1,000*l.* by fitting out either a ship of 180 tons
or a little bark that he had just built and a couple of
pinnaces.‡ Other subscriptions were readily obtained:
500*l.* from the Earl of Oxford, 300*l.* from Frobisher
himself, 300*l.* from Edward Fenton and his friends,
and 200*l.* apiece from the Earl of Warwick, the Earl of
Pembroke, Sir Francis Walsingham, Sir Christopher
Hatton, and some others, making in all 11,600*l.*§ It was
arranged that three ships and a pinnace should be

---

* RECORD OFFICE MSS., *Domestic*, vol. cxlix., No. 42; BRITISH MU-
SEUM MSS., *Cotton*, Otho viii., fol. 44.
† BRITISH MUSEUM MSS., *Cotton*, Otho viii., fol. 95.
‡ *Ibid.*, fol. 97.
§ *Ibid.*, fols. 104—106.

made ready for the enterprise, and that other ships should be added if more money could be obtained.

Frobisher was in high glee, and waited anxiously for the instructions that were issued to him in February, 1582. There was one clause in these instructions, however, which seems to have taken him altogether by surprise. Some of the new partners in the project procured a complete change in its purpose. "We will," it was said, "that this voyage shall be only for trade and not for discovery of the passage to Cathay, otherwise than if, without hindrance of your trade and within 40 degrees of latitude, you can get any knowledge touching that passage, whereof you shall do well to be inquisitive as occasion in this sort may serve."* With this order, quite at variance with the scheme which he had most at heart, Frobisher seems to have refused to comply. At any rate, his name was taken out of the instructions, and Edward Fenton's was put in its stead. The expedition which started in April was changed into an enterprise for trade or piracy in the South Seas, and accordingly all that needs to be said about it must be said in a later chapter. Frobisher had nothing more to do with it.

Of the way in which he occupied himself during the few years previous to and following this proposal for renewing the Cathayan search we know very little. In or near the year 1580, he had received from the Crown a reversionary title to the office of Clerk of Her Majesty's

---

* BRITISH MUSEUM MSS., *Cotton*, Otho viii., fols. 87—92.

ships;* but we are not told when, if ever, he really entered upon this work.† That he stood in need of some remunerative employment is tolerably clear. There is extant a curious letter, undated, but evidently written between 1576 and 1578, addressed by his wife, Dame Isabel Frobisher, "the most miserable poor woman in the world," to Sir Francis Walsingham. In it, " in her most lamentable manner," she complained that, whereas her former husband, Thomas Riggat, a very wealthy man, had left her with ample portions for herself and all her children, her present husband—"whom God forgive!"—had spent everything, and "put them to the wide world to shift." She and her children, she said, were starving in a poor room at Hampstead; and therefore she begged Walsingham to help her in recovering a debt of 4*l*. due to her husband, and so to keep them from famishing until Captain Frobisher's return.‡

It is to be feared that when Captain Frobisher returned he was not able to do very much towards restoring the money that he had borrowed from his wife.

* RECORD OFFICE MSS., *Warrant Book*, vol. i., p. 118.
† He was employed as captain of one of the Queen's ships, the *Foresight*, in preventing the Spaniards from giving all the assistance they desired to the Irish insurgents in Munster, under James Fitzmaurice, in 1580; but of this we have no useful details.—RECORD OFFICE MSS., *Irish*, vol. lxxxiii., No. 35; vol. lxxxiv., No. 56; vol. lxxxvi., Nos. 64, 71, 72.
‡ RECORD OFFICE MSS., *Domestic*, vol. cli., No. 17.

CHAPTER VII.

THE COLONIZING PROJECTS OF SIR HUMPHREY GILBERT.

[1574—1583.]

FROM active participation in the Cathayan enterprise, of which he was chief promoter, Sir Humphrey Gilbert was deterred, either by the jealousy of the men who superseded him in the work or by his own dissatisfaction at being thus superseded, or by both motives together. But he was at no loss for other and kindred ways in which to show his love of adventure and his anxiety to forward his country's welfare. While he was writing his 'Discourse to prove a Passage to Cathay,' we find him, in conjunction with other gentlemen of the west parts of England, among whom Sir Richard Grenville, Sir George Peckham, and Christopher Carlile were the principal, planning an expedition for the discovery of "sundry rich and unknown lands" in the more southern districts of America. On the 22nd of March, 1574, he and his friends addressed a petition to Queen Elizabeth on the subject, urging that this discovery was "fatally reserved for England and for the honour of Her Majesty;" and on the same day they wrote to the Earl of Lincoln, Lord High Admiral of England, bespeaking his help in furtherance of the work, and explaining more fully the advantages that would certainly come from a voyage to the parts south of the equinoctial line, which were rapidly being appropriated by Spanish adventurers.* But neither petition nor letter seems to have met with much favour, and we hear nothing more of this particular scheme.

Another abortive project is set forth in a discourse, of which there is little doubt that Gilbert was the author, showing "how Her Majesty might annoy the King of Spain" by fitting out a fleet of war-ships under pretence of a voyage of discovery, and so fall upon the enemy's shipping, destroy his trade in Newfoundland and the West Indies, and possess both regions. Gilbert offered to conduct this expedition, and begged that it might be entered upon at once, seeing that "the wings of man's life are plumed with the feathers of death."† The proposal is dated the 6th of November, 1577. It was not complied with, Queen Elizabeth having quite enough to do in keeping within bounds the schemes for annoying the King of Spain that were being enforced by Hawkins, Drake, and other men already engaged upon the business.

But in another and kindred project, which soon afterwards he propounded, he easily obtained the Queen's approval. On the 11th of June, 1578, was granted to

---

* RECORD OFFICE MSS., *Domestic*, vol. xcv., Nos. 63, 64.
† *Ibid.*, vol. cxviii., No. 12. The signature to this document is carefully erased, but it appears to have been H. GYLBERTE.

him a charter for **discovering and possessing** any distant and barbarous **lands which he** could find, provided they were not already **claimed by** any Christian prince or people, and **on condition that** all cities, castles, towns, and villages that he **might** found or conquer, were held by him **under the Crown of** England, and paid for with **the fifth that in all** such cases was claimed by the sovereign. He was authorised to plant a colony and to be absolute governor both of the Englishmen and of the natives dwelling in it, the only restriction being that his rule should be, " as near as conveniently might be," in harmony with the laws and policy of England.*

That charter Gilbert proceeded, as quickly as possible, to make use of. Towards fitting out a suitable expedition he seems to have employed the long arrears of pay lately issued to him on account of his services in Ireland. A goodly number of enterprising men, many of them destined hereafter to take famous part in the history of their country, also assisted him both with money and with personal attendance. Among them were George and William Carew, Edward Denny, Henry Nowell, Henry and Francis Knollys, and Miles Morgan. The greatest of all was his stepbrother, Walter Raleigh. †

Raleigh, now twenty-six years old, was the youngest son of Walter Raleigh, a Devonshire gentleman, by his third wife, Catharine, the widow of Otho Gilbert, and Sir Humphrey Gilbert's mother. He had studied at

* HAKLUYT, vol. iii., pp. 135—137.
† HOLLINSHED, vol. iii., p. 1369.

Oxford, had gone to France with his and Gilbert's cousin, Henry Champernon, in 1569, to fight as a volunteer in the Huguenot cause, and, after five years thus spent, had entered on a further pupilage in fighting under Sir John Norris in the Netherlands. Thence he soon returned to England. "The slender pay," says one of his old biographers, "was not encouragement sufficient to make him stay long in the service. Being restless and impatient of a narrow and low condition, and his merits not answered with a fortune strong enough to buoy up his reputation, he was resolved to leave no stone unturned nor any method of living unexperimented; and, since his land expeditions could make no addition to his fortunes, novelty, and a desire of putting himself into a better capacity, urged him to a sea voyage." *

Like or worse motives seem to have actuated several others of Gilbert's partners, all "gentlemen of good calling," and they were not calculated to bring success to the enterprise. With a fleet of eleven ships, containing five hundred gentlemen and sailors, Gilbert quitted Dartmouth on the 23rd of September.† He was hardly out of port when his "gentlemen of good calling" began to show themselves too good for their work. Concerning them, we are told by one of the number, that "their dispositions were divers, which bred a feud, and made a division in the end, to the confusion

---

* Cited in the continuation to SOUTHEY's *British Admirals*, vol. iv., p. 211.

† RECORD OFFICE MSS., *Domestic*, vol. cxxv., No. 70.

of the attempt even before it was begun."* Disputes
arose between Gilbert and Henry Knollys, which resulted in the refusal of Knollys and some others to
continue in the expedition, and the whole fleet had to
put back into Plymouth Harbour, where more than a
month was wasted in altercations and in waiting for the
decision of the Mayor of Plymouth on the subject of
variance.† At length, on the 18th of November
another start was made, the number of ships being now
reduced to seven. Then the former troubles were
repeated. It appears—though even this is not quite
certain—to have been Gilbert's purpose to plant his
colony somewhere on the North American coast, south
of Newfoundland, and as near as possible to the West
Indian possessions of Spain. But many of his comrades
had set their hearts on a preliminary attack upon the
Spanish possessions themselves, and, Gilbert being persuaded to agree to this, the ships took their course in a
south-westerly direction. That ill-advised measure
brought ruin to the whole project. Falling in with
some Spanish vessels, the fleet, which was not adapted
for warfare, was worsted in a sturdy sea fight. Many
of the adventurers were slain, and the ships, battered
and disabled, were forced to put in at Cape de
Verde. There Gilbert found that many of his associates had lost heart, and that it was impossible with
the residue to have any chance of success in carrying
on the project. Therefore, to his great chagrin, he

* HAKLUYT, vol. iii., p. 146.
† RECORD OFFICE MSS., *Domestic*, vol. cxxvi., Nos. 44, 46, 49.

abandoned it, and returned to Plymouth in May, 1579.*

In that failure Sir Humphrey had sunk all his money and all his influence, as far as his colonizing project was concerned, at Court. The project was not abandoned by him. He worked steadily for its accomplishment, and used every opportunity of collecting information and storing experience that might enable him to avoid the disasters of his first effort. But in the meanwhile he turned to other employment.

This employment was chiefly in Ireland, which, after the infinitely worthier battleground of the Netherlands, was the chief school of rough soldiership and rude statecraft for Elizabethan Englishmen. Gilbert, as we have seen, had already proved himself, both in soldiership and in diplomacy, a skilful abettor of the policy, marked by scant justice and scanter mercy, which Elizabeth and her counsellors thought fit to use towards their unfortunate dependency. While he himself was busied in other ways, Gilbert's Band, as it continued to be called, had been found a formidable instrument in restraining the lawless but patriotic attempt at recovering independence, which went by the name of rebellion; and it was a common request of those whom he had left behind, that Gilbert might be sent back to them to help in restoring order.†

The request was complied with almost immediately

---

* HOLLINSHED, vol. iii., p. 1369; CAYLEY, *Life of Sir Walter Raleigh*, Appendix, p. 6.

† RECORD OFFICE MSS., *Irish*, vol. xlvi., No. 26.

after Gilbert's return from his unfortunate expedition. In the summer of 1579 he was sent back to Ireland, and Raleigh went with him. Their first service, apparently in one or two of the ships that they had lately brought home, reinforced by others, was in resisting the attempt made by James Fitzmaurice, with the help of half a dozen Spanish ships, to promote insurrection along the coast of Munster. Sir John Perrot was the admiral in command of the Queen's ships detailed for this service, and under him Gilbert held an important position. Zealous work was soon done by him, and then he was sent home to England.*

Raleigh remained in Ireland, and outdid his stepbrother in the harshness with which he applied himself to his ugly task. He was one of the two principal officers employed in November, 1580, by Lord Grey of Wilton, then Lord-Deputy of Ireland, in capturing a fort built by the Spaniards at St. Mary Wick, commonly called Smerwick, in Kerry. This formidable and insolent measure for aiding the Irish rebellion naturally gave great offence to the English; and when the fort was captured, all the Spaniards, six hundred in number, were ruthlessly put to death, after having laid down their arms, by the troops under Captains Raleigh and Mackworth. Lord Grey, having ordered the massacre, "shed tears thereat." Raleigh seems to have done his bloody work without compunction, and the poet Spenser, who looked on at it as Secretary to the Lord-Deputy,

* RECORD OFFICE MSS., *Irish*, vol. lxvii., Nos. 40, 47, 65, 66; vol. lxix., Nos. 67, 72; *Domestic*, vol. cxxxii., No. 25.

defended it as absolutely necessary in itself if discipline was to be maintained in Ireland, and no more than wholesome vengeance due to the Spaniards for the villanies by which they had put themselves out of the pale of civilization.*

After doing other work in Ireland, Raleigh returned to England in December, 1581, or January, 1582, Barry's Island having been granted to him for his services.† He was sent back in April, with special orders from the Queen that he was to be further employed at the head of a body of horse; but, as Lord Grey reported that "he liked not Captain Raleigh's carriage or company," his stay seems to have been short.‡ Therefore he was used at Court as adviser concerning the best means of subduing the Irish rebels.§ He was also put to much other courtly use, all starting, according to the well-known tradition, from his alacrity, during his attendance upon Her Majesty in the early months of 1582, in throwing down his cloak, then almost his only property, for Queen Elizabeth to tread upon while walking over a gutter.

No such good fortune fell to his stepbrother. There is a letter written by Sir Humphrey Gilbert to Sir Francis Walsingham, in July, 1581, from his house in Sheppey, begging that he might be paid a little sum of money owing for the work that he had done in Ireland

---

* RECORD OFFICE MSS., *Irish*, vol. lxviii., Nos. 25—33; CAMDEN, *Elizabeth*, p. 243; SPENSER, *View of Ireland*.
† RECORD OFFICE MSS., *Irish*, vol. lxxxvii., No. 2; vol. lxxxviii., No. 10.
‡ *Ibid.*, vol. xci., No. 3; vol. xcii., No. 10.
§ *Ibid.*, vol. xcvi., Nos. 30, 31.

in 1579, whereby, **he said, he** had lost so much that he was reduced **to utter want.** It was a miserable thing, he added, that, after seven-and-twenty years' service, he should now **be subjected to** daily arrests, executions, and outlawries, **and have even to** sell his wife's clothes from off her back.*

He needed money, not only for his present maintenance, but also for furtherance of the colonizing scheme to which he had devoted himself. The charter conferred upon him by Queen Elizabeth stipulated that his colony should be founded within six years of the date of the document. This made him doubly anxious to continue, without delay, the work in which his first attempt had failed. Delay was necessary, however, in consequence of his poverty. During four years, Gilbert could do nothing but quicken public interest, especially the interest of his friends at Court, and collect all available information about the portion of America which was his on paper.

There was no lack of information, though it was not all very trustworthy. The island of Newfoundland, or Baccalaos, was by this time well known to Europeans. Almost immediately after its discovery by the elder Cabot trading voyages to it in search of cod had begun to be made; but in this work the Englishmen were less zealous than the Spaniards or the French. The older fishing-trade with Iceland carried on by merchants of Bristol, Hull, and other ports, was preferred to the more hazardous commerce, as it was thought, with Newfoundland. At

* RECORD OFFICE MSS., *Domestic*, vol. cxlix., No. 66.

the same time this latter was not neglected. In 1544 there were many English merchant-ships engaged in the Newfoundland fisheries. Anthony Parkhurst, an intelligent merchant of Bristol, reported, in 1578, that he had been annually to Newfoundland in the four years past, that during that time the English fishing fleet had increased from thirty to fifty sail, and that, although the French sent nearly a hundred and fifty boats, the Spaniards about a hundred, and the Portuguese some fifty, the English, by reason of the greater strength of their vessels, were masters of the trade. He urged that they should follow it in much greater numbers, seeing that it was an excellent school for trade, and a boundless source of wealth.*

This, however, was too tame a calling to be of much interest to the gentlemen adventurers of Queen Elizabeth's Court. Their projects were directed to the more southern districts on the main land adjoining the Spanish province, vaguely known as Florida, and about which, in common with Florida, many wonderful traditions were still rife, all to be traced to the credulity with which early travellers, prepared for them by their remembrance of Cathayan fables, listened to the exaggerated reports that came to them of the ancient wealth and civilization of the Aztecs in Mexico. These traditions were carefully gathered up in England, and they are set forth in a document which appears to have been drawn up for Sir Humphrey Gilbert's guidance in 1581 or 1582. There we are told of the exceeding wealth of

* HAKLUYT, vol. iii., p. 133.

the natives, and the surpassing richness of the country. Great pieces of pure gold, as large as a man's fist, were to be picked up in the heads of some of the rivers, and there were plenty of gold and silver mines that could be worked without trouble. In every cottage there was a store of pearls, and in some houses they were to be measured by the peck. There were cities traversed by streets broader and handsomer than any to be found in London, containing banqueting houses that were built of crystal, with pillars of massive silver and gold. The soldiers, who were generally women, were covered with armour plates of solid gold; and the devil whom they worshipped for a god was in the likeness of a golden calf. One traveller had received a hundred pieces of silver for a worn-out flag. In this country there were also wonderful birds and animals, "great beasts as big as two of our oxen," and fiery dragons, "which make the air very red as they fly."[*]

Of that sort were the stories derived from old travellers like Verrazano and Jacques Cartier and from living Englishmen who had lately made their way to America. Among the latter was Simon Ferdinando, a follower of Sir Francis Walsingham, who, in 1579, visited the coast in a little frigate, Andrew Thevett, and John Walker, who reported that, in 1580, he had discovered a silver mine. With the two latter, as well as with some others, we are told that Sir Humphrey Gilbert "did confer in person."[†]

Gilbert conferred with many persons. Finding it

---

[*] RECORD OFFICE MSS., *Colonial*, vol. i., No. 2. [†] *Ibid.*

impossible to raise enough money of his own, or to borrow it from his friends without due recompense, he resolved to assign some of the privileges granted in his charter to other speculators, on condition that their enterprises should be carried on under his supervision.* The result was that, in the summer of 1583, after two years occupied with "difficulties and accidents," he was able to set out on his long-cherished project.

His chief associates were Raleigh and his old friends Sir George Peckham and Christopher Carlile.† Raleigh fitted out a bark of 200 tons' burthen, named the *Raleigh*, which had lately been built for his private use. The other vessels appointed for the expedition were the *Delight*, which was also called the *George*, of 120 tons, the *Golden Hind* and the *Swallow*, each of 40 tons, and the *Squirrel*, of 10 tons. In these five ships provision was made for gentlemen, soldiers, sailors, carpenters, miners, and others, numbering two hundred and sixty. "For solace of the people and amusement of the savages," we are told, "we were provided with music in great variety, not omitting the least toys, as morris-dancers, hobby-horses, and many like conceits, to

* "Articles of agreement between Sir Humphrey Gilbert and such of Southampton as adventure with him," are among the RECORD OFFICE MSS., *Domestic*, vol. clv., No. 86.

† A request was made by Carlile, at the beginning of 1583, for the grant of a separate patent in favour of a colony to be planted at some little distance from Gilbert's settlement, towards the expenses of which he said the City of London would furnish 3,000*l.* and Bristol 1,000*l.*; but it does not seem to have been complied with.—RECORD OFFICE MSS., *Colonial*, vol. i., No. 1, where the date is erroneously given as 1574. A 'Discourse' of Carlile's, dated April, 1587, is in HAKLUYT, vol. iii., pp. 182—187.

delight the savage people, whom we intended to win by all fair means possible; and to that end we were indifferently furnished with all pretty haberdashery wares to barter with these simple people."*

If Gilbert had felt himself to be aggrieved at his hard treatment by Queen Elizabeth during the few years previous, there was now some show of royal favour to comfort him. "Brother," said Raleigh in a letter to him written shortly before his departure, " I have sent you a token from Her Majesty, an anchor guided by a lady as you see"—that is, a golden anchor with a large pearl attached to it. "And further Her Highness willed me to send you word that she wished you as great a good hap as if she herself were there in person, desiring you to have care of yourself as of that which she tendereth; and therefore, for her sake, you must provide for it accordingly. Further she commandeth that you leave your picture with me."†

If Gilbert's first expedition had been entered upon without due preparation, there was now no lack of caution. It had been at first intended that the voyagers should proceed in a south-westerly direction, and then, passing the West Indies with a curve to the north, explore the coast of America until they reached a suitable spot at which to make a settlement. From this the mishaps of the former undertaking deterred them. It was decided that they should go direct to Newfoundland, and thence pass southward in search of a convenient site for the colony. Careful arrangements

* HAKLUYT, vol. iii., p. 148.   † CAYLEY, vol. i., p. 31.

were made for the guidance of the fleet during the voyage, and it was ordered that if the ships were separated by fogs or storms, they were to proceed separately, in the first instance, to Cape Race and afterwards to Cape Breton, thence to continue their way together.*

Yet Gilbert's second expedition was even more unfortunate than the first. The fleet had hardly sailed out of Plymouth Harbour, on the 11th of June, 1583, when it was deserted by the *Raleigh*, on the plea that its captain, William Winter, and many of its crew were dangerously ill. This, of course, was only an excuse, and it is not clear that Raleigh was not in some sort a party to the foul play. "Sure I am," says Captain Hayes, the chronicler of the voyage, "no cost was spared by their owner, Master Raleigh, in setting them forth; therefore I leave it unto God." The four smaller vessels proceeded on their way. Losing sight of England on the 15th of June, they passed through a series of fogs and storms which lasted for thirteen days. Thereby the *Delight* and the *Golden Hind* were separated from the *Swallow* and the *Squirrel*; but Gilbert, sailing on, found the *Swallow*, which, being manned chiefly by pirates, had in the interval been put by them to piratical work, a month afterwards off the coast of Newfoundland. He sighted its northern promontory

* All the information about this voyage is derived from an interesting narrative by Edward Hayes, the captain of the *Golden Hind*, from a shorter narrative by Richard Clarke, and from allusions in a treatise on 'Western Plantation,' by Sir George Peckham, all in HAKLUYT, vol. iii., pp. 143—161, 163—165, 165—181.

on the 30th of July, but was deterred from landing by dense fogs through which he could see nothing but dangerous rocks. Therefore he passed on to Saint John's Harbour, there to find the *Squirrel* waiting for him at the mouth of the bay. The merchants and fishermen, who, in six and thirty vessels, were lodging there, had looked on it with suspicion and forbidden its anchoring among them. But, on Gilbert's arrival and exhibition of his credentials, they gave him welcome, and both Englishmen and foreigners readily submitted to his authority. Gilbert, being in want of provisions, levied from the merchants a small tax to supply his needs, and this they willingly agreed to and even exceeded. Gilbert and his crew were feasted, in the various trading ships, upon " wines, marmalades, most fine rusk or biscuit, sweet oil, and sundry delicacies."

On Sunday, the 4th of August, the day after his coming into the harbour, Gilbert went on shore and surveyed the neighbourhood. He was so pleased with it, and with the reports of the traders, that he at once resolved to make Saint John's the centre of his colony. On Monday he called together all his own people and all the Englishmen and foreigners who were already there, explained to them the tenor of his charter from Queen Elizabeth, and proceeded to take formal possession of the district in Her Majesty's name. In anticipation of the public laws that were to be propounded, he at once announced three cardinal rules for the guidance of all residents and visitors. These certainly were simple enough. The first appointed that all the public religion of the country should be in accordance with the practices of the Church of England. The second ordered that, if any one did or attempted anything prejudicial to the Queen's authority, he should be tried and executed for high treason. The third provided that, "if any person should utter words sounding to the dishonour of Her Majesty, he should lose his ears and have his ship and goods confiscate." Thereto all agreed, and the traders gladly consented to join with the colonists in paying rent or tax to the governor, in return for the protection to be afforded to them by the erection of a fort and the establishment of English customs and institutions. Amid the acclamation of all there was planted in a prominent place a high wooden pillar, surmounted by the arms of England engraven on lead, and the first English colony was fairly inaugurated.

For a few days Sir Humphrey Gilbert was a happy man. He saw the beginning of almost regal power to himself and a long succession of descendants; and this regal power, in the goodness of his heart, he hoped to use in the great advancement of England's welfare and in the conferment of yet greater benefits upon the natives of his adopted home. Loyalty to God, and loyalty to the Queen; these were all the laws which he deemed it necessary to make, and with them, as with a two-edged sword, he thought that he could baffle every difficulty and overcome every danger. These being obeyed, he considered that a sure road to success was before him, and that there was nothing left for him to do but to lead his comrades on to a glorious success, in which the least advantage to be expected, though that would be enough to satisfy the most rapacious, was their personal advancement in wealth and fame, and every element of worldly honour.

It was a short-lived hope. With admirable intentions, Gilbert lacked the forethought, tact, and perseverance necessary to the planter of a successful colony. Sharing the impetuous courage of the founders of Spanish rule in America, and approaching his work in a far worthier spirit than was shown by most of them, he was behind them in the capacity for quietly mastering difficulties, and patiently organizing the machinery of a new settlement in a strange region, in which even they were for the most part sadly deficient. And this was of far greater importance to the colony which Gilbert proposed to establish in the winter-oppressed island of Newfoundland than to the Spanish plantations in the West Indies, favoured with perennial summer, with ample stores of fruits that grew without cultivation, and with little need for labour in building houses, and providing against bad weather. Gilbert seems to have thought little of the preparations, without which it would have been impossible for his followers to live through the hard season of cold and rain and fog that was beginning even at the time of his arrival. All that he did was to repair his ships, to store them with food, and to make arrangements for exploration in the neighbourhood of his adopted home.

Perhaps, however, the wisest and most prudent of men would have been able to fare no better than he did. It would have been impossible to plant a thriving colony with such colonists as he had brought with him. Some were honest men who set themselves honestly to the hard work that had to be done. But most of them were raw adventurers, landsmen who did not choose to toil, and sailors who alleged that they were unable to toil anywhere but at sea and on shipboard; and many were lawless fellows, pirates and robbers, who had been taken out of prison and forced upon Gilbert in the foolish belief that, when removed from the scenes of their past misdeeds, they would change into good and peaceable servants.

The result was one that no prophet was needed to foretell. The bad men soon made converts of the weak men, and Gilbert had not been a fortnight in Newfoundland before he found himself at the head of a society which no possible machinery of government—unless, indeed, he had brought with him a little army of gaolers to rule a little colony of convicts—could turn to good, and which he had no efficient means of governing at all. Some of his people ran away into the woods and there lived as wild men. Others gave themselves up to idleness and drunkenness. The worst amused themselves with practising upon their neighbours, and especially upon the traders who were now preparing to go home with their stores of fish, the piracy and robbery in which they had previously been adepts. The best begged that they might be taken back to England, or anywhere away from the lawlessness by which they were surrounded in their new home.

To that request, with a heavy heart, Sir Humphrey Gilbert assented. Leaving the *Swallow* to carry home, as soon as they could be removed, several of his followers who were sick, and some others who wished to go direct to England, he left Saint John's with his three other ships on the 20th of August, less than three weeks after his arrival. He intended to make a careful search of the coast towards the south, believing that next year he would certainly be able to return with a better and better-furnished company to Saint John's, or to some more suitable spot, if such should be found in the course of his exploration. During eight days he made but little way, his ships being becalmed off the northern shore of Newfoundland. On the 28th they sighted Cape Breton Isle, where Gilbert intended to land. But then the crew of the *Swallow*, who had always been the most troublesome of the party, and who had been transferred at the time of starting to the *Delight*, in order that a well-behaved company might be left in charge of the sick and fainthearted, turned mutinous. They refused to follow the others into the harbour, and in the end sailed out in the direction of the open sea. Hoping to outsail the two vessels that gave them chase, they struck against a rock, and thus the *Delight* and more than a hundred men were lost, together with nearly all the provisions that had been laid up for the homeward voyage.

Thus Gilbert was left alone with the two smallest vessels of his fleet of five, the *Golden Hind* and the *Squirrel*. He himself was in the little *Squirrel*, which he preferred, both because it seemed the fittest for close following of the coast-line, and because its crew, deeming it hardly seaworthy, were afraid to be left alone. During three days the ships were sorely beaten about by storms, vainly attempting to enter the harbour, and barely saved from shipwreck amid the mountainous waves and among the treacherous rocks and sandbanks. On the last day of August, Gilbert resolved to try no longer. Summoning the chief officers of the *Golden Hind* on board the *Squirrel*, and hearing from them complaints similar to those made by his own small crew, he gave orders for immediate return to England. "Be content," he said; "we have run enough, and take no care of expenses past. I will set you forth royally next spring, if God send us safe home. Let us no longer strive here, where we fight against the elements."

Fierce winds and angry seas perplexed them still. On the 2nd of September Sir Humphrey Gilbert went on board the *Golden Hind*, and bade its people "to make merry." He could not be merry himself. "He was out of measure grieved," says Captain Hayes, who very unjustly supposed that his chief cause of grief was the loss, in the *Delight*, of some mineral which he had collected, and which he thought to be rich silver ore. Hayes could not see that there was ground enough for grief in the loss of three-quarters of his followers and the failure of his second effort at colonization. Gilbert resolved that it should only be a temporary failure, and that he would do his very utmost to retrieve his misfortunes, and that upon the scene of the disasters. "Whereas he never before had good conceit of these northern parts," we are told, "now his mind was wholly fixed upon the Newfoundland. Laying down his determination for the voyage to be re-attempted in the spring following, he assigned the captain and master of the *Golden Hind* unto the south discovery, and reserved unto himself the north, affirming that this voyage had won his heart from the south, and that he was now become a northern man altogether."

Over and over again the crew of the *Golden Hind* urged him to stay with them, instead of trusting his precious life to the ill-furnished and unsafe *Squirrel*. This he steadily refused to do. "I will not forsake my little company going homeward," he said, "with whom I have passed so many storms and perils."

With them he passed through another week of storms and perils, and then all was over. Throughout that week the voyagers battled with waves and winds so terrible that men who had been all their lives at sea declared they had never seen the like before. On the 9th of September the storm was at its highest. All day long the mariners of the *Golden Hind*, itself a mere waif upon the surging ocean, saw the little *Squirrel* tossing up and down, seeming to be engulfed by every wave as it covered the puny boat from stem to stern. But all day long Sir Humphrey Gilbert was at its helm, and, as often as the two ships came within ear-shot, the men of the *Golden Hind* heard him uttering brave words of cheer and comfort. "Courage, my friends," he shouted; "we are as near to heaven by sea as on the land!"

The noble words were ringing in their ears when, at midnight, they saw the *Squirrel* burst asunder, in a moment to be swallowed up by the waters.

The *Golden Hind* reached Falmouth on the 22nd of September, and when the dismal story of Sir Humphrey Gilbert's misfortunes and the heroic ending of them was told, Englishmen forgave him for any rashness and indiscretion that he had been guilty of, and, treasuring up his dying speech, entered with new zest upon the grand work of American colonization which he had been the first systematically to attempt.

CHAPTER VIII.

Sir Walter Raleigh's Virginia.

[1584—1590.]

Sir Humphrey Gilbert's successor in the effort to establish in North America an English colonial empire which should rival the possessions of Spain in the central and southern parts of the continent, was his stepbrother, Walter Raleigh. To him, on the 25th of March, 1584, Queen Elizabeth issued letters patent authorizing him, in terms similar to those employed in Gilbert's charter, to discover and take possession of any district not yet appropriated by Europeans, and assigning to him and his heirs perpetual governorship of any colony that he might found within the next six years.[*]

Raleigh lost no time in making use of the privileges thus conferred upon him. Keeping the business in his own hands, spending his own money, and giving his own directions, he fitted out two small vessels, which left Plymouth on the 27th of April. Their captains were Philip Amadas and Arthur Barlow.

Their instructions were to explore the eastern shores of America from Florida upwards, to note especially the

[*] Hakluyt, vol. iii., pp. 243—245.

fitness of each part of the coast for colonization, and then without delay to bring home a report of their observations. All this was done very successfully. The voyagers reached the Canaries on the 10th of May. Thence they proceeded slowly to the Bahamas, and spent twelve days on one of the islands, renewing their stores of fresh water and provisions. On the 4th of July, after sailing due north for a few days, they sighted the coast of what is now the State of North Carolina. They traversed its length for about a hundred and twenty miles, and then, entering Pamlico Sound, they landed upon one of the islands, and took possession in Queen Elizabeth's name. With this and the adjoining islands they were so charmed that they spent more than a month in exploring them and the neighbouring mainland. Their rich fruitage and the brilliance and sweetness of their flowers delighted them while they were on shipboard, and their later investigation convinced them that this was the best place for Raleigh to plant his colony in. They found it filled with oaks, cedars, cypresses, and mastics, with cinnamon trees and many others " of excellent smell and quality," and well stored with " melons, walnuts, cucumbers, gourds, peas, and divers roots, and fruits very excellent good, and corn very white, fair, and well tasted, also wheat and oats, and beans very fair, of divers colours and wonderful plenty." Everywhere the soil seemed to them to be marvellously fertile, and of the natives they formed a very favourable opinion.

Concerning these natives and their ways, Captain

Barlow furnished in his report to Raleigh much interesting information.* Here we have the first impressions of English voyagers to the homes of the red men whom English colonists were before long to drive from their fairest haunts in order that English America might be founded. Barlow tells how, very soon after their first landing, one of the natives, " never making any show of fear or doubt," came up to welcome them. "And after he had spoken many things not understood by us, we brought him, with his own good liking, aboard the ships, and gave him a shirt, a hat, and some other things, and made him taste of our wine and our meat, which he liked very well; and after having viewed both barks, he departed, and went to his own boat again, which he had left in a little cave or creek adjoining. As soon as he was two bowshots into the water, he fell to fishing, and in less than half an hour he had laden his boat as deep as it could swim, with which he came again to the point of the land, and there he divided the fish into two parts, appointing one part to the ship and the other to the pinnace. Then after he had, as much as he might, requited the former benefits received, he departed out of our sight."

* Barlow's narrative, in HAKLUYT, vol. iii., pp. 246—251, is my only guide to the story of this expedition. Most of the information given later in this chapter is also derived from HAKLUYT, vol. iii., which includes Barlow's account of the second voyage (pp. 251—253); Lane's and Hariot's memoir of the first settlement, 1585—6 (pp. 254—264; 266—280); an account of the third voyage (p. 265); an account of the fourth voyage (pp. 280—287); and an account of the fifth voyage (pp. 287—295). The authorities for information not drawn from these sources will be cited in their places.

There was like kindly intercourse between the English and the Indians all through the time of this visit. On the following day a brother of the chief of the tribe resident in the district, with about forty followers, "very handsome and goodly people, and in their behaviour as mannerly and civil as any of Europe," came in boats to the shore off which the English barks were anchored. "When he came to the place," we are told, "his servants spread a long mat upon the ground, on which he sat down, and at the other end of the mat four others of his company did the like. The rest of his men stood round about him, somewhat afar off. When we came to the shore to him with our weapons, he never moved from his place, nor any of the other four, nor ever mistrusted any harm to be offered from us; but, sitting still, he beckoned us to come and sit by him, which we performed; and being set, he made all signs of joy and welcome, striking on his head and his breast, and afterwards on ours, to show we were all one, smiling and making show, the best he could, of all love and familiarity. After he had made a long speech unto us, we presented him with divers things, which he received very joyfully and thankfully. None of the company durst speak one word all the time; only the four which were at the other end spake one in the other's ear very softly. After we had presented him with such things as we thought he liked, we likewise gave somewhat to the others that sat with him on the mat; but presently he rose and took all from them and put it into his own basket, making signs and tokens that all things ought to be delivered unto him, and the rest were but his servants and followers."

Out of that present-giving barter soon grew. The red men brought great numbers of choice skins, which they gladly exchanged for English commodities. A copper kettle was valued at fifty deer skins worth a crown apiece, and the chief's brother gave twenty skins for a bright tin dish, " which he presently took up and clapped before his breast, and after made a hole in the brim thereof and hung it about his neck, making signs that it would defend him against his enemies' arrows." The Indians bought all the hatchets and axes and knives that could be spared by the English, and offered any number of skins for the swords that could not be spared.

After further friendly intercourse on shore the chief's brother visited the ships and showed great delight at the way in which he was entertained. "And after a few days overpast he brought his wife with him to the ships, his daughter, and two or three children. His wife was very well-favoured, of mean stature, and very bashful. She had on her back a long cloak of leather, with the fur side next to her body, and before her a piece of the same. About her forehead she had a band of white coral. In her ears she had bracelets of pearls hanging down to her middle, and those were of the bigness of good peas. The rest of her women of the better sort had pendants of copper hanging in either ear. And some of the children had five or six in either ear. The King's brother had upon his head a broad plate of gold or copper. His apparel was as his wife's; only the women wear their hair long on both sides, and the men but on one."

After the natives had paid several visits to the ships, Captain Barlow and seven other Englishmen took boat and went for about twenty miles along the shore to Roanoke Island. "At the north end thereof," says our intelligent voyager, "was a village of nine houses, built of cedar, and fortified round about with sharp trees, to keep out their enemies, and the entrance into it made like a turnpike, very artificially. When we came towards it, standing near unto the waterside, the wife of the King's brother came running out to meet us, very cheerfully and friendly, her husband being not then in the village. Some of her people she commanded to draw our boat on shore; others she appointed to carry us on their backs to the dry ground; and others to bring our oars into the house for fear of stealing. When we were come into the outer room, having five rooms in her house, she caused us to sit down by a great fire, and after took off our clothes and washed them and dried them again. Some of the women plucked off our stockings and washed them. Some washed our feet in warm water; and she herself took great pains to see all things ordered in the best manner she could, making great haste to dress some meat for us to eat. After we had thus dried ourselves, she brought us into the inner room, where she set on the board standing along the house some wheat like furmenty, sodden venison and roast, fish sodden, boiled and roasted, melons raw and sodden, roots of divers kinds, and divers fruits. Their drink is commonly water, but while the grape lasteth they drink wine. We were entertained with all love and kindness, and with as much bounty, after their manner, as they could possibly devise. We found the people most gentle, loving, and faithful, void of all guile and treason, and such as live after the manner of the golden age. The people only care how to defend themselves from the cold in their short winter, and to feed themselves with such meat as the soil affordeth. Their meat is very well sodden, and they make broth very sweet and savory. Their vessels are earthen pots, very large, white, and sweet. Their dishes are wooden platters of sweet timber. Within the place where they feed was their lodging, and within that their idol, which they worship, of whom they speak incredible things. While we were at meat, there came in at the gate two or three men with their bows and arrows from hunting; whom when we espied, we began to look one towards another, and offered to reach our weapons. But as soon as she espied our mistrust, she was very much moved, and caused some of her men to run out and take away their bows and arrows and break them, and withal beat the poor fellows out of the gate again. When we departed in the evening, and would not tarry all night, she was very sorry, and gave us into our boat our supper half dressed, pots and all, and brought us to our boat side, in which we lay all night, removing the same a pretty distance from the shore. She, perceiving our jealousy, was much grieved, and sent divers men and thirty women to sit all night on the bank side by us, and sent us into our boat fine mats to cover us from the rain, using very many words to entreat us to rest in their houses. But because we were few men, and if we had miscarried the voyage had been in very great danger, we durst not venture anything, although there was no cause of doubt, for a more kind and loving people there cannot be found in the world, as far as we have hitherto had trial."

Next day the honest voyagers made some investigation of the other islands and the main land round about, and then they returned to their ships. Friendly dealings continued with the natives until they started on the return voyage to England.

From such conversation as they were able to carry on with the people, they gathered that the king or chief lived in a great city six days' journey inland, and had under him several governors like the brother from whom they received such generous treatment. There were two other kings in the neighbourhood, all three being in friendship with one another, their peoples being of kindred race. Two other kings ruled farther south, who were at constant feud with the Englishmen's entertainers. The only dark feature in the bright picture of Indian life portrayed by our travellers is in their mention of the bloody wars carried on between these two races, and in the civil dissensions that were reported to arise from time to time. The simple natives were well practised in the art of war. "Their arrows," we are told, "are of small cane, headed with a sharp shell or tooth of a fish, sufficient enough to kill a naked man. Their swords be of wood hardened. They have beside a kind of club, in the end whereof they fasten the sharp horns of a stag or other beast. When they go to war they carry about with them their idol, of whom they ask counsel, as the Romans were wont of the oracle of Apollo. They sing songs as they march to battle, instead of drums and trumpets. Their wars are very cruel and bloody, by reason whereof the people are marvellously wasted, and in some places the country left desolate."

Early in August, well satisfied with what they had seen, Captain Amadas and Captain Barlow set sail for England, bringing with them two Indians who came of their own accord. They reached Plymouth about the middle of September.

Their report, though garnished by no perversions of the old fables about Cathay and El Dorado, gave great and reasonable satisfaction to Sir Walter Raleigh and all the thousands of Englishmen to whom they were made known. And well they might. After a four months' expedition, in which there had been nothing but pleasant episode and good fortune, without loss of life or any sort of danger, a score or two of hardy seamen had discovered a region in which there was more chance of reasonably advancing the welfare of England and the wealth of its people than could be hoped for from a century of battling, as glorious as it was profitless, with the ice and ice-bound rocks by which Frobisher and his crews had been conquered. There was henceforth no lack of interest in the projects which Frobisher had been the first, in Queen Elizabeth's days, to enforce by practical experiment. But from this time prudent and matter-of-fact men, and many who were very far from prudent and matter-of-fact, determined to risk their money and their lives, if they risked them in any far-off voyaging at all, in continuance of the work which had been so successfully inaugurated by Walter Raleigh. The outcome of their enterprise appears in the United States of America.

To this new district Queen Elizabeth, as well pleased with the account of it as were any of her subjects, gave the name of Virginia; and Walter Raleigh lost no time in planning a second and larger expedition to his fortunate possession. In December a bill for confirming the charter he had already received from the Queen, and for defining the limits of his colony, passed through the House of Commons, after having been discussed by a committee of which Sir Francis Drake and Sir Philip Sidney were members.*

Sidney, famous and fame-worthy beyond all others among Elizabethan courtiers, has a place in the history of English colonization. Early in 1583, probably before Sir Humphrey Gilbert had set out on his disastrous voyage, and certainly before its issue was known, nearly a year, too, before the date of Raleigh's charter, he had been authorised by letters patent "to discover, search, find out, view, and inhabit certain parts of America not

* D'Ewes, pp. 339—341.

yet discovered, to have and enjoy so much quantity of ground as should amount to the number of thirty hundred thousand acres of ground and wood, with all commodities, jurisdictions, and royalties, both by sea and land." Having desired eight years before to go with Frobisher on his north-western voyaging, he seems now to have wished, in conjunction with his friend Gilbert, to have entered personally on the more profitable work of American colonization. That he took great interest in the work is abundantly proved, and especially by the dedication to him which another of his friends, Richard Hakluyt, prefixed to his first collection of 'Voyages,' published in 1582. But he could not be spared from Court, and there were other good reasons for his postponing and, in the end, abandoning his project. Therefore in July, 1583, while Gilbert was at sea, "for the more speedy execution of Her Majesty's grant and the enlargement of Her Majesty's dominions and government, and for the better encouragement of others in so worthy and commendable an enterprise," he made over, as a free gift, to Sir George Peckham, the title to a tenth part of his three million acres of American soil.*

Peckham does not seem to have made any practical use of his privileges, and henceforth Sidney only showed his interest in the work in encouraging other people to devote themselves to it, of which his share in the parliamentary approval of Raleigh's project was an instance. His rights being thus confirmed to him, Raleigh was

* RECORD OFFICE MSS., *Domestic*, vol. clxi., No. 44, cited in my *Memoir of Sir Philip Sidney*, pp. 367, 372.

busy, during the first three months of 1585, in organising a fleet of seven ships to go to Virginia in the summer. He thought of leading it himself, but from this he was deterred, we are told, by the fear that during his absence the Earl of Leicester, already jealous of his influence at Court, would damage his place in the Queen's regards. Therefore he entrusted the work to his cousin, Sir Richard Grenville, who was appointed Admiral of the Fleet, and to Ralph Lane, who was to be Governor of the intended colony.

Both were notable men. Grenville, now about forty-five years old, belonged to an old family in the west of England. He had gone, in 1566, to fight for the Hungarians against the Turks, and had shared in the famous battle of Lepanto, won by Don John of Austria, and so much to the satisfaction of the Pope that he could only exclaim, in the words of Scripture, "There was a man sent from God, and his name was John!" After that Grenville had done some rough service in Ireland under Sir Henry Sidney, where Gilbert had been one of his associates; and from that time he had taken a lively interest in all the schemes for Cathayan search and American plantation that had been advanced by Gilbert. He was a bold and enterprising man, too impetuous to be very persevering, and of a disposition tainted by the cruelties which Spanish example and the angry warfare carried on with Spain encouraged in nearly all the leading Englishmen of the time of Queen Elizabeth.

Ralph Lane was of the same character. Of Northamptonshire origin, he was second cousin to Queen Katherine Parr, though born only a little while before her death. He was about ten years older than Grenville, and, like Grenville, he had served both in continental wars and in Irish soldiership. At Court he was favoured by the rival Earls of Burghley and Leicester, and he was one of "Leicester's Band" of equerries to the Queen. For this he considered he was not recompensed according to his deserts. In a letter written to Burghley in July, 1583, he begged for some suitable reward, "having," he said, "served Her Majesty these twenty years, spent my patrimony, bruised my limbs, and yet nevertheless at this day not worth one groat by Her Majesty's gift towards a living." That dolorous petition brought him an appointment as Commander of Southsea Castle, with pay at two shillings a day, and to this was added, in 1584, somewhat more remunerative employment in Ireland as Governor of Kerry. On the 8th of February, 1585, Queen Elizabeth allowed him to put a deputy in that office, "in consideration of his ready undertaking the voyage to Virginia."*

The seven vessels sailed from Plymouth on the 9th of April. The largest of them were the *Tiger* and the *Roebuck*, each of 140 tons' burthen, the *Lion*, of 100 tons, and the *Elizabeth*, of 50 tons. Philip Amadas and Arthur Barlow went as chief pilots to the district which they had discovered, and Thomas Cavendish, the great

* An ample memoir of Lane by the Rev. E. E. HALE is in the *Archæologia Americana* for 1860, pp. 315—344. To this I am indebted for the particulars given above, as well as to Mr. HALE's reprint of some letters written by Lane from Virginia, in the same volume, pp. 3—33.

buccaneer, was one of the party. Following the old track, they sailed by way of the Canaries to Saint John's, one of the West Indian islands. There they waited for a fortnight, ostensibly to build a pinnace, but evidently with the hope of doing some injury to the Spaniards, work which was much more agreeable to Grenville than American colonization. Setting sail again on the 26th of May, they captured, on that and the following day, two Spanish frigates, which were taken back to Saint John's and there ransomed for "good round sums." They also seized a ship-load of salt, and did other damage to the Spaniards before proceeding to Virginia, which they did not reach till the 26th of June.

Three days afterwards the *Tiger* struck ground and was seriously damaged, and then began a series of misfortunes well earned by the unworthy method in which Grenville and Lane set themselves to perform their appointed task. As a task they seem from the first to have regarded all the duties proper to the establishment of a colony. For fierce war and lawless conquest they were well adapted; but they showed no skill, and hardly attempted to show it, in the way of peacefully organising an English settlement in the New World.

This, indeed, was never thought of by Sir Richard Grenville. He spent seven weeks in exploring the islands of the adjoining mainland of North Carolina, in receiving kindness from the natives, and in ill-using them. In the pithy report of one day's proceedings we read that "one of our boats was sent to demand a silver cup which one of the savages had stolen from us, and, not receiving it according to his promise, we burnt and spoiled their corn and town, all the people being fled."

Nor was Grenville satisfied with troubling the simple natives and laying a sure train for their ultimate extermination. He quarrelled with Lane and with most of the other leading members of his company, Thomas Cavendish among the number. "It is not possible," said Lane himself in a letter of complaint to Walsingham, written on the 8th of September, "for men to behave themselves more faithfully and more industriously in an action—the same by the General's only great default having been made most painful and most perilous—than every of these gentlemen have done, and that ever since the first to the last. Contrariwise, Sir Richard Grenville, our General, hath demeaned himself, from the first day of his entry into government until the day of his departure from hence, far otherwise than my hope of him, though very agreeable to the expectations and predictions of sundry wise and godly persons of his own country that knew him better than myself. And particularly I thought good to advise your honour how tyrannous an execution, without any occasion of my part offered, he not only purposed, but even propounded the same, to have brought me, by indirect means and most untrue surmises, to the question of my life; and that only for an advice in a public consultation by me given, which, if it had been executed, had been for the great good of us all, but most chiefly of himself. I have had so much experience of his

government, as I am humbly to desire your honour and
the rest of my honourablest friends to give me their
favours to be freed from that place where Sir Richard
Grenville is to carry any authority in chief. The
Lord hath miraculously blest this action that, in the
time of his being amongst us, even through his intolerable pride and insatiable ambition, it hath not at three
several times taken a final overthrow."*

Grenville did not wait to see that final overthrow.
In obedience to his instructions he returned to England
as soon as he had seen that the intending colonists—a
hundred and seven in number—were lodged in their
new home. Having despatched one of his vessels on
the 5th of August, he himself, with the others, left
America on the 25th of the same month. On his way
back he fought with a rich Spanish vessel, of 300 tons'
burthen, and, having seized its goods, reached Plymouth
on the 18th of October.

Lane was not able to manage the colony, even with
his rival away. He does not seem to have been chargeable, at the beginning of his career, with much cruelty,
but he was in no way fitted to be the first governor of
a settlement in which everything had to be learnt by
slow experience and close observation. His chief fault
was in seeing no difficulty in his work. "Our present
arrival in these parts," he said in another letter to Walsingham, dated the 12th of August, "hath discovered
unto us so many, so rare and so singular commodities
of this Her Majesty's new kingdom of Virginia as all

* RECORD OFFICE MSS., *Colonial*, vol. i., No. 6.

the kingdoms and states of Christendom, their commodities joined in one together, do not yield either more good or more plentiful whatsoever for public use is needful or pleasing for delight. The things that we have had time as yet to see and to send are but such as are first come to hand with very small search, and which do present themselves upon the upper face of the earth; the barrenest and most sunken plots whereof do, nevertheless, everywhere yield somewhat that either for known virtue is of price in Christendom, or somewhat at least to the smell pleasing, not having as yet found, in all our search, one stinking weed growing in this land, a matter, in all our opinions here, very strange. The climate is so wholesome, yet somewhat tending to heat, as that we have not had one sick since we entered into the country; but sundry that came sick are recovered of long diseases, especially of rheums. Not doubting, in the mercy of God, to be sufficiently provided for by Him, and most assured by faith in Christ that, rather than suffer the overthrow of us His poor servants, through famine or other wants—being in a vast country yet unmannered, though most apt for it—He will command even the ravens to feed us, as He did by His servant the prophet Habakkuk, and that only for His mercy's sake."*

Lane put his trust in God and the ravens. The fertile and pleasant island of Roanoke, which was called Plymouth, having been fixed upon as the residence of his hundred colonists, he seems to have made no attempt

* RECORD OFFICE MSS., *Colonial*, vol. i., No. 3.

to turn it into a suitable and permanent **place of settlement** for Englishmen. A fort was set **up and intrenchments** were laid round what was intended to be the town of Port Ferdinando;* but no substantial houses were built, and no preparations were made for cultivating the fruitful soil and gathering **a store of food** for future use. The colonists believed that the Indians would supply the place of ravens in furnishing them with bread and flesh, and spent all that remained of summer time in making acquaintance with the haunts and habits of these Indians, and filling them with an unwholesome dread of Englishmen.

Lane made tolerably extensive excursions, to the south-west, north-west, and north of his intended place

---

* The precise site was identified and described by Mr. Edward C. Bruce in 1859. "The island," he says, "contains nothing else of the sort, and the records of the voyagers fix the situation of the fort and village to within a mile or less. Within that circuit they must have stood, and within it lie the remains before us. The location was judiciously selected. Half a mile from the eastern, or north-eastern shore, and a little further from the northern point of the island, it was just far enough inland to be sheltered from the heavy winds by the bluffs and woods, without sacrificing facility of watch over the adjacent waters. To the north-west the position commands the broad sweep of Albemarle; to the north, Currituck; on the east, Roanoke; and on the west, Croaton Sounds,—all leading directly to this point. Opposite the narrow neck which has replaced the inlet through which Lane entered, and perhaps a mile from the fort, a fine look-out is afforded by a range of sandhills. The trench is clearly traceable in a square of about forty yards each way. Midway of one side another trench, perhaps flanking the gateway, runs in some fifteen or twenty feet; and, on the right of the same face of the enclosure, the corner is apparently thrown out in the form of a small bastion. The ditch is generally two feet deep, though in many places scarcely perceptible. A fragment or two of stone or brick may be discovered in the grass, and then all is told of the existing relics of the city of Raleigh."—Cited by Mr. HALE in the *Archæologia Americana*, pp. 24, 25.

of residence. With his boats, the stoutest of which was a four-oared barge, just large enough to hold fifteen men, he tracked the coast northwards as far as Chesapeake Bay, which he judged to be a better place than Roanoke for English settlement. "For pleasantness of seat, for temperature of climate, for fertility of soil, and for the commodity of the sea, besides multitude of bears—being an excellent good victual—with great woods of sassafras and walnut trees," he said, "it is not to be excelled by any other whatsoever."

North of Albemarle Sound, and in the direction of Chesapeake Bay, was a district call Chawanook. Its chief town contained seven hundred fighting men, and there were other towns of some size and beauty. "The king of the province," said Lane, "is called Menatonon, a man impotent in his limbs, but otherwise, for a savage, a very grave and wise man, and of very singular good discourse in matters concerning the state, not only of his own country and his own men, but also of his neighbours round about him as well near as far, and of the commodities that each country yieldeth. When I had him prisoner with me, for two days that we were together, he gave me more understanding and light of the country than I had received by all searches and savages that before I or any of my people had had conference with. Amongst other things he told me that, going three days' journey in a canoe up his river of Chawanook and then descending to the land, you are within four days' journey to pass overland north-east to a certain king's country, whose province lieth upon the sea, but his place of greatest strength is an island situated as he described unto me, in a bay, the water round about the island very deep. Out of this bay he signified unto me that this king had so great quantity of pearl, and doth so ordinarily take the same, as that not only his own skins that he weareth, and the better sort of his gentlemen and followers, are full set with the said pearl, but also his beds and houses are garnished with them. He showed me that the said king two years before brought him certain pearl, but of the worst sort. He gave me a rope of the same pearl. They were black, yet many of them very great and a few amongst a number very orient and round. He told me that the said king had great store of pearl that were white, great, and round, and that his black pearl his men did take out of shallow water, but the white pearl his men fished for in very deep water. It seemed to me by his speech that the said king had traffic with white men that had clothes as we have, for these white pearl, and that was the reason that he would not part with other than black pearls to those of the same country." This, of course, was the southern part of Chesapeake Bay.

Soon after that, Lane heard still better news. He was told that at the head of a broad river—as broad for thirty miles above its outlet as the Thames at Greenwich—which was called the Moratoc, now the Roanoke, was a famous settlement of Indians whose chief source of wealth was a goodly store of metal, either copper or gold. This he determined to seek out. He rowed for three days up the river, and found that the people fled at his approach, taking with them all the corn that he had hoped to buy or steal. Only two days' full allowance of food was left, and then he put it to his comrades "whether they should adventure the spending of their whole victual, in some further view of that most goodly river, in hope to meet with some better pass, or otherwise to retire back again." "Their resolution fully and wholly," he records, "was that while there was but one half-pint of corn for a man, we should not leave the search, and that there were in the company two mastiffs, upon the pottage of which with sassafras leaves, if the worst fell out, the company would make shift to live two days, which time would bring them down the current to the mouth of the river. This resolution of theirs did not a little please me, since it came of themselves, although for mistrust of that which afterwards did happen, I pretended to have been rather of the contrary opinion." So the journey was continued. "After two days' travel, and our whole victual spent, lying on shore all night, we could never see man; only fires we might perceive, made along the shore where we were to pass and up into the country, until the last day. In the evening whereof, about three of the clock, we heard certain savages call, as we thought, Manteo," a native servant who was taken as a guide. "Whereof we all being very glad, hoping of some friendly conference and making him answer them, they presently began a song, as we thought in token of our welcome to them. But Manteo presently betook him to his piece, and told me that they meant to fight with us. Which word was not so soon spoken by him, but there alighted a volley of arrows amongst them in one of the boats, but did no hurt, God be thanked, to any man. Immediately our other boat began to scour the place for our hands to land upon, which was presently done, although the land was very high and steep. The savages forthwith quitted the shore and betook themselves to flight. We landed fairly and easily and for a small space followed after them, but they had wooded themselves we knew not where. The sun drawing then towards the setting, and being then assured that the next day, if we would pursue them, though we might happen to meet with them, yet we should meet with some of their victual, which we then had good cause to think of, I determined the next morning before the rising of the sun, to be going back again, if possibly we might recover the mouth of the river. Unto which I found my whole company ready to assent; for they were now come to their dogs' porridge. The end was, we came the next day by night to the river's mouth, within four or five miles, having rowed in one day down the current as much as in four days we had done against the same. We lodged upon an island, where we had nothing to eat but a pottage of sassafras leaves." Thus the search for copper was abandoned.

The exaggerated reports that came to him concerning the riches of Virginia, however, made Lane very anxious to transplant his colony to Chesapeake Bay. With that object he went back to Port Ferdinando.

There he found that the rough treatment of his people had turned the Indians, whom they at first found so simple and friendly, into subtle enemies. For this the Indians were not to blame. They had received the white men with show and with hearty desire of friendship. They had freely supplied them with whatever food and furniture they needed, and had evinced great readiness to be instructed in the wonderful ways of their visitors. They were even willing to accept those visitors as masters if they might receive the protection and assistance due to servants. But when they found that they were to be treated as slaves, and as slaves who, not having been bought for money, were not even to be cared for as property, they turned rebellious. They refused to be forced into rendering those services which they had been willing to give in return for generous treatment. For that they were looked upon as rebels and traitors, and accordingly chastised.

The chastisement had begun, as we saw, some time before Sir Richard Grenville's departure. In August Lane had, in a letter to Sir Philip Sidney, complained of his trouble in having " amongst savages, the charge of wild men of his own nation, whose unruliness was such as not to give leisure to the guards to be almost at any time from them."* Very soon, though not, it must be noted in justice to Ralph Lane, until he had started on his ill-timed expedition of discovery, the guards were allowed to join with the wild men in cruel handling of the natives. Thus it happened that, while Lane was away, the news spread from tribe to tribe, and preceded him to most of the districts which he visited, that these white

* RECORD OFFICE MSS., *Colonial*, vol. i., No. 5.

men, not born of women and godlike in their strength and power, were devils, who had come to waste the land and slay all its people, unless, by subtle dealing on their part and by special favour of the Great Spirit, they were able to drive them out and kill them.

The English had had one firm friend in the chief's brother who had first made acquaintance with Barlow and the voyagers of 1584. As long as he lived he had done his utmost to propitiate the colonists and to persuade his friends that, if they themselves would deal meekly and generously with their visitors they might hope for better treatment than in any other way they could possibly receive. But he died while Lane was away from Port Ferdinando, and his son Pemisapan became leader of the steadily growing opposition to the English. His crime, certainly not a great one, was in a proposal that all the Indians in Roanoke should flee from their persecutors and seek peace in a new home in the west. This would have been fatal to the Virginian colony; "for," said Lane, not perceiving how much, in making the statement, he blamed himself and his companions, "at that time we had no weirs for fish, neither had our men skill in the making of them, neither had we one grain of corn for seed to put into the ground." Lane's return prevented this proposal from taking effect, especially as it strengthened a belief that had long been growing among the natives concerning the supernatural character of the English. They had thought that he was dead, and his coming back seemed to them to be a resurrection from the grave. They also had fresh reports of the wonderful effects of his fire-arms, which became a thousand times more wonderful in their distorted imaginations. "It was an opinion very confidently holden among them," said Lane, "that we were the servants of God, and that we were not subject to be destroyed by them; but contrariwise that they amongst them that sought our destruction should find their own, and that we being dead men were able to do them more hurt than now we could do being alive; as also that they, being a hundred miles from any of us, have been shot at in the air, and stricken by some men of ours that by sickness had died among them; and many of them hold opinion that we be dead men returned into the world again, and that we do not remain dead but for a certain time, and then we return again." Therefore the Indians, sorely against their wills and very much to their hurt, because they feared that by rebellion they would bring yet greater hurt upon themselves, continued to serve the English.

It was discontented, superstitious service, like that which Caliban yielded to Prospero in the noble drama which received many of its most poetical suggestions from the story, as it was repeated to Shakespeare, of the sufferings and conduct of the Indians in Sir Walter Raleigh's Virginia.* Many a poor red man,

---

* This is no place for Shakespearean commentary. Therefore I shall not attempt in detail to support the opinion indicated above. It is enough to say that whatever other suggestions may have come to Shakespeare from other sources, some at any rate must have come from New World history and scenery. Caliban is evidently a variation upon Canibal, itself a perversion of Caribbean. "The still vexed Bermoothes" must have been the Bermudas. Raleigh's repetition of the report concerning "a nation of people that have their eyes in their shoulders and

remembering the friendly dealings that he had with Barlow and his comrades in 1584, must have said, in rude words and phrases of his own,

> "When thou cam'st here first,
> Thou strok'dst me, and mad'st much of me, wouldst teach me how
> To name the bigger light, and how the less,
> That burn by day and night: and then I lov'd thee,
> And show'd thee all the qualities o' th' isle,
> The fresh springs, brine-pits, barren place and fertile;—
> Cursed be I that did so!"

or, in moments of resolution to shake off the tyranny to which he was now subjected,

> "No more dams I'll make for fish;
> Or fetch firing
> At requiring,
> Nor scrape trencher, nor wash dish."

But a thraldom as heavy as Prospero's over Caliban oppressed him—the thraldom of his own superstitious belief in the superhuman powers of his master; and so he slaved on unwillingly, hoping, amid despair, that some yet greater power would rid him of his trouble.

The Indians shared none of Caliban's brutalities, however, and, unlike Caliban, they were able to bring upon their tyrants, no peers of Prospero's, sufferings almost equal to their own. After long submission,

---

their mouths in the middle of their breasts" must have suggested Gonzalo's exclamation—

> "When we were boys,
> Who would believe that there were mountaineers
> Dew-lapped like bulls, whose throats had hanging at 'em
> Wallets of flesh? Or that there were such men
> Whose heads stood on their breasts? which now we find
> Each putter-out of one for five will bring us
> Good warrant of."

they organized a plot with their friends on the mainland for a general attack upon the intruders. Ralph Lane, hearing of this, and having still some friends, or allies who had not been turned into open enemies, among the natives about Chesapeake Bay, prepared for a counter attack. Hitherto he had found it necessary to postpone his intention of exterminating the people whose supplies of food and other services had kept alive the colonists. For this he took great credit to himself. "Pemisapan," he said, "was afraid to deny me anything; neither durst he in my presence but by colour and with excuses which I was content to accept for the time, meaning in the end, as I had reason, to give him the jump, once for all; but, in the mean whiles, I and mine bare all wrongs and accepted of all excuses."

At length, at the close of May, 1586, when his colony was about ten months old, the Indians showed him that the time for patient endurance of wrongs was over. In the night they stole into Port Ferdinando, and broke up the fish-weirs and the woolen huts that they had constructed for their masters; and they crossed over to the mainland, or to island fastnesses in which they could not easily be reached. Lane had to divide his hundred men into parties of fifteen or twenty apiece, and send them to different parts of the island, to keep themselves from starving by catching such fish and oysters as they could, while he made preparations for a massacre. This was not possible, since Pemisapan had already made preparations for an overwhelming assault of natives upon the white men. "They," said Lane, "privy to their own villanous purposes against us, held as good espial upon us, both day and night, as we did upon them." Therefore on the 1st of June something like a battle ensued. As many Englishmen as their boats could hold were conveyed across the strait, and then they marched against Pemisapan. The ugly story can only be told in Lane's own words. "I gave the watchword agreed upon, which was 'Christ our victory!' and immediately his chief men and himself had, by the mercy of God for our deliverance, that which they had purposed for us. The king himself being shot through with a pistol, lying on the ground for dead, suddenly started up and ran away, as though he had not been touched, insomuch as he overran all the company, being by the way shot thwart the buttocks by my Irish boy. In the end an Irishman serving me, one Nugent, and the deputy provost, following him into the woods, overtook him; and I, in some doubt lest we had lost both the king and my man, met him returning out of the woods with Pemisapan's head in his hand."

The Indians were more than a match for their tyrants in running, at any rate, and they escaped without very much slaughter. Their pleasant home in Roanoke had been despoiled; but they had succeeded also in ruining the English colony that had brought them so much misery.

Nothing but a fortunate accident saved the colonists themselves from being utterly ruined. Lane could find no red men either to kill or to rob of the food of which his people were in sore need. He waited in despair from the 1st to the 8th of June. On that day he heard that a great fleet of three-and-twenty ships was in sight, and this proved to be the fleet of Sir Francis Drake on his way home from his famous West Indian expedition of 1585. In this Ralph Lane, always most pious when his work was most impious, saw "the very hand of God stretched out to take them." Another of the party thought, more reasonably, that "the hand of God had come upon them for the cruelty and outrages committed by some of them against the inhabitants of that country." Theologians must decide in which way the hand of God had worked.

Drake's arrival, however, was propitious. Hearing of the sad condition to which his brother Englishmen had been reduced, he offered them a ship, a pinnace, and some boats, either to be left at Roanoke, with a month's supply of provisions, and there used by Lane in furtherance of his colonizing or conquering work, or to be taken home, with the colonists on board, under protection of the fleet. Lane was inclined to choose the former alternative, but before the provisions could be landed there arose so violent a storm that Drake had to save his ships by again hurrying out to sea, leaving only the detachment that had been offered to his distressed fellow-countrymen. In these Lane embarked on the 19th of June, and overtaking his deliverers, sailed with them into Portsmouth Harbour.

The troubles that had befallen the colonists screened

them from the blame that they deserved. With the stories of their woes, moreover, they brought over an article for which all England soon was grateful to them. Thomas Hariot, one of the number, in a long account of the various productions of Virginia, describes one in particular. "There is an herb," he says, "which is sowed apart by itself, and is called by the inhabitants uppowoc. In the West Indies it hath divers names, according to the several places and countries where it groweth and is used. The Spaniards generally call it tabacco. The leaves thereof being dried and brought into powder, they are to take the fume or smoke thereof, by sucking it through pipes made of clay into their stomach and head, from whence it purgeth superfluous phlegm and other gross humours, and openeth all the pores and passages of the body. This uppowoc is of so precious estimation among them that they think their gods are marvellously delighted therewith; whereupon sometime they make hallowed fires and cast some of the powder therein for sacrifice. We ourselves, during the time we were there, used to suck it after their manner; as also since our return; and have found many rare and wonderful experiments of the virtues thereof, of which the relation would require a volume by itself. The use of it by so many of late, men and women of great calling, as else, and some learned physicians also, is sufficient witness." Only a few years after that Edmund Spenser, in his 'Faerie Queene,' spoke in praise of the "divine tobacco."

Ralph Lane laid the blame of his failure upon Sir

Richard Grenville, who had promised that he would return to Roanoke early in the spring with fresh colonists and ample stores of provisions. He excused himself for not having turned Port Ferdinando into a permanent and well-built town on the score that his visit to Chesapeake Bay had convinced him that that was a very much better site than Roanoke for the headquarters of the colony. He believed that the river which he had partly navigated would lead him to the copper district of which he had heard, and perhaps afford an easy route to the Pacific Ocean. "The discovery of a good mine, by the goodness of God, or a passage to the South Sea," he said, "and nothing else, can bring this country in request to be inhabited by our nation." "I resolved with myself," he added, in his report to Raleigh, "that if your supply had come before the end of April, and that you had sent any store of boats, or men to have had them made in any reasonable time, I would have sent a small bark with two pinnaces about the sea to the northward. I would there have raised a main fort, both for the defence of the harbour and our shipping also, and would have reduced our whole habitation, from Roanoke and from the harbour and port there, which by proof is very naught, unto this other." Not receiving his reinforcements, he considered himself quite justified in abandoning the whole enterprise, which indeed, considering the state to which mismanagement and ill-treatment of the natives had brought the colonists, was the only thing possible.

Only a fortnight after his departure, Grenville arrived with the promised supplies in three ships; the sending of which from England appears to have been delayed by Raleigh's difficulty in raising money enough for the undertaking. Finding Roanoke deserted, and "all things left confusedly, as if they had been chased from thence by a mighty army," Grenville spent a little time in scouring the neighbourhood and making inquiries from the natives as to the fate of the colonists. Then, leaving fifteen men on the island, with provisions for two years, "to retain possession of the country," he made his way back to England, turning the voyage to profit, and affording some rough sport to himself and his followers by attacking the Spanish possessions in the Azores, and seizing a large quantity of booty.

This was sufficient consolation for the disasters that had befallen the settlement in Virginia. Raleigh shared with all other brave Englishmen in the growing jealousy and hatred with which Spain was regarded during the years previous to the Great Armada Fight. He had been rising steadily in royal favour while his colony was being built up and broken down. As member for Devonshire he had taken important part in the work of the Parliament of 1584 and 1585. He had been knighted by the Queen, and received more substantial proof of her liking in a grant of wine licences, and another grant of twelve thousand acres in Ireland. His Virginian expedition had cost him and the friends who joined in the adventure much money,—

according to one estimate about 40,000*l*. His Spanish prizes, however, had more than compensated for that outlay. Therefore he had no difficulty in fitting out a fourth expedition, furnished with the materials for another colonization, in 1587.

In this instance the conduct of the enterprise was entrusted to a Captain John White, of whose previous history we are ignorant, but who proved himself, in spite of his misfortunes, a much better deputy than either Grenville or Lane. With three vessels, the largest of which was the *Admiral*, of 120 tons burthen, and with a hundred and fifty colonists on board, including seventeen women and nine children, he left Plymouth on the 8th of May. He proceeded to Virginia in the usual curve by way of the West Indies. He, however, was not in search of Spanish prizes, and the only capture during the voyage was of "five great tortoises, some of them of such bigness that sixteen of the strongest men were tired with carrying but one of them from the sea-side to the cabins," near Vera Cruz.

The mainland of America was not reached till the 16th of July, when White anchored in the neighbourhood of Roanoke. There he halted, intending to pick up the fifteen Englishmen who had been left behind by Grenville in the previous year. He found nothing but the bones of one man. He saw the ruins of Port Ferdinando, "overgrown with melons of divers sorts, and deer within feeding on those melons." One of his company was killed by some of the natives, who had learnt to hate every Englishman. "The savages, being secretly hidden among high trees, where oftentimes they find the deer asleep, and so kill them," we are told, "espied our man, wading in the water alone, almost naked, without any weapon, save only a small forked stick, catching crabs therewithal, and also being strayed two miles from his company. They shot at him in the water, where they gave him sixteen wounds with their arrows, and, after they had slain him with their wooden swords, they beat his head in pieces, and fled over the water to the main." Within three short years the pleasant region in which Captain Barlow had been generously entertained by "a people most gentle, loving, and faithful, void of all guile and treason, and such as live after the manner of the golden age," had become a wilderness, haunted only by a few Indians turned into savages by English cruelty, and so filled with detestation of all Englishmen that when they saw one undefended they must kill him with arrows, and then hack his corpse with their swords and break his head in pieces.

Still in search of the fifteen missing men, or, at any rate, of some clue as to their fate, Captain White, on the 30th of July, staying himself with the ships which were at anchor off the southern edge of Roanoke, sent some of his people to Croatan, a neighbouring island, the home of Manteo, the Indian who had been found useful to the English as an interpreter, and therefore had been kindly treated by them and taken to England, in Lane's company, in 1586. "At our first landing," says one of the party, "the people seemed as though they would fight with us, but, perceiving us begin to march with our shot towards them, they turned their backs and fled. Then Manteo, their countryman, called to them in their own language, whom as soon they heard they returned and threw away their bows and arrows, and some of them came unto us, embracing and entertaining us very friendly, desiring us not to gather or spill any of their corn, for that they had but little. We answered them that neither their corn nor any other thing of theirs should be diminished by any of us, and that our coming was only to renew the old love that was between us and them at the first, and to live with them as brethren and friends; which answer seemed to please them well. Wherefore they requested us to walk up to their town, where they feasted us after their manner, and desired us that there might be some token or badge given them of us, whereby we might know them to be our friends when we met them anywhere out of the town or island."

From these simple people of Croatan was heard the story of the fifteen missing colonists. They had been set upon by a party of the natives whom Lane and his followers had persecuted. These Indians, hiding themselves in the wood, sent two of their number, with arms concealed, to make show of friendly intercourse with the Englishmen, and thus coaxed two of them, really unarmed, to go into the wood out of reach of their friends. One Englishman was then killed, and, though the other was able to escape and give warning of the danger, he only succeeded in bringing his comrades out of the hut which they had built and in which all their provisions were stored, before they were attacked by their assailants. They fought stoutly, and, with the exception of one who received a fatal shot in the mouth, defended themselves from any but slight wounds, while they succeeded in killing some of the Indians. But during the scuffle the hut and its contents were burnt. The thirteen survivors were forced to take their only boat, and in it put to sea. They were never heard of afterwards.

This account of their misfortunes being repeated to Captain White, had an unfortunate result. White had intended, instead of staying at Roanoke, to go in search of a suitable place on the borders of Chesapeake Bay, and there, with firm resolve to live on friendly terms with the Indians who, having no grudge against the English, might be expected to reciprocate the friendship, to try and make a prosperous settlement. Now, however, he considered it his duty to be revenged upon the natives of Roanoke and their kinsmen on the mainland for the more excusable vengeance which they had wreaked upon his fifteen unhappy countrymen. He was also much incensed at the brutal murder of his own follower ten days before. But the time appointed by Raleigh for the return to England of the ships that had brought him out was nearly at an end; and Simon Ferdinando, their chief pilot, who seems to have been on bad terms with White, refused to prolong it. Therefore it was resolved that the ships should set down their passengers and cargoes, that a temporary settlement should be made on the site of the old colony, and that afterwards the English should make their way leisurely and by land to Chesapeake Bay.

While the ships were unloading, Captain White began the ungracious work of retaliation which he had marked out for himself. Attended by twenty-five of his men and Manteo, the interpreter, he crossed over to the mainland in the early morning of the 9th of August. "We landed, while it was yet dark, near the dwelling-places of our enemies," says one of the party, "and very secretly conveyed ourselves through the woods to that side where we had their houses between us and the water, and having espied their fire and some sitting about it, we presently set on them. The miserable souls, herewith amazed, fled into a place of thick reeds, growing fast by, where our men, perceiving them, shot one of them through the body with a bullet, and therewith he entered the reeds, among which we hoped to acquit their evil-doing towards us." Fortunately no great harm was done. One of the poor creatures had the boldness to come out, and, at the risk of being killed, explain that they were all people of Croatan and friendly towards the English. It seems that the tribe which White meant to punish, foreseeing his intention, had fled inland, and that the Croatan Indians had only come over to collect the ripe corn and tobacco which had been left in the fields. White made amends for the blunder and, with help of his native friends, gathered in the harvest. Then he took both it and them back to Roanoke, postponing his vengeance until a later day.

That day never came. No sooner were the colonists landed than they began to quarrel with one another and show signs of mutiny. It was necessary that two able messengers should accompany the ships to England, to acquaint Sir Walter Raleigh as to the proceedings of the party, and to arrange with him for the proper sending of such fresh supplies as were required; and Captain White was forced to be one of these. Sorely against his will,—for he honestly desired to bring the plantation of Virginia to a successful issue, and he was bound to it by strong personal ties as well as by feelings of honour and duty, his daughter, Eleanor Dare, being one of the colonists, and her infant child, christened Virginia because she was the first native of the colony and of English America, having been born on the 18th of the month,—he yielded to their imperative request, and left Roanoke on the 27th of August.

His homeward voyage was altogether disastrous. On the day of starting, the little vessel in which he went was nearly disabled and many of its crew were lost. Ferdinando, in charge of the *Admiral*, being instructed to do what he could towards reimbursing Sir Walter Raleigh for the expenses of the expedition, by trade or piracy among the Spaniards of the West Indies, refused to take his general by a direct route to England. Therefore White resolved to make the best of his way home by himself in the little broken-down vessel Gentle winds helped him onwards during twenty days, by which time nearly all his fresh water was exhausted and the provisions were brought very low. Then, as he says in his doleful narrative, "there arose a storm which for six days ceased not to blow so exceedingly that we were driven further in those six days than we could recover in thirteen days. In which time others of our sailors began to fall very sick and two of them died. The weather also continued so close that our master, sometimes in four days together, could see neither sun nor star, and all the beverage we could make, with stinking water, dregs of beer, and lees of wine which remained, was but three gallons, and therefore now we expected nothing but famine and to perish at sea." By good fortune, however, they kept afloat and alive for a few days longer, and at the end of that time they drifted up to the south-western corner of Ireland. There they were picked up by a Southampton pinnace and taken by it into port. After being more than ten weeks at sea, White reached Southampton on the 8th of November, and learnt that the *Admiral*, " in such weakness by sickness and death of their chiefest men, that they might all have perished if a small bark by great hap had not come to them to help them," had arrived at Portsmouth, without a shilling's worth of booty, some three weeks before.

England was too full of excitement about the public and private war then being waged with Spain, and of preparations for the expected coming of the Great Armada, for the poor Virginian colonists to be much thought of, or for Captain White's entreaties on their behalf to receive serious attention. Sir Walter Raleigh, indeed, seems to have grown weary of his North

American possessions. Already his adventurous spirit had been attracted by the fables of El Dorado, and he was resolved, as soon as more pressing occupations allowed him time and opportunity, to apply himself to the work of discovery and conquest in South America. Accordingly, after doing no more than listen to John White's petitions during a year and a half, he formally abandoned the colony out of which, five years before, he had hoped to construct an empire which was to prove as helpful to his own fortunes as it could be to the welfare of England. On the 7th of March, 1589, he transferred his Virginian patent to a company of merchants and others, himself tendering a subscription of 100*l.*, " in especial regard and zeal of planting the Christian religion in those barbarous countries, and for the advancement and preferment of the same, and the common utility and profit of the inhabitants."* White eagerly became a member of this company; and he seems to have been its only active member.

After a year of further effort on behalf of the unfortunate colonists who had been waiting for assistance from home since the summer of 1587, he managed, with Raleigh's assistance, to persuade the owners of three ships intended for piracy in the West Indies to take him back to Virginia and do something on behalf of his neglected friends. It was at first intended that several other Englishmen and abundant stores of necessary articles should go with him; but this arrangement

---

* SOUTHEY, *The British Admirals*, vol. iv., p. 238.

was overruled, and he was allowed to take nothing but his own personal property.

The three vessels, the *Hopewell*, the *John Evangelist*, and the *Little John*, with two shallops, left Plymouth on the 20th of March, 1590. " Both governors, masters, and sailors," says White, " regarding very smally the good of their countrymen in Virginia, determined nothing less than to touch at those places, but wholly disposed themselves to seek after purchase and spoils, spending so much time therein that summer was spent before we arrived at Virginia; and, when we were come thither, the season was so unfit and the weather so foul, that we were constrained of force to forsake that coast, having not seen any of our planters."

Some search, however, was made for the planters. On the 1st of August, after much hunting and some spoiling of Spaniards, the mainland of the Virginian district was sighted. The ships were kept at sea, by bad weather, for a fortnight, and on the 15th they anchored off the southern edge of Roanoke. " At our first coming to anchor on this shore," says White, " we saw a great smoke in the isle, near the place where I left our colony in the year 1587; which smoke put us in good hope that some of the colony were there expecting my return out of England." That hope was soon dispelled. On the morning of the 16th, two boats were sent to examine the part from which the smoke had been seen to rise; but no men and no signs of white men's residence were found. Next day a more careful search was begun in two boats with crews of nineteen persons. Let the story be told in Captain White's own words. "Before we could get to the place where our planters were left, it was so exceeding dark that we overshot the place a quarter of a mile. There we espied, towards the north end of the island, the light of a great fire through the woods, to which we presently rowed. When we came right over against it, we let fall our grapnel near the shore, and sounded with a trumpet a call, and after many familiar English tunes of songs, and called to them friendly. But we had no answer. We therefore landed at daybreak, and coming to the fire, we found the grass and sundry rotten trees burning about the place. From hence we went through the woods to that part of the island over against the mainland, and from thence we returned to the water-side, round about the north point of the island, until we came to the place where I left our colony in the year 1587. In all this way we saw in the sand the print of the savages' feet of two or three sorts trodden the night before; and, as we entered up the sandy bank, upon a tree, in the very brow thereof, were curiously carved the fair Roman letters C R O Which letters presently we knew to signify the place where I should find the planters seated, according to a secret token agreed upon between them and me at my last departure from them. I willed them that if they should happen to be distressed in any of those places, they should carve over the letters or name a cross. And having well considered of this, we passed towards the place where they were left in sundry houses; but we found the houses taken down and the place very strongly inclosed with a high palisado of great trees, with curtains and flankers very root-like, and one of the chief trees or posts at the right side of the entrance had the bark taken off, and five feet from the ground in fair capitals was graven, CROATAN, without any cross or sign of distress. This done, we entered into the palisado, where we found many bars of iron, two pigs of lead, four iron fowlers, iron rack shot, and such-like heavy things thrown here and there, almost overgrown with grass and weeds. From thence we went along by the water-side, towards the point of the creek, to see if we could find any of the boats or pinnace, but we could perceive no sign of them, nor any of the last falcons and small ordnance which were left with them. At our return from the creek, some of our sailors, meeting us, told us that they had found where divers chests had been hidden and long since digged up again and broken up, and much of the goods in them spoiled and scattered about, but nothing left, of such things as the savages knew any use of, undefaced. Presently I went to the place, which was in the end of an old trench, made three years past by Captain Amadas. There we found five chests that had been carefully hidden of the planters, and of the same chests three were my own, and about the place many of my things spoiled and broken, and my books torn from the covers, the frames of some of my pictures and maps rotten and spoiled with rain, and my armour almost eaten through with rust. This could be no other but the deed of the savages our enemies, who had watched the departure of our men to Croatan, and, as soon as they were departed, digged up every place where they suspected anything to be buried. But, although it much grieved me to see such spoil of my goods, yet on the other side I greatly joyed that I had safely found a certain token of their safe-being at Croatan, which is the place where Manteo was born, and the savages of the island our friends."

White of course greatly desired to go to Croatan and try to recover the colonists, among whom were his own daughter and grand-daughter. But, after one feeble effort, the captain of the fleet refused to assist him further in his search. Virginia and its English residents were abandoned, and the unworthy people who thus deserted them made a disastrous voyage to Plymouth, which they reached on the 24th of October.

That was the last of Sir Walter Raleigh's Virginia The patent which he had transferred to a company of merchants in 1589, and which apparently was never used by them, passed, in 1602, into the hands of a new and more enterprising company, which, in the following year, sent two small barks to explore the district. The report brought home being satisfactory, the new company was formally incorporated in 1606, and thereupon the real colonization of Virginia was promptly begun. Thence sprang the famous series of English settlements in the United States of America under the Stuarts in the seventeenth century. The first successful colonizing party was led by Captain Christopher

Newport in 1607, who heard from the natives that "the men, women, and children of the first plantation at Roanoke had been miserably slaughtered;" but that some of the English escaped from the slaughter, and going far inland lived peaceably with the natives. In 1607 it was reported there were "seven of the English alive, four men, two boys, and one maid." Perhaps this "one maid" was Virginia Dare, the first English native of America, at that time nearly twenty years of age.*

* STRACHEY, *History of Travaill into Virginia Britannia*, ed. by MAJOR for the Hakluyt Society (1849).

CHAPTER IX.

JOHN DAVIS'S THREE VOYAGES IN THE DIRECTION OF CATHAY.

[1585—1587.]

IN 1497 and 1498 John and Sebastian Cabot, searching for a passage to Cathay, sailed northwards, past Newfoundland and Labrador, up to the entrance to Baffin's Bay, and appear to have reached the westernmost promontory of Cumberland Island in $67\frac{1}{2}$ degrees of north latitude and about 61 degrees of west longitude. During his three voyages in 1576, 1577, and 1578, Martin Frobisher visited the southern edge of Greenland, and then, crossing over to the broken districts north of America, confined his researches to the western half of the bay known after him as Frobisher's Straits, in 62 and 63 degrees of north latitude, and between 62 and 64 degrees of west longitude, just discovering, without defining, the mouth of Hudson's Straits. It was reserved for an abler and more fortunate voyager to follow up his exploration of Greenland as far as 72 degrees of north latitude, a hundred and fifty miles further north than the Cabots' furthest point, to trace the rugged coast-line of Cumberland Island between the districts visited by the Cabots and by Frobisher, and to indicate the broad channel known by his name as Davis's Straits, the only entrance to Baffin's Bay, and the route followed by most later arctic voyagers in search of a passage to the Indies.

He fared better than one of Frobisher's comrades, Charles Jackman, who in company with Arthur Pet, an old associate of Willoughby and Chancelor, set out on the 31st of May, 1580, in pursuit of that north-eastern quest of Cathay which had cost Willoughby and Chancelor their lives. This expedition was organized by the Muscovy Company, being the first of its appointment since the voyage of 1556, in which Stephen Burroughs had sailed along the northern coast of Russia, and passed between Nova Zembla and Vaigats, into the Sea of Kara. Pet and Jackman left Harwich, with two barks, one of forty the other of twenty tons' burthen. At Wardhus in Lapland, they parted company on the 24th of June. Pet reached the upper part of the more southern of the two Nova Zembla islands on the 4th of July, and then, sailing downwards, tried to enter the straits found by Burroughs. Failing therein, he followed the coast of Russia and discovered, on the 17th of the month, the channel between it and Vaigats, henceforth known as Pet's Straits. Thus he entered the Sea of Kara, and after vainly attempting to proceed further westwards through the pack of ice, fell in with Jackman, who had made a passage into the same waters by way of Burroughs' Straits. The partners met on the 24th of July and made another effort to continue their voyage to China. "Winds we had in plenty," says the chronicler, "but ice and fogs much against our will, if it had pleased the Lord God otherwise." For nearly three weeks they were locked in the ice, and then, abandoning the work, turned back to Vaigats, which they reached on the 15th of August. There and along the Russian coast the approach of winter bringing fresh stores of ice, caused many fresh delays. Pet arrived in England on the 26th of December. Jackman wintered in Norway and died on his way home in the following spring.*

The expedition added very little to geographical knowledge, and its failure increased the reasonable distrust that was growing in nearly all men's minds with reference to the project of a north-eastern passage to Cathay. There was quite as much reason for doubt as to the possibility of safely reaching the same district by a north-western route. But here, at any rate, was more room for enterprising search, and neither active seamen nor stay-at-home adventurers were long deterred from it by the disastrous incidents of Frobisher's third voyage. While the voyage in which it had been intended that Frobisher should make a fourth attempt was diverted from its original purpose and turned into a piratical attack upon the Spanish possessions in the southern seas, and while Frobisher himself was in disrepute by reason of the bursting of his golden bubble, schemes for carrying on the work to which he had devoted himself were as rife as ever.

* BRITISH MUSEUM MSS., *Cotton*, Otho E., viii., fols. 67—77, and a shorter account in HAKLUYT, vol. i., pp. 445—450.

The first man of note who tried to bring them to an issue was Adrian Gilbert, a younger brother of Sir Humphrey Gilbert. In 1583 he petitioned Queen Elizabeth for permission to found a new company to be called " The Collegiate of the Fellowship of New Navigations, Atlantical and Septentrional," which, with powers to travel and settle in any hitherto unoccupied parts, was in the first instance to devote itself to the search and discovery of the north-west passage to China. That request was partly acceded to in letters patent which were issued to Adrian Gilbert, on the 6th of February, 1584. By them a " Fellowship for the Discovery of the North-West Passage" was authorised, provided that a sufficient number of such adventurers "as should venture their money and not their names" could be brought together; and as chief managers of the enterprise were named Adrian Gilbert, Walter Raleigh, and John Davis, who were " to be custom free for their proper goods, which during the space of sixty years they should bring from those lands to be discovered." *

It is probable that Adrian Gilbert himself was one more ready to venture his name than his money; and Raleigh was sufficiently occupied with his Virginian colony. Therefore the pretentious " Fellowship of New Navigations Atlantical and Septentrional " came to nothing. But John Davis was in earnest, and being deserted by his friends at Court, he found friends in the

* RECORD OFFICE MSS., *Domestic*, Addenda; *Ibid.*, vol. cxxx., No. 20; HAKLUYT, vol. iii., pp. 96—98.

City, who enabled him, in 1585, to set out on a new Cathayan search.

Of his previous history we know nothing, save that he was known to be "a man very well grounded in the art of navigation;" and of the steps by which his employment in this special work of navigation was brought about we know very little. He tells us himself that he had an excellent patron in Sir Francis Walsingham. But his chief supporter was a London merchant named William Sanderson, "who was so forward therein that, besides his travail, which was not small, he became the greatest adventurer with his purse." With him were associated several other merchants of London and the west of England, and especial care seems to have been taken in fitting out the expedition with suitable provisions and trustworthy men.

Two barks, the *Sunshine*, of 50 tons' burthen, and the *Moonshine*, of 35 tons, left Dartmouth on the 7th of June. In the *Sunshine* were Captain Davis and seventeen officers and sailors, besides four musicians, and John Jane, a merchant, who went as Sanderson's deputy, and who has written the history of the voyage.* In the *Moonshine* were Captain William Bruton, and eighteen others. Bad winds and weather caused three short delays, and the vessels had to put in once at Falmouth and twice by the Scilly Islands. They fairly left the English coast on the 28th of June and sailed on, amid frequent storms and fogs, for two-and-twenty days without

* HAKLUYT, vol. iii., pp. 98—103. There is also a brief memoir of the voyage by Davis himself, in HAKLUYT, vol. iii., p. 119.

seeing land. They saw, however, plenty of porpoises and whales. The porpoises Davis tried hard to capture with harpoons, with pikes, and with a boat-hook. Some were wounded, but only one, which they called a "darlie head," could be brought on board. It was cooked and "did eat as sweet as any mutton." The whales they did not attempt to catch or trouble.

On the 19th of July they were becalmed off the coast of Greenland, which a fog hindered them from seeing, though they heard "a mighty great roaring of the sea, as if it had been the breach of some shore." On the 20th, after sailing further northward, they passed out of the fog and beheld the shore. "The land," said Davis, " was very high and full of mighty mountains, all covered with snow; no view of wood, grass, or earth to be seen, and the shore two leagues off into the sea so full of ice as that no shipping could by any means come near the same. The loathsome view of the shore and irksome noise of the ice was such that it bred strange conceits among us, so that we supposed the place to be waste and void of any sensible or vegetable creatures." "It seemed," we are also told, "to be the true pattern of desolation;" and therefore Davis fitly named it the Land of Desolation. This was not the modern Cape Desolation, but the south-eastern part of Greenland, now called Cape Discord,—another apt name by reason of the contrary currents with which its coast is vexed.

Davis turned southwards and passed round Cape Farewell on the 25th of July, whence, after vainly trying to land, he directed his course towards the north-

DAVIS'S STRAITS

west, in good hope that thus he should sail on to Cathay. On the 29th, after having lost sight of Greenland for four days, he was tempted by the absence of ice to approach the shore again, and was able to make an easy landing upon one or two of the small islands in the south-western bay to which he gave the name of Gilbert's Sound. They were "green and pleasant isles," but the mainland was still covered with great quantities of snow. In this bay the travellers rested and refreshed themselves. They also made some acquaintance with the natives. "The people of the country," says Davis, " having espied our ships, came down unto us in their canoes, and, holding up their right hand to the sun and crying *Iliaout*, would strike their breasts. We doing the like, the people came aboard our ships, men of good stature, unbearded, small eyed, and of tractable conditions." "I shook hands with one of them," we read in Jane's fuller record, "and he kissed my hand, and we were very familiar with them. We were in so great credit with them upon this simple acquaintance that we could have anything they had. We bought five canoes of them. We bought the clothes from their backs, which were all made of seals' skins and birds' skins, their buskins, their hose, their gloves, all being commonly sewed, and well dressed; so that we were fully persuaded that they have divers artificers among them. We had a pair of fine buskins of them, full of fine wool like beaver. We had of their darts and oars, and found that they would by no means displease us, but would give us whatsoever we asked of them, and would be satisfied with whatsoever we gave them. They took great care of one another, for, when we bought their boats, then two others would come and carry him away between them that had sold his. They are a very tractable people, void of craft or double dealing, and easy to be brought to any civility and good order; but we judge them to be idolaters and to worship the sun." It was always a wonder to European travellers in those days that the simple people whom they visited did not share with them the complicated system of theology that had been developed by long centuries of mysticism and scholasticism out of the oriental fancies and traditions on which it had been founded.

These Greenlanders by signs gave Davis to understand that there was a great and open sea to the northwest, and he renewed his voyage in search of it on the 1st of August. But the search was very soon abandoned for that year. He entered the broad channel which is named after him Davis's Straits, and, sailing right across it in a northerly direction, on the 6th of August reached its opposite shore in sixty-six and a half degrees of latitude. "We anchored," says the chronicler, "in a very fair road under a brave mount, the cliffs whereof were as orient as gold." The mountain they called Mount Raleigh. The bay which led up to it they named Exeter Sound; to its northern and southern shores were given the titles of Dyer's Cape and Cape Walsingham. "So soon as we were come to an anchor under Mount Raleigh," says Jane, "we espied four white bears at the foot of the mount. Supposing them to be goats or wolves, we manned our boats and went towards them; but when we came near the shore, we found them to be white bears of a monstrous bigness. Then we being desirous of fresh victuals and the sport, began to assail them, and, I being on land, one of them came down the hill right against me. My piece was charged with hail shot and a bullet, which I discharged and shot him in the neck. He roared a little and took the water straight, making small account of his hurt. Then we followed him with our boat, and killed him with boar-spears; and two more that night." Next day was slain another bear. "When we came up to him he lay fast asleep. I levelled at his head, and the stone of my piece gave no fire. With that he looked up, and laid down his head again. Then I shot, being charged with two bullets, and struck him on the head. He, being but amazed, fell backwards. Whereupon we ran all upon him with boar-spears, and thrust him in the body. Yet, for all that, he gripped away our boat-spears, and went towards the water. Then he came back again, and our master shot his boar-spear and struck him in the head, and made him take the water and swim into a cove fast by, where we killed him and brought him aboard. The breadth of his fore foot, from one side to the other, was fourteen inches."

Bears and a raven were all the inhabitants that the voyagers saw in their new halting-place. They found no signs of human life, no wood or grass or earth, nothing but a mass of rock, which, they said, was "the bravest stone that ever they saw," with here and there a flower like a primrose blossoming in the midst of barrenness.

Here they could not rest, and they had no safe place in which to leave their ships if they had wished to search inland. Some of the sailors, moreover, began to grumble at the smallness of their rations, and the store of food was getting scanty. "Therefore," says Davis, "considering the year was spent, and not knowing the length of the strait and the dangers thereof, we took it our best course to return with notice of our good success for this small time of search."

The success had really been good. Davis had, for the first time, explored the southern coast of Greenland or Desolation, had proved the existence of the great channel known as Davis's Straits, and had visited the eastern side of Cumberland Island, very near to the most northern limit of old John Cabot's voyage, and at the narrowest part of the Straits, which were there nearly two hundred miles broad.

He turned homewards on the 9th of August. After coasting Cumberland Island for two days, he reached its southern corner, which he called the Cape of God's Mercy. A fortnight was spent in visiting some small islands in its neighbourhood and exploring the entrance to Cumberland Sound in which they were situated. The discovery of these straits, while giving great delight to Davis, caused him some confusion. He thought that here, too, was a passage to the Indies, and he had some difficulty in giving up a plan for next year attempting to sail through them instead of following the course he had previously marked out. But the season was too far advanced for him to attempt any new work then; and, therefore, he left Cumberland Sound and its islands on the 26th of August. On the 10th of September he reached the Land of Desolation, where he was prevented from anchoring by a violent storm and the fog that succeeded it. In that storm the *Moonshine* disappeared and was given up for lost. It was recovered on the 13th and missed again on the 27th. Both *Sunshine* and *Moonshine*, however, safely reached Dartmouth on the 30th of September, within two hours of one another.

The light thrown by them upon an important section of the Arctic world, and the excellent way in which they had been carried through their dangerous voyaging, gave such satisfaction to the merchants who had sent them out that they at once resolved to prepare another expedition for the following year. In this many other merchants, especially from Exeter and the west of England, and a few courtiers and statesmen, following the lead of Sir Francis Walsingham offered to take part. The result was, that on the 7th of May, 1586, Davis was able to leave Dartmouth with four vessels, a goodly ship of 120 tons' burthen named the *Mermaid*, his old *Sunshine* and *Moonshine*, and the *North Star*, a little pinnace of 10 tons.*

He was near Iceland on the 7th of June, and there resolved to divide his party. Going himself, with the *Mermaid* and the *Moonshine*, in the direction of his former voyage, he sent the *Sunshine* and the *North Star*

* There are two accounts of this expedition by Davis himself, in HAKLUYT, vol. iii., pp. 103—108, 119, 120. In pp. 109, 110 is also a short memoir of the exploits of the *Sunshine*, by Henry Morgan.

to explore Iceland and the eastern side of Greenland, and to see if there was any hope of a direct northern passage to Cathay. This mission was not very successful. Richard Pope, who had charge of it, sailed round the southern and western sides of Iceland, and, landing on its North Cape, had some intercourse with its people. "Their dwelling-houses," we are told, "were made on both sides with stones and wood laid over them, which was covered over with turfs of earth, and they are flat on the tops. Their boats were made of wood and iron all along the keel, like our English boats; and they had nails for to nail them withal, and fish-hooks and other things for to catch fish, as we have in England. They have also brazen kettles, and girdles and purses made of leather, and knops on them of copper, and hatchets, and other small tools as necessary, as we have." Off Iceland Pope met an English fishing-vessel and two others, and then he crossed over to Greenland, reaching it on the 7th of July. "It was very high and looked very blue," but a firm block of ice prevented him from landing. Then coasting southwards and passing, on the 17th of July, the part of Desolation Land which Davis had visited in 1585, he cleared Cape Farewell on the last day of the month. Thence he proceeded to Gilbert's Sound, there, according to his orders, to wait for Davis's return and to tell how very little he had done in the way of Arctic voyaging. He waited for a month, which he and his people were satisfied to spend in discovering the corpses of three Greenlanders, in firing upon some who were alive, and once or twice in playing football with them after a fashion of their own, the wit and merit of which consisted in tripping up the natives as they ran after the ball. "Thus much," says the complacent historian of the undertaking, "of that which we did see and do in that harbour where we arrived first."

A little more they saw and did. Tired of waiting for Davis, they resolved to make their own way back to England. First, however, they worked up a quarrel with the natives, and, having captured three of them on shipboard, indulged in a little butchery. "Two of them were hurt with arrows in the breasts, and one was shot with an arrow, and hurt with a sword and beaten with staves." After that it was a matter of surprise to them that the Greenlanders refused to have any more intercourse with their civilised and Christian visitors. The *Sunshine* and the *North Star* sailed homewards on the 31st of August. The *North Star* was wrecked on the 3rd of September, and the *Sunshine* entered the Thames on the 6th of October.

Davis reached home before them, after doing much worthier work. Having parted from Pope on the 7th of June, he had gone as directly as bad weather would allow to Gilbert's Sound, meeting on the way a great iceberg which he mistook for an island, and being troubled all along by the great blocks of ice which the weak summer sun had not yet broken up, or had only so far broken up as to make them especially dangerous. He did not reach his intended halting-place till the 29th of June, but then his honest heart had reward enough in the welcome given to him by his native friends. "The ships being within the sounds," he says, "we sent our boat to search for shoal water, where we might anchor, and, as the boats went sounding and searching, the people of the country, having espied them, came in their canoes towards them with many shouts and cries. But after they had espied in the boat some of our company that were here the year before with us, they presently rowed to the boat and took hold on the oars, and hung about the boat with such comfortable joy as would require a long discourse to be uttered. They came with the boats to our ships, making signs that they knew all those that the year before had been with them. After I perceived their joy and small fear of us, myself with the merchants and others of the company went ashore, bearing with me twenty knives. I had no sooner landed but they leapt out of their canoes, and came running to me and the rest, and embraced us with many signs of hearty welcome. At this present there were eighteen of them, and to each of them I gave a knife. They offered skins to me for reward, but I made signs that they were not sold but given them of courtesy, and so dismissed them for that time, with signs that they should return again after certain hours." They did return in plenty, coming up in as many as a hundred canoes, and bringing with them loads of skins and fish, fat boars and birds just killed, the best of everything they had, to offer to the white men who came to them as friends.

Foul weather and a desire to see more of the pleasant district which he had reached, in which, too, he thought of building a fort for winter residence, if that should seem necessary to the prosecution of his Arctic quest, caused Davis to spend a fortnight in Gilbert's Sound. Giving strict orders that during his absence no injury should be done to the natives, and that no gun should be fired even in sport, he sent one of the boats to explore the coast in one direction and himself proceeded in another. Within the wall of snow-capped rocks and mountains that lined the shore he found open and inviting country, "with earth and grass, such as our moory and waste grounds of England are," but he sought in vain for villages or any signs of settled life. Only a big grave was discovered, with many corpses in it, and a movable covering of seal-skins.

Wherever he went Davis reports that he was followed by a wondering and respectful crowd of Greenlanders, "very diligent to attend them and to help them up the rocks and likewise down." "At length," he continues, "I was desirous to have our men leap with them, which was done; but our men did overleap them. From leaping they went to wrestling. We found them strong and nimble, and to have skill in wrestling, for they cast some of our men that were good wrestlers. They are of good stature, in body well-proportioned, with small, slender hands and feet, with broad visages and small eyes, wide mouths, great lips, close-toothed, and the most part unbearded. Their custom is, as often as they go from us, still at their return to make a new truce, in this sort; holding his hand up to the sun, with a loud voice he crieth *Iliaout*, and striketh his breast, with like signs. Being promised safety, he giveth credit. They are idolaters, and have images, great store, which they wear about them and in their boats, which we suppose they worship. They are witches, and have many kinds of enchantments, which they often used, but to small purpose, thanks be to God. They eat all their meat raw; they live most upon fish; they drink salt water and eat grass and ice with great delight. They are never out of the water save when dead sleep taketh them, and then under a warm rock, laying their boats upon the land, they lie down to sleep."

There were only two faults found in these simple people, faults shared by all rude races, and only faults at all by reason of their ignorance of the ways of putting the same tendencies to decent use that come, or are supposed to come, with civilization. They were too inquisitive and too acquisitive. Their wonder at the strange things that they saw induced mischievous handling of them, and their desire to have for their own more than was given or sold to them caused them to try and steal what they could not obtain as presents or purchases, and, when this was objected to, pettishly to attempt to destroy them. "They are very simple in their conversation," says Davis, "but marvellously thievish, especially of iron, which they have in great esteem."

The unfortunate result was rapid growth of ill-feeling between the Greenlanders and their visitors while Davis was away on his little explorations. "They cut away the *Moonshine's* boat from her stern," he tells us; "they cut our cables and our cloth where it lay to air, though we did carefully look to it; they stole our oars, a caliver, a boat, a spear, a sword, with divers other things, which so grieved the company that they desired me to dissolve this new friendship." Good and honest Davis was very loth to do this, or to punish the natives for offences that in them were hardly culpable. As he told his grumbling sailors, the Greenlanders could not be expected in so short a time "to know their evils." He tried, first, to frighten without hurting them by firing into the air, whereat they all ran away. "Within ten hours," he says, "they returned and entreated a peace, which being granted they brought us seal-skins and salmon-peal; but, when they saw iron, they could not forbear stealing, which when I perceived, I commanded that in no case they should be any more hardly used, but that our own people should be more vigilant to keep their things."

In his kindly efforts Davis only half succeeded. On the 7th of July he went off on another little boat-journey. "On the 9th," he says, "we returned to our ships, where our mariners complained heavily against the people, that they had stolen an anchor from us, had cut one of our cables very dangerously, and spared not to fling stones at us of half a pound's weight. The next day I went ashore and used them with much courtesy, and when I returned they followed me on board, whom I used kindly, and let them depart; but as soon as sun was set they began to practise their devilish nature, and with slings threw stones very fiercely into the *Moonshine* and knocked down the boatswain. Whereupon we pursued them with our boats and shot at them, but they rowed so swiftly that we could not reach them. On the 11th five of them came to make a new truce. The master acquainted me with their coming and desired they might be kept prisoners until we had our anchor again, and when he saw the chief ringleader and master of mischief was one of the five, he was very urgent to have him seized. So it was determined to take him. He came crying *Iliaout*, and, striking his breast, offered a pair of gloves to sell. The master offered him a knife for them. So two of them came to us: one we dismissed, but the other was soon made captive among us." Davis made signs to him that he should be released as soon as the anchor was returned. That was soon done; but Davis broke his promise, the only piece of treachery or unkindness that can be charged against him through all the period of his Arctic voyaging. He held his prisoner and took him to sea with him. "One of his companions, following our ship in his canoe," we read in the charmingly quaint narrative, "talked with him and seemed to lament his condition. At last he aboard spake four or five words to the other, and clapped both his hands on his face. The other did the like, and so they parted. We used him well. After some time he became a pleasant companion among us. I gave him a new suit of frieze of the English fashion, of which he was very fond. He trimmed up his darts and all his fishing-tools, and would make oakum and set his hand to the rope's-end."

Davis left Gilbert's Sound on the 11th of July, three weeks before the arrival of the unworthy mariners of the *Sunshine* and the *North Star*. Some of his own mariners were not worth very much. Sailing westward the *Mermaid* and the *Moonshine* fell in, on the 17th, with an iceberg, so large and so curiously marked along its edge with bays and capes that it was supposed to be an island wrapped in snow which hitherto had not been seen. The discovery that it was ice, and only a fragment of the vast pack of ice along which the voyagers had slowly and painfully to work their way for a fortnight, amid fogs which changed the day into worse than night, and, fastening on the shrouds, ropes, and sails turned all into a frozen mass, filled most of them with despair. They loved and honoured their brave captain too much to turn mutinous; but though Davis saw that they did their work "very orderly and discreetly," they did it without heart. At length they gathered round him and openly declared their fears. They begged that he would show pity on their forlorn condition; that, if he set no store on his own life, he would at any rate have some regard for theirs, and not, "through his over-boldness, leave their widows and fatherless children to give him bitter curses."

In that trouble Davis did the wisest thing that was possible to him. He pitied rather than blamed his faint-hearted sailors. He did not choose to listen to their entreaties and go home with them; but he saw that if he forced them to accompany him, their unwilling attendance would only impede his movements. Therefore, turning eastward again and making for the nearest land, which happened to be the coast of Greenland, in 66½ degrees of latitude, about five hundred miles to the north of Gilbert's Sound, he there rearranged his crews and his provisions. The bravest of his followers he collected, with a sufficiency of food and other furniture, in the little *Moonshine*, of 35 tons' burthen, determined in it to voyage on " as God should direct him." The larger *Mermaid* he assigned to those who wished to go home.

With those arrangements he was occupied between the 2nd and the 12th of August. Even then, however, he found time for cultivating, in his characteristic way, some friendship with the natives of this central part of Greenland. "On one day," he says in his diary, "I went to the top of a hill, and, espying three canoes under a rock, went unto them. There were in them skins, darts, and divers superstitious toys, whereof we diminished nothing; but left upon every boat a silk point, a bullet of lead, and a pin." Thereby the natives were encouraged to approach their visitors, and a small trade was carried on with them in skins and other articles.

Leaving this shore on the 12th of August, and saving his little vessel from destruction by anchoring it to an iceberg throughout one night, Davis crossed over to Cumberland Island, and made his way into the Cumberland Sound which he had desired to explore when he was forced to return from his former voyage. "I followed the same eighty leagues," he says, "until I came among many islands, where the water did ebb and flow six fathoms upright, and where there had been great trade of people to make train. But, by such things as there we found, we knew that they were not Christians of Europe that had followed that trade." Perhaps Davis, in his hasty observations overestimated the importance of this native commerce.

He was not long in Cumberland Sound. In it he thought there was great hope of finding a passage to Cathay. But he wisely judged, as he had done the year before, that it was impossible to prolong the search for it so near the end of the brief summer season, and he saw that his little *Moonshine*, with no other vessel to take refuge in in case of mischance, was quite unequal to the work. Therefore he turned back on the 20th of August, resolved to spend the next few weeks in exploring the coast-line to the south. He passed Frobisher's Meta Incognita and Hudson's Straits, apparently failing to discern the importance of that great channel, if indeed, amid the blocks of ice that hindered him from entering it, he even perceived that it was a great channel, larger and more propitious than Cumberland Sound. He skirted the shores of Labrador and discovered Davis's Inlet, now usually called Esquimaux Bay, where bad weather caused him to take shelter between the 28th of August and the 1st of September. In that neighbourhood he saw bears and deer, as well as a great number of pheasants, partridges, wild ducks, and other birds. Yet more plentiful was the fish. "We being unprovided with fishing furniture," he says, "with a long spike-nail made a hook and fastened the same to our sounding-lines. We took more than forty great cod, the fish swimming so abundantly thick about our bark as is incredible to be reported; of which, with a small portion of salt that we had, we preserved some thirty couple or thereabouts." Then he continued his explorations down to what is now known as Ivuctoke Inlet, in $54\frac{1}{2}$ degrees of latitude, which he thought might be another passage to the Pacific Ocean.

Thus Davis was occupied till the 10th of September, when a sudden storm nearly took away his only anchor and did much damage to the *Moonshine*. He had already lost two of his men, who had been attacked by the natives of an island off Labrador, and he decided that, if he was to reach England at all, he must return at once. Accordingly he set sail on the 11th of September, and arrived at Dartmouth on the 1st or 2nd of October, having crossed the Atlantic in three weeks.

Besides adding much to his discoveries along the coast of Greenland, he had thus, during his five months' absence, traced the western side of Davis's Straits from Cape Walsingham down to nearly the most southern parts of Labrador, following, with curious exactness, the track made by John Cabot eighty-nine years before. His employers, however, were not satisfied with the report of his discoveries. They saw that Cathay was nearly as far off as ever, and the only circumstance that pleased them in the whole voyage was the abundant fish-taking about two hundred miles above the already much-frequented cod district of Newfoundland. The west-country merchants and several in London refused to be partners in another voyage in the direction of the Indies. Sanderson, still as zealous as ever, could only obtain subscriptions for the equipment of three vessels, the *Sunshine*, the *Elizabeth*, and the *Helen*, on the understanding that two of them were to go no further than Labrador, and there to be applied in cod-fishing, while Davis continued his Arctic researches in the third. It was hoped that the cod brought home would pay for the doubtful voyaging towards Cathay.

The vessels left Dartmouth on the 19th of May, 1587.* Davis took them in the direction of Gilbert's Sound, intending thence to send the two fishing-vessels across to Labrador and himself to go northwards. Even Gilbert's Sound was too northern a part for the timorous dispositions of many of his sailors. On the 12th of June, when the Sound was almost in sight, there were threats of a mutiny on board the *Sunshine*, and Davis could hardly persuade the crews to keep together for a few days longer. His old halting-place was safely reached, however, on the 16th of June, and there the ships waited till the 21st, while the stores were divided and other arrangements were made for the separation of the fishing and the exploring parties.

* All my information touching this voyage is derived from HAKLUYT, vol. iii.,—containing a tolerably full account by John Jane, in pp. 111—114; Davis's own short memoir, p. 120, and a very precise log-book, also by him, pp. 115—118.

One chief work was the setting up of a pinnace which had been brought out in pieces, and which Davis had hoped to find very useful in the prosecution of his search. This was spoiled by the Greenlanders, whose thieving and mischievous propensities had given trouble enough in July, 1586, and who had been made very much more troublesome by the evil treatment to which they had been subjected in the following August. No sooner had the pinnace been put together on the shore of a little island, than they took advantage of the nighttime and pulled it to pieces again, took all the nails out of the wood, and stole every bit of iron they could lay hands on. Detected in the act, they very deftly turned the broken boat into a barricade, and so saved themselves from punishment. Orders were given that they should be fired at, but the gunners, out of regard for the pinnace, and, as they said, also in pity for the natives, put no shot with their powder. The Greenlanders were frightened away by the smoke, and all the pieces of iron that they could not carry off as they ran down to their canoes were recovered along with the woodwork. But so much harm was done to the pinnace that, when put together again, Davis found it useless for his purpose, and had to convert it into a clumsy and not very safe fishing-boat for the *Elizabeth*.

That done, the fishing party was despatched from Gilbert's Sound on the 21st of June. In the vessel assigned to him—we are not told which of the three—Davis proceeded on his work. Many of his comrades were out of heart, even at the time of starting. They asked to be taken home, or at any rate no further than Labrador. But Davis, says one of them, "by whom we all were governed, determined rather to end his life with credit than to return with injury and disgrace, and so, being all agreed, we proposed to live and die together, and committed ourselves to the ship."

The first part of the voyage was without much peril. Coasting the western side of Greenland, Davis was met by successive parties of natives, who came out to him in their canoes, and bartered their rude commodities for whatever the English were willing to give them. "For a knife, a nail, or a bracelet," we read, "they would sell their boats, their coats, and everything they had, although they were far from the shore." One "unicorn's horn," as it was considered, was exchanged for a knife, and with a few trinkets were bought a great number of skins, which proved very serviceable to the English in their cold journeying.

On the 24th of June, when he was opposite to Cape Walsingham, and when he was really in the narrowest part of the straits, though then nearly two hundred miles broad, Davis saw a great iceberg with deceptive show of mountains, cliffs, and bays, and fancied that it was part of Cumberland Island. "When I saw the land of both sides," he says, "I began to distrust it would prove but a gulf." But he sailed on, and soon, passing the iceberg and passing out of his straits, entered the wider channel into the Polar Sea, which is known as Baffin's Bay.

On the 30th of June he was in 72 degrees of latitude,

two hundred and fifty miles further north than any previous Arctic voyager had reached. He was near the modern Danish settlement of Uparnavik, and to the little promontory which he discovered he gave the name of Sanderson's Hope. The people came out in their canoes to meet him, sometimes as many as a hundred at once, and gladly sold to him a good store of dried fish and flesh, and some freshly-killed birds as well. He made no stay among them, as his eager eyes, looking northwards, discerned "no ice, but a great sea, free, large, very salt, and very blue," through which, he said, "it seemed most manifest that the passage was free and without impediment towards the north."

There was plenty of impediment. On the same day a dense fog arose, precursor of the rush of icebergs that the summer sun and a north wind just set in were driving down the channel. On the 1st of July Davis found his course blocked up by a great island of ice, and passing round that, he fell in with another and another. The whole sea was full of icebergs, large and small, through which he vainly tried to work his way during nearly a fortnight. Sailing first in one direction and then in another, he could do nothing but save his little bark from destruction, and made no progress at all. On the 13th of July he was again near Sanderson's Hope. The natives came out to meet him as they had done before, "pointing to the shore," we read, "as though they would show us some great friendship; but we, little regarding their courtesy, gave them a gentle farewell, and so departed." Good-hearted

Davis was afraid that further intimacy would lead, as it had done in Gilbert's Sound, to quarrelling and mutual injury. He preferred the perilous sea, and made a fresh attempt to pursue his northern voyage. The ice, however, growing every day more plentiful, formed an impenetrable barrier. Finding it impossible to go further north, he slowly worked his way westward, and, as the ice bore down to the south, he was forced to go with it.

Thus driven, Davis found himself, on the 19th of July, in the neighbourhood of Mount Raleigh. He took shelter in Cumberland Sound, and then, during three days, tried to make a passage through that smaller channel, which, in both his former voyages, had seemed to him as likely as Davis's Straits to lead on to Cathay. But Cumberland Sound was altogether frozen over, and six days were spent in ploughing back through the troubled waters which, in entering, had been traversed in three days.

On one of these six days, the 25th of July, Davis landed on Cumberland Island. He saw some Esquimau dogs which were too fat to run. He also saw a number of graves, or mounds that looked like graves, and traces of visits paid by natives for the extraction of whale oil. He was much astonished at the unusual heat that prevailed amid all the snow and ice. His three voyages had not made him familiar with the mysteries of Arctic climatology.

Reaching the mouth of Cumberland Sound on the 29th of July, Davis wisely concluded that it was not possible for him, in his one little bark, leaky from the time of quitting Gilbert's Sound, and much damaged by recent battles with the ice, to attempt any further northern voyaging. Therefore he travelled south with the icebergs. On the 30th he crossed the entrance to Frobisher's Straits, and approached Warwick's Headland, which was the name given to Resolution Island. On the 31st he passed Hudson's Straits, where, he says, "to our great admiration, we saw the sea falling down into the gulf, with a mighty overfall and roaring, and with divers circular motions like whirlpools, in such sort as forcible streams pass through the arches of bridges." The corner of Labrador opposite to Resolution Island he called Cape Chidley, and thence, on the 1st of August, a "frisking gale" helped him on his southward voyage. On the 12th he touched at a place which he named Darcy's Island, and there had some sport in hunting bears and deer and hares, which formed a timely addition to his scanty remnant of provisions. On the 13th his worn-out little ship struck a rock and was further disabled. He had already passed the neighbourhood in which he expected to find the two ships which, a couple of months before, had left him to go fishing on the coast of Labrador, with instructions to await his return from the north. These ships, however, had long before made their way back to England. It is not clear whether their crews, tired of voyaging even before they parted from Davis in June, ever went to Labrador at all. At any rate they were not there in August. By the 15th of the month, Davis had traversed the whole coast and was almost within sight of Newfoundland. "Then," he says, "being forsaken and left in this distress, referring myself to the merciful providence of God, I shaped my course for England, and, unhoped for of any, God alone relieving me, I arrived at Dartmouth." That was on the 15th of September.

Davis never went north again. The day after his arrival, he sent a report of his expedition to Sanderson, and urged continuance of the search in a better vessel than the one in which he had been able to do so much. "The passage is most probable," he said, "and the execution easy." Few people seem to have shared this belief with him. "This Davis," they said, "hath been three times employed, why hath he not found the passage?" Therefore, in spite of the countenance still given to him by Sir Francis Walsingham and some others, he found it impossible to arouse interest enough for the appointment of a fourth voyage.

For this want of interest in Arctic voyaging there was just then special reason in the demands made upon the energies of all patriotic Englishmen by the threatened coming of the Spanish Armada. But when this great peril was safely overpast, and men were able to give their thoughts to other work, Davis still failed in gaining the support that he desired. In a memorial which he addressed to Walsingham, he repeated all the old arguments with a new one to the effect that even in the case of failure in reaching Cathay, England and Queen Elizabeth would gain by the employment in good naval work of "many of those busy and fiery spirits that, by their factious stirrings at home, served only to create confusion in Church and State." He represented that it must certainly be of great service to the nation to keep up a constant succession of Arctic enterprises, as by them the northern regions would gradually be explored and probably colonized. If they were cold, he had proved by his own experience that they were adapted for healthy residence; and if they were barren, he had shown that they furnished, at any rate, some articles of trade that were sought for and held valuable. The furs which he had brought home, he said, yielded a higher price than those obtained from Muscovy, and were more esteemed at Court. If the fashion of wearing them at Court were further encouraged, he added, some fresh interest might thus be roused in favour of the voyaging by which they were to be procured,—" For you know right well, most honourable sir, that it is a great secret in policy to make the follies of the extravagant and the vanity of the ambitious contribute to the maintenance of industry, so that even the vicious and the lazy may, of their own accord, furnish the rewards of labour and virtue."*

But all Davis's persuasions were of no avail, and after Sir Francis Walsingham's death, in 1590, he seems to have ceased from offering them. " When his Honour died," he said, " the voyage was friendless, and men's minds alienated from adventuring therein."† Therefore he himself turned to other work.

* HARRIS, *Collection of Voyages*, vol. ii.
† HAKLUYT, vol. iii., p. 120.

CHAPTER X.

THE END OF THE CATHAYAN QUEST.

[1579—1603.]

WITH John Davis's third voyage the English search for Cathay was brought to a close. Through the two centuries and a half ensuing, from his day to Sir John Franklin's, the work of north-western discovery, in which he had better success than any of his forerunners, was continued, and besides its great services to geographical science, provided an excellent school for English seamanship. But with that noble work the old fables about Cathay were no longer, or only to a very small extent, associated. Travellers by land and sea, and map-makers and prudent thinkers who stayed at home, had come to the conclusion that, though India and the islands beyond it, from Java to Japan, were worth all the pains that could possibly be taken in exploring and trading with them, there was no such region of wonderful splendour and stupendous riches as Friar Rubruquis and Marco Polo and Friar Odoric had represented. Davis's successors, therefore, sought only to break through the icy barriers of the Arctic Sea and find a passage to the real wealth of India. Entering upon their work with less extravagant hopes, and with better knowledge of the dangers and difficulties incident to it, they were prepared for the disappointments that befell them, and satisfied with the comparatively small results that, from generation to generation, attended the heroic work to which they devoted themselves.

In the meanwhile, for those whose only object was to reach the Indies in the easiest way, another route was being opened up. The route was an old one. From 1498, when Vasco de Gama first doubled the Cape of Good Hope, and sailed across the Indian Ocean up to Calicut, it had been followed with growing interest and profit by the fleets of Portugal. But through more than three quarters of a century the East Indies had been reserved as exclusively for Portuguese adventurers as were the West Indies for the hidalgos of Spain; and when, in 1580, Philip II. seized the throne of Portugal, both East and West Indies became the common property of Spaniards and Portuguese. While England was Catholic, it dared not interfere with the monopolies which the southern nations of Europe held under sanction of the Pope; and for some time after Englishmen had learnt to disregard all papal interdicts, they had not naval strength enough to venture upon the seas in which Portuguese and Spanish galleys protected the rich freights of Portuguese and Spanish galleons coming from the East and the West Indies. At first, as we shall see in later chapters, they forced their way into the mid Atlantic Ocean, and began to wrest from Spain some of its West Indian treasures, and then, gaining courage therein, they pressed on across the broad Pacific, and came into collision with its forces in the East Indies. Thus while Frobisher and others were attempting to reach the Indies by what was thought to be the shortest passage, the same end was being attained, through the longest passage that could possibly be taken, by Drake and his followers.

India being once reached by Englishmen, they determined to pursue their traffic with it; and the great triumph which British prowess, favoured by an accident, secured in the overthrow of the Spanish Armada, made their new enterprise far easier than it could otherwise have been.

But one Englishman, at any rate, had sailed round the Cape of Good Hope, and thus made the voyage to India, long before the time of the Great Armada Fight. He was a native of Wiltshire, and a Jesuit missionary, Thomas Stevens by name. In company with others of his order, he left Lisbon in a Portuguese ship on the 4th of April, 1579. "The setting forth from the port," he said, in a lively letter to his father, "I need not to tell how solemn. It is with trumpets and shooting of ordnance. You may easily imagine it, considering that they go in the manner of war." Off the coast of Africa the voyagers met an English ship, "very fair and great," that offered some fight, but was soon driven back by a broadside from the Portuguese galley, which after that met with no resistance, save from the elements, during the rest of her six months' voyage. Near the equator she was becalmed for a long time. "Sometimes," said Stevens, "the ship standeth there almost by the space of many days; sometimes she goeth, but in such order that it were almost as good to stand still."

In the Gulf of Guinea Stevens had some amusement in watching the Medusa, or Portuguese man-of-war, as the sailors still call it. "Along all that coast," he says, "we oftentimes saw a thing swimming upon the water like a cock's comb, but the colour much fairer; which comb standeth upon a thing almost like the swimmer of a fish in colour and bigness, and beareth underneath, in the water, strings, which save it from turning over." He was also delighted with the sea-birds which met the galley as it neared the Cape of Good Hope. "As good as three thousand fowls of sundry kinds followed our ship; some of them so great that their wings, being opened from one point to the other, contained seven spans, as the mariners said;—a marvellous thing to see how God provided so that in so wide a sea these fowls are all fat, and nothing wanteth them." These were probably albatrosses. Stevens also saw sharks, pilot fish, and sucking-fish. "There waited on our ship fishes as long as a man. They came to eat such things as from the ship fall into the sea, not refusing men themselves; and if they find any meat tied in the sea, they take it for theirs. These have waiting on them six or seven small fishes, which never depart, with guards blue and green round about their bodies, like comely serving men; and they go two or three before him, and some on every side. Moreover, they have other fishes, which cleave always unto their body, and seem to take such superfluities as grow about them. The mariners in times past have eaten of them; but since they have seen them eat men, their stomachs abhor them. Nevertheless, they draw them up with great hooks, and kill of them as many as they can, thinking that they have made a great revenge."

Stevens told his father more about the birds and fishes that came in his way during his voyage than about the people whom he saw at its termination, when he reached Goa on the 24th of October. "The people," he says, "be tawny, but not disfigured in their lips and noses, as the Moors and Caffres of Ethiopia. They that be not of reputation, or at least the most part, go naked, save an apron of a span long; and thus they think themselves as well clothed as we, with all our trimming."*

Stevens lived many years in India, and was able to be of good service to four other Englishmen, Fitch, Newberry, Leedes, and Storey, who made their way overland to Goa in 1583. They were sent thither by the Levant Company, and bore letters from Queen Elizabeth to the great Akbar and to the Emperor of China. They conveyed some cloth and tin, as samples of English commerce, from Aleppo to Bagdad, thence down the Tigris to Ormuz, and so by sea to Goa, where they arrived near the end of the year, to find it frequented by traders from all parts—" Frenchmen, Flemings, Germans, Hungarians, Italians, Greeks, Arme-

* HAKLUYT, vol. ii., part ii., pp. 99—101.

nians, Nazarenes, Turks, Moors, Jews and Gentiles, Persians and Muscovites," people of every nation except England, as Newberry reported.

These Englishmen, chiefly in consequence of the rude treatment which the Portuguese had lately received from Sir Francis Drake, were roughly handled by the masters of the European colony. Father Stevens and two other Jesuits, whom he interested on their behalf, were their only protectors. "Had it not pleased God," says Newberry, "to put into their minds to stand our friends, we might have rotted in prison." But, with Stevens's help, they escaped with only a short captivity, and were able to extend their journey to many inland parts of India, to Ceylon, Malacca, and Pegu. Storey became a priest at Goa; Leedes entered the service of Akbar; Newberry died on his way home, in the Punjab; and Fitch travelled about till 1591, when he returned to England to write a full account of his adventures and observations, which had already, in brief reports, caused great stir in England, and were soon to encourage much more extensive action on the part of his countrymen in the way of Indian trade and travel. "Who ever heard," said Richard Hakluyt, "of Englishmen at Goa before now?"* Not long after that Englishmen were heard of very frequently, both in and out of Goa.

In October, 1589, a number of London merchants sought permission of Queen Elizabeth to send out three ships and two or three pinnaces on a voyage to India,

* HAKLUYT, vol. ii., part i., pp. 245—268.

there to seek out the ports best fitted for trade in English cloths and other wares, and to lay the foundations of future trade.* The project was approved, and on the 10th of April, 1591, the *Penelope*, the *Merchant Royal*, and the *Edward Bonaventure* left Plymouth with a view to its fulfilment. George Raymond was captain of the *Penelope*, and leader of the expedition. Abraham Kendal had charge of the *Merchant Royal*, and James Lancaster, the ablest seaman of the three, who seems to have had much practice in voyaging to the Spanish main and elsewhere, was captain of the *Edward Bonaventure*.

A month was occupied in sailing from England to Cape Verde Islands, and between the 13th of May and the 1st of June the ships were becalmed near the equator. In that neighbourhood they captured a Portuguese caravel, well stored with wine, oil, olives, and, according to the report of one of the voyagers, "divers other necessaries fit for our voyage, which were better to us than gold." At that time, however, began the misfortunes that attended the expedition through nearly all the rest of its course. Great tornadoes and bad weather of all sorts harassed the fleet, and produced much sickness among its crews. The ships, instead of proceeding in a straight line to the south of Africa, sailed in a curve past the coast of Brazil, and did not reach the Cape of Good Hope till the 28th of July. There they were troubled with contrary winds and currents, which, as well as the prevalence of scurvy

* BRUCE, *Annals of the East India Company*, vol. i., p. 109.

and other diseases among the sailors, made it necessary that they should put in at Saldanha Bay. There they waited for six weeks. At first great difficulty was experienced in procuring the fresh meat of which the voyagers were sadly in need. They had to content themselves with such shore-birds as they could kill, with mussels and other shell-fish; but afterwards they had dealings with the "black savages, very brutish," who brought their cattle for sale, and gladly disposed of as many as the Englishmen required for very small payment. The usual price of an ox was two knives, and a large sheep was valued at one.

But this cheap food does not seem to have been of much service. Early in September Raymond had to send home the *Merchant Royal* with fifty invalids on board. The *Penelope*, with a hundred and one men, and the *Edward Bonaventure*, with ninety-seven, proceeded on their voyage. The Cape of Good Hope was safely passed; but soon after that, on the 14th of September, there arose a violent storm, by which the *Penelope* was wrecked, or at any rate parted from Lancaster's ship, never to be heard of afterwards.

Thus Captain Lancaster and the crew of the *Edward Bonaventure* were left sole representatives of the goodly company sent out from England five months before. They, too, were very nearly wrecked by another terrible storm which came upon them on the 18th of September. Four men were killed by lightning, and nearly all the others were more or less injured. The mainmast of the *Edward Bonaventure* was split and much other damage was done. The mischief was sufficiently repaired, however, for Lancaster to make a passage along the southwestern coast of Africa and through Mozambique Channel, despoiling three or four local trading vessels of their very serviceable cargoes of provisions on his way up to Comoro Island. Halting there he found it "exceeding full of people of tawny colour and good stature, but very treacherous and diligently to be taken heed of." The treachery does not seem to have been exhibited until it was provoked by the bad conduct of the English. Sixteen of the crew of the *Edward Bonaventure* went on shore on three separate occasions, were well treated by the natives, and provided with the fresh water which they were specially sent to obtain. After that, William Mace, the master of the vessel, and thirty others, much against Lancaster's wishes, crowded into the only boat that they had and again went on shore. Their object was only idle curiosity, and they gave such offence to the people of the island that they were all of them murdered within sight of their comrades, who, having no other boat, were unable to go to their assistance.

Leaving Comoro, Lancaster and his scanty crew proceeded to Zanzibar, which they reached near the end of November. There they rested for nearly three months. They strengthened their shattered vessel, built a new boat, and did all else that was possible towards preparing for further voyaging towards India. They prudently kept aloof from the Portuguese, who had a small factory in Zanzibar, and made friends of the natives, who, like all the other people of those parts, are called Moors by the chronicler of the expedition. "The Moors," he says, "informed us of the false and spiteful dealing of the Portuguese towards us, which made them believe that we were cruel people and men-eaters, and wished them, if they loved their safety, in no case to come near us." Captain Lancaster produced a better impression, and, in the course of his friendly intercourse with the people, received from them good supplies of food before parting with them on the 15th of February, 1592. Even the Portuguese looked upon him, from a distance, with some respect. Just before he set sail they sent a negro to ask him for some wine, oil, and gunpowder, of which they stood in need. Lancaster gave them what they asked for, but kept the negro, who, being well acquainted with the Portuguese settlements, and a fair linguist to boot, proved a very useful servant during the next nine or ten months.

In those nine or ten months Lancaster met with a wonderful combination of troubles and good fortune. He intended to sail direct to Cape Comorin, and there, or among the Maldive Islands, to lie in wait for passing vessels laden with Portuguese or Spanish treasures, on which he might with advantage exercise his privateering skill. Contrary winds and currents, however, drove him much farther north than he had planned, and he therefore first visited Socotra, where, says the historian, "we never wanted abundance of dolphins, bonitoes, and flying-fish." Cape Comorin was doubled in May, and then Lancaster deemed it advisable to sail on at once through the Straits of Malacca into the China Sea. He anchored off Pulo Panjang early in June, and there the sickness of his men, too few when they were well properly to navigate the vessel, caused him to lie idle for more than two months. At the end of August he found that in Pulo Panjang "the refreshing was very small." Scanty food and bad climate had killed twenty-six of the men who had escaped with him from Cape storms and the murderous purpose of the natives of Comoro. Only thirty-three men and a boy were left, and of these eleven were invalids, and no more than seven or eight were efficient sailors.

Even with this small crew, however, Lancaster was able, in the Straits of Malacca, to attack three little Portuguese ships, conveying pepper and other articles to Pegu, and to capture one of them. Another Pegu ship was also captured a few days afterwards, but, its cargo being of slight value, it was released. The food taken in the first prize proved very serviceable to the weary and half-starved men of the *Edward Bonaventure*. At the end of ten days they were all described as "lusty," and Lancaster was able, as he passed through the Straits of Malacca, to seize two other Portuguese vessels, well stored with spices, rice, and other commodities, useful either for consumption or for sale. He stayed at Malacca till the 1st of October, on which day he captured a far more valuable prize than any of the previous ones. This was a great galleon, of 700 tons burthen, laden with wine, brass, haberdashery wares, and the like, newly brought from Portugal or Spain. The crew of this vessel all escaped in boats as soon as it was captured, and it was therefore left to founder at sea after the most valuable part of its cargo had been transferred to the *Edward Bonaventure*. Lancaster proudly cruised about until the 3rd of December, when he reached the eastern side of Ceylon, and proceeded to Point de Galle, there intending to lie in wait for other prizes.

At Point de Galle his exploits in the East Indian waters came to a close. Lancaster himself, though so ill that he seemed "more like to die than to live," was willing to carry on the privateering work through another year. But his crew were tired of it. They had already been twenty months absent from England, and of the three hundred men or so who had started on the voyage only about a tenth part remained. They refused to continue it any longer than could be helped, and insisted upon being taken home. Lancaster was forced to comply with their request, and therefore, on the 8th of December, he started for the Cape of Good Hope, which, after four or five weeks' waiting in Algoa Bay, was doubled about the middle of February, 1593. At Saint Helena the voyagers halted on the 3rd of April, and enjoyed its fruits and game during nineteen days. There they found one of the men who had been ordered home in the *Merchant Royal*, and who, left by some accident on the island, had been leading a Robinson Crusoe life for a year and a half. "At our coming," says one of the chroniclers, "we found him as fresh in colour and in as good plight of body to our seeming as might be, but crazed in mind and half out of his wits, as afterwards we perceived; for whether he were put in fright of us, not knowing at first what we were, whether friends or foes, or of sudden joy when he understood we were his old consorts and countrymen, he became idle-headed, and for eight days' space neither night nor day took any natural rest, and so at length died for lack of sleep."

From Saint Helena Lancaster attempted to sail direct for England. But his ship was becalmed for five weeks a little to the north of the equator, and thereby the old mutinous spirit of the crew was aroused. At starting each man had received his allowance of provisions for the homeward voyage. Some, with feasting and drinking, nearly used up their allowance in the course of the five weeks, and their jealousy of their more prudent comrades led to discontent among them all and gave great trouble to Lancaster. Judging it impossible to go home with such a crew, and without fresh supplies of food, he determined to sail westward in the direction of Trinidad, from which he was not very far distant. This he did, but missing Trinidad, he entered the Gulf of Paria and was there very nearly shipwrecked. For five months he and his discontented comrades, in their worn-out vessel, wandered about in the Caribbean Sea and among the West Indian islands. They dared not seek help from the Spaniards, and could barely pick up food enough to keep them alive from day to day. At length, on the 20th of November, they landed at the little island of Mona, between San Domingo and Porto Rico. There they had previously been kindly entertained, and they hoped now to **obtain food** enough to last them on their homeward voyage. Lancaster and eighteen men, all but the six or eight who were needed to look after the vessel, spent a few days in the forlorn search. Having brought together all the provisions they could find, they went down to the shore, intending to return to the *Edward Bonaventure*. But while they were waiting for the sea to be quiet enough for their little boat to traverse it, they saw the vessel sail off, to be seen no more. The food they had collected did not last them for many days, and then they had to keep themselves alive on boiled weeds, "and now and then a pumpkin." Twenty-nine days were spent in this dismal way. At the end of that time a French ship fortunately put in at Mona. Seven of the Englishmen, wandering about on another part of the island, could not be found; but Lancaster and eleven others were taken on board by the French vessel and conveyed to San Domingo, thence to be brought to England, on the 24th of May, 1594, by way of Dieppe.*

Lancaster had been more than three years at sea, and in the expedition much money and more than two hundred lives had been lost. But these losses were thought little of in comparison with the report brought home concerning the wealth of the East Indies

* The foregoing details are from an account by Edmund Barker, lieutenant of the *Edward Bonaventure*, in HAKLUYT, vol. ii., part ii., pp. 102—110. A somewhat different report, by Henry May, purser, is in PURCHAS, vol. i., p. 110.

and the ease with which the Spanish and Portuguese could be discomfited by English privateers. A kindred and yet more unfortunate expedition was fitted out in July, 1596, at the instigation of Sir Robert Dudley, when three ships, the *Bear*, the *Bear's Whelp*, and the *Benjamin*, left England under the command of Captain Benjamin Wood. Two years afterwards they captured two Portuguese vessels on their way from Goa to China; and they seem to have carried on a prosperous piracy for some time in Indian and Chinese waters, but neither the ships nor any of their crews ever returned to England.*

The English merchants, however, were not deterred by these misfortunes from their purpose of boldly competing with the Portuguese and Spaniards in their prosperous eastern trade. They determined that, where others had so notably succeeded, they too would force their way to success. Fresh strength also came to this determination from the bold efforts made at the same time by the Dutch in rivalry with Portugal.

In these efforts, destined, when the Portuguese were virtually driven out of India, to issue in long jealousy and contest between Dutch and English trading companies, Englishmen had much to do. In the spring of 1598, Captain John Davis, the great Arctic navigator, went as pilot-major with the first trading or piratical fleet equipped by the Netherlanders. Thereby he was

* Purchas, vol. i., pp. 110—113; Sainsbury, *Calendar of State Papers, East Indies*, vol. i., pp. 98, 99.

made personally acquainted with the long and perilous route by way of the Cape of Good Hope to the Indies, and with the great opportunities of wealth which it afforded. He shared in the taking of some Portuguese prizes, and, coming home in July, 1600, did much to encourage his countrymen in prosecuting the work of East Indian trade and conquest.*

That work was soon entered upon in good earnest. A famous meeting of London merchants was held on

* PURCHAS, vol. i., pp. 116—124. The curious adventures of William Adams, who, in June, 1598, went as pilot-major to a fleet of five Dutch ships equipped for the Indies, are tolerably well known. The ships passed through the Straits of Magellan, which they did not reach till the 6th of April, 1599. There, says Adams, "with cold on the one side and hunger on the other, our men grew weak;" and there they halted till the 24th of September, seeking food with such poor success that great numbers died of hunger. They visited Chili, and there had some comfort, though they were prevented, by fear of the Spaniards, from staying as long as they wished. A few weeks afterwards, however, having shaped their course for the East Indies, they were nearly all murdered at some island in the Pacific Ocean. The survivors proceeded in two ships to Japan, and reached it on the 19th of April, 1600, "at which time," says Adams, "there were no more than six, besides myself, that could stand upon his feet." The crew then numbered twenty-four, of whom six died soon afterwards. Adams was summoned to the Emperor's presence, and put in prison for a few weeks at the instigation of "the Portuguese and Jesuits;" but ultimately he rose high in favour with the Emperor, for whom he built a ship, of 80 tons burthen, after the English fashion. "He, coming aboard to see it, liked it very well; by which means I came in more favour with him, so that I came often in his presence, who from time to time gave me presents, and at length a yearly stipend to live upon, much about seventy ducats, by the year, with two pounds of rice a day." He taught the Emperor mathematics and other things, and built other ships, in which he traded about. In 1611 he wrote a letter to his "unknown friends and countrymen," which was transmitted to the East India Company, and led to some attempt by the English, under James I., at trade with Japan.—RUNDALL, *Memorials of the Empire of Japan* (Hakluyt Society), pp. 18—32.

the 24th of September, 1599. It was there resolved to apply to Queen Elizabeth for permission, "for the honour of our native country, and for the advancement of trade of merchandize within this realm of England, to set forth a voyage this present year to the East Indies and the islands and countries thereabouts;" and in proof that they were in earnest, a sum of 30,133*l.* 6s. 8*d.* was at once subscribed by a hundred and thirty-one influential Londoners, headed by Sir Stephen Soame, the Lord Mayor, and including nearly all the foremost merchants of the day, Baptist Hicks, Richard Staper, Richard Cockayne, and the Garways, among the number.* On the 10th of October the merchants were informed that the Queen had graciously accepted their proposal. That was the beginning of the East India Company, and great preparations were promptly made for carrying out the enterprise. Just then, however, there was talk of a peace between England and Spain, and the Privy Council decided that it was better to run no risk of hindering the negotiations for peace by sanctioning the immediate carrying out of the merchants' project.† Therefore the project was delayed for a year, the year being well spent in collecting information and laying plans for future action. In the summer of 1600, a fresh petition was addressed to the Queen, and in answer to that, the merchants were commanded by her " to proceed in their purpose and accept of her certificate as an earnest of a further warrant to be after-

---

* SAINSBURY, vol. i., pp. 99—101 ; BRUCE, vol. i., pp. 111—113.
† BRUCE, vol. i., p. 114.

wards granted to them."* The further warrant appeared in a charter of incorporation of "The East India Company, by the name of the Governour and Company of Merchants of London trading into the East Indies," with two hundred and fifteen members. This charter was dated the 31st of December, 1600.†

In anticipation of that formal document, all things had been put in readiness for the great work to be entered upon. Sir Thomas Smythe had been chosen first Governor of the Company. Court influence had been used for the appointment of Sir Edward Michelborne as admiral of the fleet to be sent out; but the merchants had wisely decided to have nothing to do with courtiers, and had asked for leave " to sort their business with men of their own quality." The result was the appointment of Captain James Lancaster to the coveted post, with Captain John Davis as pilot-major and second in command. Like wisdom had been shown in the appointment of factors and deputies, the buying of ships and provisions and other necessary preparations, not the least being the selection of Richard Hakluyt as geographical adviser of the Company and "historiographer of the voyages to the East Indies."‡

All things were prepared for the first voyage by

---

* BRUCE, vol. i., p. 126.   † PURCHAS, vol. i., pp. 139—147.

‡ SAINSBURY, vol. i., pp. 106—115. The terms made with Davis will illustrate the method usually pursued by the old East India Company, which generally made partners of all its principal servants. He received 300*l.* before starting, and was promised 500*l.* more if the profits of the voyage were 100 per cent.; 1000*l.* if they were 150 per cent.; 1500*l.* if they were 200 per cent.; and 2000*l.* if they were 250 per cent. or upwards.

the 20th of April, 1601. On that day four stout ships, the *Dragon*, of 600 tons burthen, the *Hector*, the *Ascension*, and the *Susan*, sailed from Torbay under the leadership of Captain Lancaster. He took with him several copies of a letter addressed by Queen Elizabeth to "the great and mighty King of ———, our loving brother, greeting," with instructions to fill in the blanks and present one to each monarch whom he visited. In these letters Queen Elizabeth represented that, God having ordained that no place should enjoy all the things appertaining to man's use, but that one country should have need of another, and that thus men of remote districts should have commerce one with another, and by their interchange of commodities be linked together in friendship, she had sent out these her subjects to visit the territories of the east and offer commerce according to the usage of merchants. She promised that her merchants should conduct themselves in a better way than had been followed by those of Spain and Portugal, who vaunted themselves to be kings of the East Indies. Therefore she requested that her people might be kindly entertained, and that while some of them were allowed to bring home a report of their discoveries and negotiations, others might be permitted to remain in each king's territory, there to learn the language, and direct themselves according to the fashions of the country.*

Lancaster's whole company numbered four hundred and eighty men. After sailing comfortably down to

* Bruce, vol. i., pp. 147—150.

the neighbourhood of the equator, he was there, as was usual, becalmed for some weeks. On the 21st of June, however, he fell in with a Portuguese vessel, which was soon caught and despoiled of a goodly store of wine, oil, and meal. Much sickness befel the crews as they sailed slowly towards the Cape, and Lancaster was obliged to put in at Saldanha Bay early in August. There he built huts for the sick, and conversed with the people in "the cattle's tongue, which was never changed at the confusion of Babel," that is, shouted *moo* and *baa*, to show that he wanted to buy cows and sheep. Keeping on good terms with the Caffres, and to that end issuing strict orders to his men, he procured more than a thousand sheep and forty or fifty oxen, a piece of iron six inches long being the price paid for each of the former, and one eight inches long for each of the latter. The Caffres were anxious to sell him land as well, and to induce him to settle among them; but two months' careful management served to restore the sick men to health, and on the 29th of October he put to sea again. The Cape of Good Hope was doubled on the 1st of November, and the stormy seas to the east of it were traversed without damage. Fresh sickness among the crews made necessary another and longer delay, apparently on the coast of Madagascar, the waiting time being well employed in the construction of a little pinnace, which proved very useful as a pioneer during the rest of the voyage. Halting at an island near Sumatra, Lancaster saw what he supposed to be a religious service of the natives, in which the priests, wearing horns and tails like devils, appeared to be worshipping the prince of the devils. He is also reported to have seen a wonderful tree, growing from a worm which gradually dies as the tree grows, the branches of the tree itself, when cut off and dried, being turned into white coral.

Sumatra was reached on the 2nd of June, 1602, more than thirteen months after the departure from England. On the 5th, Lancaster entered the Road of Acheen, and there found sixteen or eighteen ships of various nations. Two Dutch merchants came on board the *Dragon*, and told him that he was sure of a hearty welcome from the King of Acheen, who had heard of the English victories over the Spaniards. Therefore John Middleton, the captain of the *Hector*, was sent with a friendly message to the King. He was generously received, and two days afterwards Lancaster himself went to Court, accompanied by a guard of honour, including six elephants, that had been sent to receive him. He delivered a copy of the Queen's letter with which he had been provided, also a present of a silver basin and cup, some looking-glasses, and other articles. He was sumptuously entertained at a feast in which all the dishes used were of gold or other costly metal, and after the feast, as a great honour, the King's dancing-women came to entertain him. He made a treaty with this friendly monarch, who therein allowed English merchants to settle in his territory, to trade with his subjects and other natives, and to observe their own laws and customs. That done, the merchants who had come out with Lancaster immediately proceeded to buy pepper, which was the chief produce of Acheen. On Lancaster himself other work devolved in over-reaching the treachery of the Portuguese. He heard from an Indian slave that the Portuguese were arranging for the bringing of a sufficient number of ships from their large settlement in Malacca to destroy the English fleet, and, by using the Indian as a spy, he was able to learn all the movements of his enemies and to make preparations for checkmating them. The King of Acheen, when informed of this state of affairs, told Lancaster that the Spaniards and Portuguese were as hateful to him as they could be to the English, and promised to help him to the utmost of his power. With his assistance, the Portuguese were prevented from carrying out their treacherous project; and on the 7th of September, Lancaster was able safely to sail towards Malacca, and in its neighbourhood to capture a Portuguese vessel, and appropriate all the costly merchandize that he found on board. He cruised about for six weeks, and returned to Acheen on the 24th of October. There he renewed his friendship with the King and received from him a courteous letter to Queen Elizabeth. He also took on board the merchants whom he had left to carry on their trade, and all the pepper, cloves, and cinnamon which they had collected during his absence.

Leaving Acheen on the 9th of November, Lancaster sent the *Ascension* home, with a report of his achievements, and went with the other ships along the south-western side of Sumatra to the Straits of Sunda and

Java. In that neighbourhood the *Susan* received a full cargo of pepper and cloves, bought at a much lower price than was charged at Acheen, and was also sent with it direct to England.

On the 6th of December Lancaster reached Bantam. He had a friendly interview with its boy King and his " protector," to whom one of the Queen's letters was given, leading to an alliance for trade and mutual assistance. The English merchants brought their goods ashore, and sold great quantities both to the King, who by law had the first choice of everything that came into the country, and to his subjects. In return they bought an abundance of pepper. Some of the natives proved thievish; but Lancaster was authorized to kill any one he might find about his house at night time; and, it is said, " after thus killing four or five they lived in peace." Enough pepper to fill both the remaining ships was collected by the 10th of February, 1603. All the English goods that remained in them were transferred to the pinnace that had been built during the voyage out, and it was entrusted to twelve sailors and some merchants, with orders to visit the Moluccas, and, if possible, to establish there a trading settlement. A dozen merchants were also left at Bantam; and then Lancaster started on his homeward voyage on the 20th of February.

This was performed with hardly greater trouble than was usual in those times. A furious storm assailed the ships in the Straits of Sunda, and did damage which could never be repaired; and two months afterwards, when they were near the Cape of Good Hope, another storm almost wrecked the *Dragon*. Her rudder was lost, and, after vainly attempting to fix another, or some substitute for another, Lancaster thought his case so desperate that he proposed to send home the *Hector* alone, and, in the *Dragon*, either to follow more at leisure or to try and find some resting-place at which the mischief might be retrieved. The men of the *Hector*, however, refused to desert their brave admiral, and so the ships pushed slowly on together, a mast being hung from the keel of the *Dragon* in place of the lost rudder. After much beating about the Cape of Good Hope was passed, and the troubles of the voyagers were brought to an end. They halted at St. Helena, and there made a new rudder, besides remedying some other injuries. They entered the English Channel, and completed their expedition, which had occupied nearly two years and a half, on the 11th of September, 1603.*

By his successful management of this voyage Captain Lancaster made a memorable beginning to the famous career of the East India Company. The pepper and spices that he brought home realized profits enough to satisfy the merchants who had sent him out, and encouraged them to set forth other expeditions, some of them disastrous, but all conducing to the ultimate prosperity of the Company. The treaties of trade and alliance made by Lancaster with the Kings of Acheen and Bantam

---

* The foregoing account of Lancaster's voyage is derived from the narrative in PURCHAS, vol. i., pp. 147—164.

led the way to other treaties, issuing in the establishment of our great Indian empire. Lancaster himself lived on for nearly thirty years, adding to his fame as a brave sea-captain much useful service as a stay-at-home adviser. But the sequel to his personal history, and the achievements of the East India Company after this first successful enterprise, do not belong to the story of English seamanship under the Tudors. Therefore we have not here to deal with them.

During its brief three years' existence under the reign of Queen Elizabeth, however, the East India Company did some other memorable work. Lancaster had only been gone a few months on his south-eastern voyage to the Indies when, in July, 1601, George Waymouth, who is described as "a navigator," though we are not told of what sort were his navigations, wrote a letter to the Company, urging the importance of making another attempt to reach the Indies by a north-west passage.

The project was well entertained, and arrangements were promptly entered upon for carrying it out. In September it was determined that 3,000*l.* should be spent in fitting out two pinnaces, with about thirty men between them. To Waymouth 100*l.* were granted to be expended on instruments and other necessaries; and it was agreed that if he found the passage he should have 5,000*l.* in payment. He was so sure of success that he asked for no remuneration in the event of his failure. The right of searching for Cathay by northern voyaging having long before been assigned to the Muscovy

Company, a message was sent to its Directors, asking them to transfer their privileges to the new association. This the Muscovy Company at first refused to do. It also refused to conduct the enterprise in partnership with the East India Company, and announced its intention of undertaking the voyage itself, without specifying any time for the enterprise or giving any token of immediate action. At a meeting of the East India Company Directors in November it was agreed that "an enterprise of such importance should not be slacked;" and a fresh message was sent to the Muscovy Company to the effect that if it would really take the work in hand it should be left to do it in its own way, or that the East India adventurers were still willing to enter upon it in conjunction with the Muscovy traders; but that, if the Muscovy traders refused either of these plans, an appeal would be made to the Privy Council. That threat was enforced, and the Muscovy Company was in December ordered by the Queen to take its part in the projected voyage. It appears to have been still obstinate, and to have transferred its privileges to the rival association.

This, however, gave no annoyance to the East India Company. Its object was gained, and the few following months of winter were spent in completing the preparations that had been begun in the summer. On the 10th of April, 1602, the formal articles of agreement with Waymouth were signed; and on the 24th John Cartwright, a London preacher, who had already travelled in Persia, and written an account of his journey,* was chosen to go with Waymouth as his chief adviser. All the preparations were completed by the end of April, and the East India Company was in "great hope that there is a possibility of discovery of a nearer passage into the East Indies, by seas by the way of the north-west, if the same be undertaken by a man of knowledge in navigation, and of a resolution to put in execution all possibility of industry and valour for the attaining of so inestimable benefit to his native country and his own perpetual honour."† Perhaps Waymouth was such a man; but the work to which he applied himself, almost sure to have failed in any case, was brought to premature failure by his chief adviser, John Cartwright, and his inefficient crew.

With two little vessels, the *Discovery*, of 70 tons burthen, and the *Godspeed*, of 60 tons burthen, victualled for sixteen months, and having thirty-five men and boys on board, he started from Ratcliffe on the 2nd of May.‡ He was instructed "to sail towards the coast of Greenland, and pass on unto the seas by the northwest towards Cathay or China, without giving over proceeding on his course so long as he found any possibility to make a passage through those seas, and not to return for any let or impediment whatever until one year had been bestowed in attempting the passage." He was, in fact, to avail himself of all the experience

---

* *The Preacher's Travels*, in OSBORNE's *Harleian Collection of Voyages*.
† The preceding account of the preparations for Waymouth's voyage are from SAINSBURY, vol. i., pp. 128—133.
‡ The following details are from Waymouth's Journal in PURCHAS, vol. iii., pp. 809—814.

attained by Davis fifteen years before, and to do his best in realizing the hopes which Davis, for want of support, had been forced to abandon. Had the work been entrusted to Davis himself, it might have had a different issue.

Following Davis's track Waymouth reached the north-western part of Greenland on the 18th of June. Thence he sailed almost due west, and on the 29th he had sight of the northern part of Frobisher's Meta Incognita, then generally known as Warwick's Foreland. It was covered with snow, and along the coast were snow-covered masses, of which no one could say whether they were icebergs or rocks. Waymouth attempted to enter Frobisher's Straits, judging that therein he would find the coveted north-western passage to India. But contrary winds kept him at sea during sixteen or seventeen days, which he spent in sailing up and down the neighbouring coast, and that short time sufficed to sicken his sailors of their arctic voyaging. They were all puzzled by the numerous islands that they saw dimly through the fogs that oppressed them, and by the conflicting currents, formed of melting ice, that pressed upon them with a force which, in the darkness, was especially alarming. They were sorely frightened, too, by the distant rumble and turmoil of cracking ice and shivering icebergs, and yet more by the intense cold which froze their sails, ropes, and tackling, so as to render them almost unmanageable. At length, on the 19th of July, says Waymouth, "all our men conspired secretly together to bear up the helm for England while I was asleep in my cabin, and there to have kept me by force until I had sworn unto them that I would not offer any violence unto them for so doing." Waymouth woke up in time to prevent the full accomplishment of this mutinous purpose; but having all or nearly all his men in league against him, with John Cartwright, the parson, at their head, he was forced in the end to give way to them. They insisted upon being taken out of this icy region, alleging that their demand was "a matter builded upon reason, and not proceeding upon fear or cowardice." All Waymouth could do was to induce them to carry him in a southerly direction as far as the great channel discovered by Frobisher in 1578, but first properly explored by Henry Hudson in 1610. Waymouth entered Hudson's Straits on the 25th of July, and sailed along it for about three hundred miles. Then he was forced to turn back. He touched the coast of Labrador between the 5th and the 17th of August. On the 18th a violent storm nearly destroyed his ships, and the sailors thereupon obliged him to return at once to England. He reached Dartmouth on the 5th of September.

In the stringent inquiry which the East India Company instituted as to the cause of this unfortunate ending of Waymouth's expedition, it appears that Cartwright "did confess and justify that he was the persuader and mover of the company to return for England and give over the voyage." Waymouth was not blamed, and it was proposed that, in the following year, a new and better-manned voyage to Davis's

Straits should be intrusted to him.* But the proposals came to nothing. The East India Company found more profitable work in southern voyaging to India, after the plan initiated by Lancaster; and the task of arctic searching, in succession to John Davis, was left to Henry Hudson, in the reign of James I.

* SAINSBURY, vol. i., pp. 135—138.

END OF VOL. I.

www.ingramcontent.com/pod-product-compliance
Lightning Source LLC
Chambersburg PA
CBHW030731230426
43667CB00007B/677